Praise for *Delusions and Grandeur*

"*Delusions and Grandeur* is about what it means to be a man in the west—but if that conjures images of steely-eyed cowboys and oilmen, put those out of your mind. What struck me most is just how gorgeously tenderhearted, vulnerable, and emotionally engaged these essays and their characters are. If a smallish group of men have been the main perpetrators of the destruction of our planet, a larger group, including many of those in this fine book, have been their victims—and survivors."—Vauhini Vara, Pulitzer Prize finalist and author of *The Immortal King Rao*

"This is the West as seen through the eyes of ordinary people with extraordinary connections who have explored politics, literature, environment, and the act of being human. Sundeen has an uncanny knack for finding himself in the thick of things. Once there, he dives deep and reports back with an unerring eye. As a writer, I'm exhausted imagining what he went through to get these stories, but as a reader I'm carried along and come away feeling like I've been everywhere."—Craig Childs, author of *Tracing Time: Seasons of Rock Art on the Colorado Plateau*

"A riveting and powerful collection of essays that asks the reader to reconsider the connection between landscape, culture, and the past, Mark Sundeen's latest book arises from a lifetime of experience not only in western places but with those who build their lives amid the boom and bust born from a region marked as much by beauty as a lack of it. It's the people that matter to Sundeen, those passing through, those staying on, those leaving, longing, coming, touring, hawking, and forever hoping. Long disabused of any romantic notion of what it means to live in the West, Sundeen stands beside all those who populate his essays, bewildered, angry, but never without wonder roped to tenderness. *Delusions and Grandeur* frames a window through which we see how we far we have traveled, why we have arrived at this moment, and how much farther we still must go."—Jennifer Sinor, auth- *Meditations on Loving a Broken World*

DELUSIONS *and*
GRANDEUR

Also by Mark Sundeen

The Unsettlers
The Man Who Quit Money
The Making of Toro
Car Camping

MARK SUNDEEN

*Dreamers of the
New West*

delusions and **grandeur**

UNIVERSITY OF NEW MEXICO PRESS

ALBUQUERQUE

Library of Congress Cataloging-in-Publication Data

Library of Congress Cataloging-in-Publication Data
Names: Sundeen, Mark, 1970– author.
Title: Delusions and grandeur: dreamers of the new
    west / Mark Sundeen.
Description: Albuquerque: University of New
    Mexico Press, 2025.
Identifiers: LCCN 2024032519 (print) | LCCN
    2024032520 (ebook) | ISBN 9780826367648
    (paperback) | ISBN 9780826367655 (epub)
Subjects: LCSH: Men, White—United
    States—Psychology. | White people—United
    States—Attitudes. | Masculinity—United States.
    | United States—Civilization—21st century. |
    LCGFT: Essays.
Classification: LCC HQ1090.3.S86 2025 (print) |
    LCC HQ1090.3 (ebook) | DDC 305.31—dc23/
    eng/20241030
LC record available at https://lccn.loc.
    gov/2024032519
LC ebook record available at https://lccn.loc.
    gov/2024032520

Founded in 1889, the University of New
Mexico sits on the traditional homelands of the
Pueblo of Sandia. The original peoples of New
Mexico—Pueblo, Navajo, and Apache—since time
immemorial have deep connections to the land
and have made significant contributions to the
broader community statewide. We honor the land
itself and those who remain stewards of this land
throughout the generations and also acknowledge
our committed relationship to Indigenous peoples.
We gratefully recognize our history.

Cover photograph by Andrew Charney via Upsplash
Designed by Isaac Morris
Composed in Garamond Pro and Proxima Nova

The land knows you, even when you are lost.

—Robin Wall Kimmerer

I have seen all the works that are done under the sun,
and behold, all is vanity and a striving after wind.

—Ecclesiastes

Hey, I'm not braggin' or complainin'
Just talkin' to myself man to man.

—Merle Haggard

Contents

DELUSIONS and
GRANDEUR

Introduction

My wife who was born and raised in Whitefish, Montana, a railroad and timber town turned ski resort, population 8,500, sixty miles from the Canadian border, tells me that the colonized West is the teenager of America: all beauty and body, prone to outbursts, boom and bust, brain not fully formed, driven by passionate beliefs about the self that later turn out to be dubious. This may explain why it attracts a certain type, me for example, who showed up not as an actual teen, but only a few years older, hellbent on remaking myself in the image of the gorgeous things I saw: brown riverwater pouring over black rock, ravens circling on the canyon updrafts, a lone yellow cottonwood quivering on slickrock.

But this is not one of those books about nature where the solitary man connects to the earth. Calling the West a wilderness is a bit like calling the teen singing in the mirror a pop star. It could be true. But of course the continent was inhabited for millennia before the Europeans arrived and declared it a virgin land untouched by the hand of man. And between the zones now rigorously managed as parks and wilderness for our solitude, there are roads, and on those roads rise outcroppings of the tourist-industrial apparatus: burgers and shakes and zip-lines and curios and four-wheelers for rent. Sure, you can play cowboy or scout for a week or two, but what interested me more was the people who live here year round, decade after decade, linked in some way to the sprawling industry that sells the boots, maps, gasoline, and cowboy hats—the product called self-reliance—to one visitor after the next. The historian Patricia Limerick has written about this paradox, the heap of tin cans rusting behind the cabin in the woods, just outside the camera's frame: "Living out of cans, the Montana ranchers were typical Westerners, celebrating independence while relying on a vital connection to the outside world." I was drawn to the cans more than the cabin, and more acutely, to the mental and spiritual energy required for a culture to labor year after year to convince its customers that it doesn't really exist, that the reality is a mirage while the curated experience is what's authentic.

I should recount how I arrived here. I came of age in the 1980s in shiny Southern California with a sense that someone had replaced America with a second-rate imitation. On the flickering screen I was told by a twinkly-eyed president that ours was a nation of moral strength and innovative spirit, but when I flipped through the channels, it was more preening singers and weeping preachers and huffing wrestlers and hustling idols, all of them—including the president—actors remarkable only for their hairstyles.

Resistance to this fakeness propelled me first to become a literature major at a fancy university, then a sunbaked dropout in a desert trailer. When I finally arrived in the middle of nowhere, free from that artifice, I encountered the people who occupy these essays. They were like me: driven and haunted by a sense that something in our culture, our economy, our cities was terribly wrong.

I arrived at college with the conviction that my suburban upbringing on the beach in Los Angeles County was phony and materialistic. Just seventeen years old, I was a budding Man of Letters. Exhibit A: I had read the entire oeuvre of Albert Camus. In the rare event that a pretty girl spoke to me, I whispered that I was an *existentialist*. What I presumed to mean was that I defined myself by my actions, not my thoughts. The opposite was true. I was timid, a straight-A student, and a mediocre athlete, who like most American teenagers had performed few actions of significance.

The one hobby that might have qualified—rockclimbing—was a slight embarrassment. I had scaled a number of Yosemite's cliffs, yet when I tried to frame these mystical adventures within my worldview—that is, the worldview of a 1940s French intellectual—they didn't fit. My climbing friends passed me the books of Edward Abbey, but I thought his hymns of nature the stuff of simpletons. If I wanted to read about rocks, I'd take *The Myth of Sisyphus*.

The first threshold on the path to authenticity would be the writing of fiction. To imbue my artificial American life with European angst, I depicted a teenager from a beach town who planned to shock the indifferent world into pathos, and also punish a girl who had rejected him by hanging himself from El Capitan in Yosemite Valley. It's clear now that what I wanted more than the Letters was the Man—I felt trapped in adolescence, and yet my teenage self had already shitcanned the ambition of *becoming a man* as too earnest and trite.

But somewhere along the way to becoming a Man of Letters, I made a discovery. My fellow students had not come to plumb the mysteries of the human heart. Instead, they majored in econ to become day traders or lawyers. That phoniness I'd left on the beach descended, stronger than ever.

My disaffection manifested in the most predictable ways: I grew my hair long, briefly dropped out of college, sulked around France in the dead of winter, fell in love with a cutter. I forswore rockclimbing. I could not connect with nature outside but neither could I connect with ideas in classrooms. I barricaded myself in my room with Great Books and alcohol and tobacco until truth presented itself.

Placing a paper square on my tongue, my dilemma turned critical. After the fun part, in which I imagined myself a giant reptile whose ten-foot tongue unfurled across the bed to snatch slices of pizza, I got claustrophobic and wanted to go outside. But when my friends and I stumbled into the courtyard, I felt an equally oppressive agoraphobia. We went back in. Then back out. This went on all night. If I couldn't stand the inside, and I couldn't stand the outside, then I was doomed.

This sickening dread—the fear that I could never be satisfied, that I'd destroyed my mind—these were the most real emotions I had ever felt.

Amid the metaphysics, I needed new socks. I did not have a car. My bicycle had been ripped off (I refused to lock it based on some anti-capitalist notion that now eludes me), and riding my skateboard was beneath a Man of Letters. The nearest place to buy clothing was the mall four miles away. I borrowed a cruiser and pedaled across the sunny campus and past the stucco apartments.

I became aware of a dopey grin on my face. The mere sensation of moving my body through space, of pumping my legs and gripping the handlebars, sweat evaporating from my forehead—it was delicious. My heart had not pounded from anything besides fear in months. What if the solution were this simple: instead of just reading about action, you had to *take* action.

Racing through the parking lot, I hopped the curb. The front wheel dislodged, and I sailed over the handlebars onto the concrete. It hurt, but I howled in delight. Pain was the result of action! Better than the paralysis of endless thinking. I lay laughing. There was a great big world out there, and I wanted a piece of it.

I took my situation to my writing professor, a woodchopping fellow from Montana. I'd scored high with my fiction, but now I wanted to live a life as big as the ones in books. He looked me over and then peered out his office window at the tree branches fluttering over grass. Finally he said, "Have you considered doing some manual labor?"

One of my old climbing friends told me of a place in the Utah desert where you could get paid to row a boat eighty-four miles downriver without seeing any roads, bridges, or buildings. Desolation Canyon became my beacon, a place where theory and intellect would prove meaningless, and where action would win the day.

Some months later, I stood in 105-degree heat in the gravel yard of a raft outfitter. Rusted jeeps idled in the heat, along with big steel jet boats hauled on trailers. A whiff of raw sewage rode the wind. I handed my resume to a man wearing a faded red jumpsuit embroidered with the words Marlboro Adventure Team. BluBlocker sunglasses could not conceal a pink face swollen by the sun. I applied for a job rowing rafts down the Colorado River near Moab, Utah, a stretch known as the Daily, bereft of whitewater but crowded with European tourists and buffeted by upstream gales. It was perhaps the lowest rung in the rafting industry: a thankless hauling of boats heavy with Frenchmen who don't leave tips, and yet for an existentialist such as myself who couldn't tell the stern from the back of a rubber raft, it was the route to Desolation Canyon. The man in the jumpsuit glanced at my vita and muttered over the idling engines, not exactly to me, "Speaks some French, so that's good." If he was impressed by the literature degree he did not say. He asked if I could start the next week. Another guide, a bearded fellow with a braid down his back, sized me up as he hefted an ice chest across the yard.

"More fresh meat for the Daily."

·+·

I did not set out to write a book about men. I am unqualified to hold forth on masculinity. My friends mock my delicate constitution. I'm useless under the hood but love to pin clean wet laundry to a line and watch it ripple in the wind. I have been the sole man in one hundred yoga classes. In a line of bicyclists or backcountry skiers I'm at the back, wheezing at the one in front, usually my wife, to wait up. I enjoy lotions that smell like flowers and coconuts. Nonetheless here it is: a book about landscape populated by men. Let me explain.

I rowed boats for fifty dollars a day plus tips, sinking into the ancient canyons that seemed to touch the earth's core. The bedrock, like the Yosemite granite that I'd quit at nineteen, was telling me something important that I still could not understand. I did this supposedly seasonal job for eleven years, which left winters for writing. I became a reporter of sorts, unable to make things up, delighted by the shocking weirdness of real life.

What interested me, at first, was a type of extreme escapist, who like me had hitched himself to some vision and defied common sense to pursue it. A drunken sculptor sets out in the 1930s to the Utah canyons to build a monument on the scale of Mount Rushmore but ends up instead dynamiting a hole in the rock which becomes first a speakeasy and then a roadside tourist trap. An Elvis impersonator takes up residence in a windblown casino beside the airfield where crews trained to drop atom bombs on Japan. A middle-aged Californian hardware man devoutly transforms himself into the swashbuckling author, Jack London. I felt kinship with those who believed in America's former greatness, and could not quite grasp why things had turned out crummy.

This collection spans the first two decades of this century, a period of continuous foreign war that transformed us back here in the United States: a fifty-year-old environmental crusader and desert river guide ventures east of the Mississippi for the first time to protest the Iraq War in the Capitol; a Marine struggles to readjust to the civilian world after combat, then disappears into the Montana wilderness; my own call to action in an anti-war presidential campaign.

What unites these dreamers and pilgrims and hucksters is the freedom of landscape, the sense of infinite spirit and possibility in the canyons and deserts and mountains, which reflects back at us our own longing for freedom. Later

I found in those grand empty vistas their own brand of delusion, rooted in the widespread yet false belief that one can outrun one's former self.

The men I profiled held a certain outsider charm, having exiled themselves to the fringe. They were the inarticulate rebels lionized by Ed Abbey and Ken Kesey, strong-willed and politically aloof. But as the nation split into red and blue, the flyover country where I'd settled drifted farther from the wealthy coasts, and the men around me resented the elites, and wanted their share of the boom. Now the dreamers of dubious dreams amassed power: town fathers in southern Utah scheming to build a new metropolis in the desert (and stick it to Californians) by running a 150-mile water pipe down the canyon walls to the dammed Colorado River; clean-cut men and boys hoping to transform North Dakota into a start-up hub for drones, gleefully embracing the unmanned aircraft that elsewhere triggered fears about spying and war; Utah hotel owners taxing tourists to advertise to more tourists, selling a packaged version of the desert's solitude.

Just as I'd become deeply skeptical about the environmental politics of the West, the tug of war between factions of white people over lands bearing Indigenous place-names, my skepticism was upended by Native Americans who journeyed from all over the continent to Standing Rock Sioux Reservation in North Dakota. I embedded with Oklahoma Pawnee elders who came to the Dakotas to stop an oil pipeline and save their tribe from a centuries-long genocide.

While my intent was never to write about men, it may have been inevitable. I could not see that my search for the authentic was also a kind of retreat into maleness, white maleness in particular. I had relocated from one of the most diverse and expensive cities in the world to a place that was white and cheap, where even with the unofficial vows of poverty inherent to a life of writing and guiding, I could live in humble comfort, oblivious to tectonic shifts in technology, economy, and demographics that might have made me feel irrelevant, or obsolete. I didn't ask, until later, if our malaise was related to guilt and shame that came from sitting at an unearned perch in an unjust society.

When I began to investigate the halls of power in the rural West, it was no surprise to find them inhabited by mostly white guys. Barriers persist that make even such lowly vocations as ski bum and dirtbag and park ranger accessible, still, mostly to whites.

Meanwhile, the coasts have become strange to me: pricey, crowded, fast—nice places to visit but frankly unlivable. I complain about property taxes and leash laws and parking spaces too small for my truck. After thirty years in Utah, Montana, New Mexico, Colorado, and Alaska, I suppose the provincial man upon whom I'm most expert is myself.

In the dashed dreams of these men who appear in the early essays, I now see seeds of the white male grievances that have since usurped the country. In the later essays I was able to reckon in real time with how that perceived loss of stature played out politically. I would not mistake the men in this book for those who went on to storm the Capitol, and this tract will not explain the rise of the right. Rather, these are rural white men who reveal a tenderness, brokenness, and complexity that I didn't see in print back then, and I don't see now.

Today I cherish seeing them lifted from flimsy pages of magazines—or published for the first time—into a book, which still strikes my naïve heart as the stamp of the real. As I have tried to find my way in the world, these fools and heroes have been my guides, showing me in their fashion the way to act, and the way not to.

Green Green Grass of Home

Let us now praise southern Utah!

I moved here the high-water spring of 1993, everything I owned in the car, and my savings whittled to three hundred cash. The hitchhikers said Moab, so I dropped anchor in the red rock oasis and spent the next decade dowsing: mossy seeps, wind-chime waterfalls, pollywog potholes. I guided the rivers—the Green, the San Juan, the Colorado—splashed up the slots of Canyonlands and Escalante, and finally bought my own acre of promised land along a lazy creek sweet with Russian olives and fluffy with cottonwood duff. I loved the small scale of the desert towns. The Mormon pioneers did not develop the land for tourists, loading it with bars and resorts, but for themselves, placing a premium on self-sufficiency and community. The sandstone labyrinths, swaths of public land, and fine-just-the-way-it-is locals precluded it from becoming the California I had fled.

Turns out that my own migration to Utah wasn't unique. I was part of a historical exodus—let's call it the Golden Diaspora—beginning in the 1990s, when hordes of Californians split for the interior, jacking up home prices and residents' ire. By 2012, a whopping 12 percent of people born in California had moved to other western states. Seventeen percent of Utahns were born in California—that's more than half a million of us asking the waitresses at Mom's Diner to sub avocado on that.

We'd also like some water, please. Utah is the second-driest state in the nation, and all that growth has strained the limited supply. The influx of newcomers has been most dramatic in sunny Washington County, where the average summer temperature hovers above one hundred and the ground sees just eight inches of rain a year. Home of Zion National Park and the golfy sprawl of St. George, the county has jumped in population from 26,000 to 191,000 since 1980, St. George is now the fastest-growing metropolitan area in America. The state forecasts that in forty years the county will boom to half a million, which is like plunking down a whole new Albuquerque in the canyons.

Thirteen golf courses bloom green amid desert cliffs. Capillary culs-de-sac pulse with turf. Plans are underway for a Caribbean-slash-Polynesian water park with a 900-foot lazy river, a seven-story slide, and an artificial wave pool for surfers. Bulldozers broke ground on a master-planned tract called Desert Color, where 33,000 souls will dwell near the shores of—get this—man-made lakes! The drawings show denizens tanning on white-powder beaches and SUPing across waters that glisten like chunks of turquoise in the 300 days of annual sunshine. Washington County, in fact, guzzles more water per capita than any metro area in the Southwest.

To keep the water flowing, the state plans to dip a six-foot-diameter straw into Lake Powell—a reservoir of the Colorado River 140 miles to the east—then suck the water 2,000 vertical feet through five pumping stations and six hydroelectric plants, crossing the Paria River and what used to be Grand Staircase–Escalante National Monument. The pipeline is mired in bureaucratic proceedings, but when it caught my attention, state leaders were pushing to get it permitted while President Trump is still in office, because his administration has proven friendly to industry. Ultimately, boosters predicted, the Lake Powell Pipeline would deliver 86,000 acre-feet of water per year, enough to support a third of a million people. The price tag for that big hose: between $1.1 billion and $2.2 billion, more than twice as much in today's dollars as the Golden Gate Bridge.

Utah has every legal right to its acre-feet, but the Colorado River is already overallocated. It waters seven states, including the megalopolises of Los Angeles, Phoenix, and Las Vegas. Plus, the river is suffering from decades of drought and rarely reaches the sea. If its two main reservoirs, Lake Powell and Lake Mead, remain low—Powell is at 40 percent of capacity, Mead at 30 percent—everyone will have to start cutting back.

"There is no lack of water here," Edward Abbey mused about the arid West, "unless you try to establish a city where no city should be."

·+·

As I set out to investigate the proposed pipeline, I sped northeast on Interstate 15 from the Las Vegas airport. My wife and I lived in Albuquerque at the time, but we would never give up our singlewide trailer in Utah. Crossing the Mojave, I thought of the dozens of times I'd driven between Los Angeles, where I grew up and my parents still live, and Moab. I climbed the Virgin River Gorge to my beloved jumble of stone and sand, green mountains jutting up from the horizon. Coasting into St. George, the white steeple of its Mormon temple pushing toward heaven, I embraced my LA roots and followed the signs to an In-N-Out Burger, where I housed a Double-Double with fries. It was February, seventy degrees, blue skies, and infinite sun. From my umbrellaed picnic table, I had direct line of sight on Del Taco, El Pollo Loco, Jack in the Box, Bed Bath & Beyond, and Best Buy.

The battle over the pipeline is a proxy for the debate on growth: Can towns decide how big they want to be, or are they beholden to the same global market forces that have replaced mom-and-pop shops with big-box chains? Growth is something every town grapples with, but here in the desert it's strictly limited by available water.

From my hotel Jacuzzi, I phoned Mike Noel, a state legislator and pipeline booster, and asked how he felt about St. George growing to the size of Albuquerque or Tucson.

"I don't like Albuquerque, and I don't like Tucson," he snapped. "Albuquerque has a lot of asphalt lawns." Washington County has a similar climate, but it consumes far more water. In 2015, it used more than 49 million gallons of publicly supplied water per day, or 317 gallons per person per day. By comparison, that same year, Clark County, Nevada, which surrounds Las Vegas, used 204 gallons per person per day, and the counties surrounding Phoenix, Tucson, and Albuquerque used even less: 186, 174, and 129, respectively. Santa Fe County, up the road from Albuquerque, used only seventy-one gallons per person per day. "Utah has yards and trees and gardens," Noel told me. "Our kids don't want to play on green-painted gravel lawns."

The town fathers agree. Dean Cox is a fifth-generation St. Georgian, a descendant of the town's original Mormon settlers, and serves as a Washington County commissioner. Clad in jeans and a blazer, he recounted the founding of the town, starting with the Paiutes who irrigated crops along the Santa Clara River. When the Latter-day Saints arrived in 1861, directed by Brigham

Young to forge a southern outpost of their Kingdom of Zion, they diverted a spring to "green up the grounds of the temple," as Cox put it, and hand-dug canals and reservoirs to allow the settlers to eke out a living. But St. George didn't grow into more than a hot, dusty outpost on a two-lane highway where drivers filled their tanks and radiators for the sweltering haul between Vegas and Salt Lake.

"What I'm trying to impress upon you is that it was small and poor," Cox said. In 1965, when he was a boy, St. George's leaders resolved to convince those travelers to spend the night—and some money, Cox recalled. They built the Dixie Red Hills Golf Course, a rug of turf nestled among the bluffs.

"Since then the population of Washington County has more or less doubled every decade," he said, unable to contain a smile. "That's what people do: use our ingenuity and innovation to improve our lives."

It was easy to like Dean Cox and his tale of entrepreneurial grit. He welcomes the new growth. In the past, most local kids were forced to leave St. George—or Dixie, as it's nicknamed—if they wanted a career. The area became a haven for retirees, the first wave arriving in the 1970s. One big achievement of this early boom, Cox told me, is the expanded new hospital. Instead of a handful of country doctors, they have a first-rate medical center with a roster of specialists. His daughter works there. "She wouldn't be here—that job wouldn't be here—" he said, "without the previous water projects."

Old-timers like Cox say they have no right to shut the door behind them. He believes that the county needs the water for the next generation. "If we don't have the pipeline, we don't have the growth, and we can send our kids somewhere else," he said. "We'll water grass until the price of water prohibits it—I think the free market, supply and demand, will provide the solution."

Cox made some good points. I'm that guy who will raise an interminable fuss to the county council if they even suggest paving the road where I park my singlewide. I like southern Utah fine the way it is and hope Moab never reaches the size of St. George, much less Albuquerque. But the reason my wife and I don't live in Moab anymore is that there aren't many jobs except in tourism. Even Ed Abbey didn't stick around, spending his final years on the outskirts of Tucson.

Cox shrugged off growing pains like traffic and not knowing your neighbors. "They said if we ever got to 100,000, it would cut the head off the golden goose and ruin our quality of life," he said. "But it hasn't. You either believe that technology will make things better or that we're doomed. I believe the world is getting to be a better place. And I'd rather import water than export children."

If importing water saves children, then the man responsible for retaining the most local offspring is Ron Thompson, general manager of the Washington County Water Conservancy District (hereafter, the District). Another descendant of settlers, Thompson may be the William Mulholland of southern Utah: since he took charge thirty-five years ago, the population has jumped 600 percent, and the town has two new reservoirs. I met him at District headquarters, a three-story faux-dobe castle perched on a ridge overseeing the dominion below. Thompson is six foot eight, with a shock of disheveled white hair and a toothy grin. In a blazer that didn't match his slacks, and with an orthopedic boot on one foot, he ambled the plush conference room like a buffalo.

Thompson told me that the situation is dire. The county's sole source of water is the fickle Virgin River, a tributary of the Colorado that he predicts, given population-growth estimates, will be depleted in just ten years. "You can't stick your head in the ground and do nothing or you end up like Cape Town," he said, referring to the South African city of four million whose water shortage threatened municipal taps to run dry within a year. "They're looking at a doomsday scenario right now." (Cape Town eventually avoided the dreaded "day zero" of empty taps through conservation and engineering.)

Thompson is not worried by the price tag. "Water always pays for itself, every time. But lack of it can destroy economies and societies," he said. Indeed, all the major cities of the Southwest, whether you consider them enlightened centers of culture or object lessons in blight, rely on elaborate waterworks delivering the Colorado River.

"If we don't have an adequate water supply, why are we spending billions for education and highways?" Thompson asked. "We can't have any of that without water."

To understand why St. George wants this water so badly, one must exit the debate of practical policy and enter the realm of centuries-old grievances. Mormons arrived in Utah after years of persecution, seeking not to join the United States but to escape it. Even as they've assimilated, many still fear that the forces of federalism will encroach. Instead of laying out more than a billion dollars, I asked Cox, why not let the water flow down to California as it always has?

"How many congressmen does California have?" he asked. "How many does Utah have?" The correct answers were fifty-three and four, but the questions were rhetorical; he meant that if Utah does not develop its water and multiply its population—and with it, its political clout—Californians will rewrite the law to benefit themselves. This isn't paranoia. Western water law has long encouraged rights holders to use their share—or lose it.

When the Colorado River was divvied up nearly a century ago, yearly flow was estimated at 17.5 million acre-feet. The river was divided into the Upper Basin and the Lower Basin, with each half getting an annual 7.5 million acre-feet. In the Lower Basin, California got 4.4 million, Arizona 2.8 million, and Nevada a meager 300,000. Upper Basin states each received a percentage of their half, with Colorado getting 51.75 percent, Utah 23, Wyoming 14, and New Mexico 11.25. To further cloud things, Mexico was left out entirely, as were Native American tribes, although both were addressed in later agreements.

The big winner so far has been California. The so-called Law of the River—the collection of federal guidelines, legal compacts, and court decisions that govern the Colorado—states that in the event of a shortage in the Lower Basin, water will first satisfy California and any federal Native American reservations.

But the natural flow of the Colorado has proved to be smaller than anticipated, closer to 15 million acre-feet. In 2012, in fact, annual flow dipped to 7.5 million acre-feet. In the meantime, as the drought came to be called a "megadrought," Upper Basin states—which haven't built the dams and canals to claim their full share—send their surpluses downstream.

·+·

Paul Van Dam is also a fifth-generation Utahn. He descends from George Smith, first cousin of Mormon Church patriarch Joseph Smith and one of the founders of the town. He's eighty now, retired, and I met him and his partner, Lisa Rutherford, in their comfortable home twenty minutes northwest of St. George, set beneath a spectacular array of red cliffs.

"I moved down here ten years ago because the air in Salt Lake City was unacceptable," he told me, tugging at his glasses and rubbing his temples.

Van Dam served as the Salt Lake County district attorney, then was elected state attorney general. While some retirees take up golf or bridge, Van Dam became an activist, joining the board of a local group called Conserve Southwest Utah. A widower, he met another young-at-heart retiree who'd joined the cause, and they've been a couple ever since. They've spent a decade battling the Lake Powell Pipeline. As Van Dam and I reclined on sofas, Rutherford pored over sheaves of documents.

"We fight the fight, but we don't let it get us too upset," Van Dam said with a laugh.

Rutherford disagreed. "Oh, I'm pretty nasty, hon."

Van Dam and Rutherford dispute Ron Thompson's premise that the county will run out of water. The District had more than 67,000 acre-feet per year for its 2018 population of 160,000; by comparison, Albuquerque served 677,000 county residents with just 100,000 acre-feet. In other words, if St. George conserved water like Albuquerque, its population could almost triple without depleting its source.

The pair point to a 2013 report by the environmental group Western Resource Advocates, which claims that by transferring agricultural water rights from farms as they're turned into subdivisions, and by reducing current water use by 1 percent per year, the county could grow to half a million people by 2060 without piping in any extra.

They also question whether the Colorado River can even provide the promised water, given population growth and the drought. They and other critics allege that the pipeline is just an excuse for Utah to maximize its allotment. "There's a mentality of, we need to use this water because quote-unquote, It's ours," says Zachary Frankel, of the nonprofit Utah Rivers Council. "It's not about the need for water. It's about keeping another state from using it. Who's using it? You know, California has used more than its share." Basically, he says, "It's a water project whose purpose is to build a water project."

Van Dam and Rutherford also dispute the line that growth makes the city more affordable for future generations. They showed me a report by a panel of university economists forecasting that, if the pipeline is built, it could raise water rates more than 500 percent. Eventually, Van Dam said, St. George will have to reckon with the fact that it's living beyond its natural means. "They'll keep building until you have more people here than God ever intended," he said. "They are passing the hard decisions they should be making now onto their grandkids."

The two sides do not agree on the basic facts, and Thompson has little patience for naysayers. That report from the economists predicting skyrocketing water rates? "The authors are heavily involved with Utah Rivers, which has a different agenda," he said. (The study's lead author is a pro bono consultant for the group.) The District hired a consulting firm to prepare a rebuttal, which concluded that the pipeline would raise water rates only 68 percent. The economists stood by their findings.

While Thompson was keen to compare St. George to Cape Town, he rejected comparisons to desert cities like Las Vegas and Tucson that made St. George look wasteful. "It's not that simple," he told me. "What do you do with our six million tourists? Tell them they can't have a drink of water? What do you do with the college that has ten thousand students in it? Say they can't drink water?"

District officials told me again and again that comparisons to other desert cities are misleading, because of factors as far ranging as density, income level, and local soil composition. They pointed out that much of the new construction is drip-irrigated, with native gardens of cactus, mesquite, yucca, and cholla, and that St. George reduced its water use by a quarter in the past decade. But they did not provide figures that refuted the basic premise that greater St. George uses more municipal and domestic water per capita than other southwest cities. Both Las Vegas, with its forty-two million tourists, and Tucson, with its ninety thousand college students, still used less per capita than St. George. Tucson receives more rainfall than St. George, with similarly high temperatures, which I took as another reason for drier Utah to kick the bluegrass habit. But Thompson interpreted the data the opposite way: since Tucson has its lawns watered by summer monsoons, it doesn't need to import as much water.

Thompson had another theory. In 2011, he told the *St. George Spectrum and Daily News*, "Tucson is primarily a Latin culture, and we're fundamentally a European-descent culture." I asked him if Latinos use less water.

"You tell me," he said. "They're incredibly social people, great people, and they have tremendous family values. The countries I've been in where they have that influence, they don't recreate in the backyard. They recreate in the front street. I can remember walking down Latin American streets, and they're filled with people till clear after dark, socializing, kids playing ball in the streets, barbecues going on, and people sharing. In the European culture, we tend to be in many ways not as social. We socialize in our homes, in our backyards. There's fundamental differences—I don't mean that negative at all. If all your recreation is in the front, you're not worried about a half-acre of turf or a pool in the backyard. And you probably see some of that in Albuquerque, I suspect."

The truth might be less exotic. The District provided me with a typical water bill for a single-family household in St. George. For thirteen thousand gallons they paid thirty-one dollars. I checked my most recent bill, and for nine thousand gallons I paid eighty-three dollars. My gallon costs four times as much.

Had some miracle of the free market delivered this bargain? No. The District achieves its rates through a trusty old trick of European descent called socialism. Most water suppliers in the West, including Las Vegas, Albuquerque, Tucson, and Phoenix, do not collect property tax. But the District raises more revenue through taxing property than selling water. So there's no incentive to choose, say, a xeriscaped concrete courtyard over an above-ground splash pool.

Utah, in fact, ranks second in the nation in per capita water use, behind Nevada. In a twenty-seven-page report subtitled "Why do we use so much water, when we live in a desert?" the Utah Division of Water Resources emitted a collective duh when it arrived at this stupefyingly obvious conclusion: "Today, Utah citizens enjoy irrigated green lawns on relatively large lots, primarily because of the large quantities of inexpensive water."

The deeper I delved into the District's case, the weaker it looked. In a pamphlet called "Top Ten Reasons Why Utah Needs the LPP," the District claimed that the water would benefit "primarily the children and grandchildren of current residents." But only 5 percent of Utahns live in the counties that will draw that water. And the growth is not driven by bunny-like fertility but by migration, much of it from out of state.

Perhaps the pamphlet's most peculiar claim is that the pipeline "provides more water at a lower cost than other alternatives." Thompson told me that reducing water use by 1 percent per year and transferring farm water to towns would cost more than $1.5 billion—about as much as building the pipeline. Three-fourths of that figure, a cool $1.1 billion, is the cost of replacing lawns with something else. The District calculated that homeowners would shell out an average $10,000 for new professional landscaping. Even if everyone could afford that, it's apples and oranges—a private decision, as opposed to a pipeline financed by state taxpayers.

·+·

After a few days in Dixie, my head was spinning with circular logic: we must grow grass, therefore we need water, therefore we must get more water, therefore we can grow more grass. In what sounded to me like the last gasp of Manifest Destiny, this frugal state may break the bank to grow bluegrass on red rock.

But I assumed that the free market would settle things. If bond investors are willing to risk $2 billion to water this rock, more power to them. This is how the city of Colorado Springs financed its own $825 million pipeline. If Thompson's math is correct, those investors will earn a fortune on interest; if Van Dam is correct, they'll lose their shirts.

But here's where the story gets strange. No banks or private investors are financing this project. The lender for the Lake Powell Pipeline will be Utah taxpayers.

"The state came down to us in the 1990s and said, Look, you'll never be able to provide the water for the people coming here," Thompson told me. "They asked us to look at a pipeline. That idea did not originate in St. George. It originated in the state capitol."

This explained a lot. The District does not provide convincing arguments to reporters or opponents because it doesn't have to. The decision to build the pipeline had already been made by the Utah legislature, which in 2006 authorized the treasury to lend the District the funds. According to a *Salt Lake Tribune* story last January, the state has already spent $33 million just on plans and permits.

As for opposition, Utah is essentially a one-party state. Republicans hold an eighty-two to twenty-two supermajority in the legislature. Its four US representatives are Republican. Though Salt Lake City has had a long procession of Democratic mayors, no Democrat has been elected governor since 1980, and there hasn't been a Democratic senator since 1970. State leaders have all lined up behind the pipeline. In February 2017, after President Trump ordered approval of Dakota Access and Keystone XL, Utah governor Gary Herbert wrote to the White House requesting that the Lake Powell Pipeline "be determined a 'high priority' infrastructure project, with environmental reviews and approvals expedited." The Utah congressional delegation followed suit with its own letter, urging that the review process be completed by 2018. When Trump approved the decision to slash Grand Staircase–Escalante National Monument, a section of the excised land contained the proposed route of the pipeline.

Still, I knew enough about land and water to surmise that the true beneficiaries of those master-planned exurbs would be the developers. What surprised me was that the unbuilt tracts didn't belong to ranchers or farmers. The largest landowner in St. George is the State of Utah, which has been selling off a tract totaling sixty-eight thousand acres—roughly 15 percent of the city—projected to one day house forty thousand people. This includes Desert Color, with its future sunbathers on fake lakes. In all, development of the tract could boost the city's population by 50 percent.

As much as I appreciated a bootstrapping tale of local pluck, or the idea that a golf course launched an entire region, what caused this desert to blossom in the 1970s was the interstate highway system—I-15 passes right through St. George—and air-conditioning fueled by cheap electricity, both of which were delivered by massive public projects. Like many Sunbelt cities, this one would barely exist without the faraway reign of tax-and-spenders. And the current boom isn't the result of individuals developing their property, or of citizens exercising their personal freedom by moving here. It's engineered by the State of Utah, irrigating its own desert metropolis. If they build it, people will come.

.+.

Who is this oasis for? I drove up the Santa Clara River to the west side of Washington County. The subdivisions advertised themselves with petroglyphic fonts and Kokopellis: Lakota Ridge, Anasazi Hills, Chaco Bench, Kachina Cliffs. None of the golf-cart pilots I saw appeared to belong to the above-listed peoples.

But then what a shock—at a roundabout on Wapatki Trail, my eye spied an Indian! He clung, twenty feet off the ground, to a slab of sandstone that protruded from the xeriscape. He was nude but for a loincloth, jute sandals, and a feather in his hair. Lashed to his back were three more slabs of sandstone.

Alas, the Native American was a bronze statue, and if he were to summit his crag, he would peer down at pueblo-style mansionettes. But as I reached the westernmost village in the county, a plain metal sign proclaimed: Shivwits Paiute Indian Reservation. Out here the houses were stucco rectangles—no green grass or, for that matter, exotic cactus, just sagebrush and cheatgrass and tumbleweeds. I stopped at the one place of business, a gas station, to get a Coke. The actual Paiute working the register looked nothing like his ripped bronze ancestor. For starters, he wore clothes.

I knocked on the door of the home of Lawrence Snow, the band's land-resource manager. As we stood in his yard, he looked downvalley and said, "The houses are coming closer and closer. It's like Las Vegas. If they all lived up here, I'd feel crowded. Everything they love about the place, you can kiss it goodbye."

Snow didn't think the pipeline would affect the Shivwits band, who had negotiated a water settlement with the federal government a few years back. He said that the biggest problems here were the same ones facing many other rural parts of the country—unemployment, poverty, the opioid epidemic. With his finger, he scratched pie charts into the dust on the hood of his minivan. "When there are so few of us, the problems seem bigger."

The Shivwits band is small indeed: just 305 members, of which only about 100 live on the reservation. In 1954, at the urging of Utah senator Arthur Watkins, the United States "terminated" the Utah Paiute bands, rescinding their recognition as a tribal nation. It was an attempt to force the Paiutes to assimilate and resulted in a spike in disease, malnutrition, and alcoholism. The tribe, which includes five bands, was finally able to reverse the termination in

1980. Its official website puts a fine point on the ordeal: "The Paiute Indian Tribe of Utah is engaged in the long, slow climb back from near destruction by the invasion of European settlers and Mormon Pioneers. Their numbers, once in the thousands, dwindled to less than 800."

The history of this continent is one of colonists pushing indigenous people off the land. A decade ago, author Rich Benjamin noticed that, while the country at large is becoming more diverse, small cities in the West are filling mostly with more white people. He concluded that they were fleeing larger cities for what he called Whitopia: towns that were at least 85 percent non-Hispanic white and booming with more new white arrivals. Places like Bend, Oregon; Coeur d'Alene, Idaho; and Fort Collins, Colorado. His prime example was St. George, which in 2006 was 89 percent non-Hispanic white. In the previous six years, it had jumped 40 percent in population; of those new arrivals, 84 percent were white.

"Most whites are not drawn to a place explicitly because it teems with other white people," he wrote in *Searching for Whitopia*. During three months of research in St. George, Benjamin, who is Black, found residents to be exceedingly polite, with strong anti-immigrant views. They look for neighborhoods with "higher property values, friendliness, orderliness, hospitality, cleanliness, safety, and comfort. These seemingly race-neutral qualities are subconsciously inseparable from race and class in many whites' minds," he wrote.

The effect is that Whitopia is only getting whiter. This is not an accident of the free market; it's engineered by public policy. Last century, as whites fled cities for the suburbs, public money flowed into those suburbs for freeways, police departments, and schools. Now, as whites rush to the Intermountain West, public money flows toward projects like the Lake Powell Pipeline that benefit them.

·+·

I drove east out of Washington County along the proposed path of the pipeline, dropping down from Utah into the Arizona Strip—the parched land of Paiutes and fundamentalist Mormons cut off from the rest of their state by the Grand Canyon. I stopped at Pipe Springs National Monument, a watering hole that has supported the Kaibab Paiutes for millennia. One could argue that Native Americans were treated better by Mormons than by other settlers, but in any case the Kaibab band of Paiutes numbered more than five thousand before contact with Europeans; now the tribe has 335 members.

The Kaibab Indian Reservation consists of a smattering of homes just a few miles from the springs. As I puttered down a stretch of two-lane blacktop through sagebrush, I came across a parking lot filled with cars. Outside, what looked like any blocky municipal office but turned out to be a basketball gym, a dancer in feather regalia exited a sedan. I skidded to a stop in the gravel and within ten minutes was feasting on fry bread and hamburger stew. The powwow was in honor of veterans, and I met a Marine who had served in the corps for twenty years, from Vietnam to Iraq. As the dance began, he carried the medicine staff while his brothers hoisted the Paiute tribal flag and the Stars and Stripes. A circle of men beat a drum and wailed a victory song while a half-dozen vets, most in gray braids and black leather vests, pounded their feet in place. The eldest danced with a cane.

Because of drought and new wells, the flow at Pipe Springs has dwindled from fifty gallons per minute to five. One proposed path of the Lake Powell Pipeline crosses the reservation, but since the pipeline is exclusively for Utah counties, the Paiutes won't get any of its water.

Another hundred miles up the Colorado River canyon, where the pipeline would dip into Lake Powell, sits the Navajo Nation, home of the country's second-largest tribe (after the Cherokees), with more than 360,000 enrolled members. About half of them live on the reservation, which spans parts of New Mexico, Arizona, and Utah.

I talked to Mark Maryboy, a former commissioner in San Juan County, located in the southeastern corner of Utah, and the first Native American elected to office in the state. "I always felt like it was just a joke," he said of the pipeline. "It's very expensive. But Utah is a Republican state. They're in control. And they get to do whatever they want."

The Navajo Nation has water rights to the Colorado that it has not developed, but of the eight thousand or so Navajos living in the Utah portion of the Nation, I found that more than three thousand did not have running water. Let me say that again: in the year 2018, American citizens did not have water to drink in their homes.

"Hauling water is a way of life on the Navajo reservation and has enormous economic and social costs," Navajo Nation president Russell Begaye testified before Congress in December of 2017. "The only way to improve this situation is through water infrastructure."

Begaye was speaking in support of a bill introduced by Utah senator Orrin Hatch that would authorize the Navajo Nation to develop about the same amount of Colorado River water as the Lake Powell Pipeline would carry. The US government would pay $200 million for the project, and Utah would pitch in $8 million.

When compared with the Lake Powell Pipeline, the Navajo settlement loses some of its luster. First off, it must be approved by Congress, which could take years or might simply never happen. And for roughly the same amount of water, the Lake Powell Pipeline will cost nine times more. Either the Navajo project has been shortchanged, or the LPP is an extravagant boondoggle.

"Western water pork barrel has always focused on diverting water away from reservations, not to them," said Dan McCool, a professor emeritus of political science at the University of Utah, who has written two books on Indian water rights.

Says Melanie Yazzie, a professor at the University of Minnesota, who studies Navajo water rights, "Whether or not they want to be hauling water, Navajo people have a prior right to the water. This is another case of colonial dispossession and the exploitation and extraction of our resources."

What's happening in St. George may be the result of state water priorities, or it may be part of the great morass of federal policy that has forever bogged down Indian affairs. Either way, the optics of white people frolicking on water slides while Natives haul drinking water in pickups looks to some a lot like apartheid.

·+·

I kept driving east along the pipeline's future route to find Mike Noel, the Utah state legislator I'd spoken with from my hotel hot tub. Noel is one of the pipeline's loudest proponents and the archnemesis of public land advocates. He has said that the US Forest Service has been taken over by "the bunny lovers and the tree huggers and the rock lickers." Representing the counties that contain Grand Staircase and Bears Ears, he helped persuade the president to slash them, then tried to rename the road through Zion the Donald J. Trump National Park Highway.

I drove to his ranch outside Kanab, a town of 4,700 on the Arizona state line. With a smattering of hotels and bungalows ringed by red cliffs, Kanab reminded me of the Moab I moved to twenty-five years ago and is perhaps what St. George would look like without the interstate. I left the pavement, crossed a dry wash and an alfalfa field, then wound up a dirt lane to a handsome home overlooking the canyon. Noel met me at the door in jeans, running shoes, and a black sweatshirt.

He plopped down on the couch and yawned. Fifth-generation, pioneers, etc. His wife brought glasses of ice water. If I'd expected a fist-pounding ogre, I found instead a kindly grandfather with deeply held beliefs. Noel lit up when I mentioned that my wife and I had a baby on the way. "That's what life is all about," he said. "It's a wonderful thing, a spirit coming down from heaven." Noel is a widower, and he and his new wife have forty-eight grandchildren between them.

"It's part of our heritage as a state," he said of the pipeline. "We're not giving up that water. It goes back to the way Utah was founded. Brigham Young left Nauvoo, Illinois, in the greatest single migration in the history of the continent. He came to a place, it had open land, it had room to grow, it had freedom from oppression because it was outside the United States, and it had water. For us to give up water would be like giving up our firstborn.

"I want there to be farmers," Noel told me. "I produce 100,000 pounds of beef every year. I don't give it any growth hormones. I grow hay and sell it to the dairy farmers, for milk for children. I feel I'm doing what God wants me to do. He wants me to be a good steward of the land. He wants me to produce food and fiber for people."

Noel conceded that the pipeline will not help farmers. "That water's too expensive for agriculture," he said. I suggested that the second-home resort growth in St. George was actually destroying his pastoral way of life. "It is," he agreed. Nonetheless, he supported the right to build lakes and lakefront condos. "We shouldn't use water as a zoning mechanism," he said.

When I suggested that the Colorado River might not have enough water for the pipeline, he scoffed. "If it went down by 80 percent, our water will still be sitting there." I brought up California and the other states downstream.

"The people in California, at least they have an ocean," he said. "They have lawns. Should people in Utah not even be allowed to drink?"

I took a sip of ice water.

"You know more about this than I probably do," he said.

I set the glass down.

"If we could sit and reason together, I think we'd be better off," he said. "I'm pretty bombastic in the things I say, maybe less so since my wife died. But it's very annoying, this whole harangue: no growth, no growth, no growth. They would say to you: There's too many people on the planet, Mark, you should have chosen to have a dog, not a child. It's an amazing thing—that's what people get married for, but for these guys it's like doomsday."

The next week, the Utah Rivers Council would file a complaint against Noel, accusing him of conflicts of interest over the pipeline. Noel denied all wrongdoing and announced that he'd been planning to retire from the legislature anyway.

"What do you say to the critics?" I asked him at his house. "The people who wonder if we're spending a billion dollars so people in St. George can water their lawns?"

He let out a sigh, the kind an adult gives a child who insists Santa Claus isn't real.

"Don't they like lawns?" he said, grinning, sinking deeper into the cushions. "I like lawns."

Why Noah Went to the Woods

Vern and Donelle Kersey aren't the type of parents satisfied with hauling their kids to a national park and pitching a tent beneath the floodlights of someone's motor home. Both raised in Montana, when they go to the great outdoors they get all the way there. In the summer of 2010, when Vern's only week of vacation was pushed into September, the couple were not cowed by the threat of early snow. Along with their two youngest kids, sixteen-year-old Shelby and eleven-year-old Trevor, they set out to hike thirty miles to the Chinese Wall, one of the most magnificent and remote features in the country: a one-thousand-foot-high, twenty-six-mile-long spine splitting the Rockies of western Montana.

The Bob Marshall Wilderness Complex—known in these parts as the Bob—is thirty miles wide by eighty miles tall, accessible only by foot and horse (and, in dire circumstances, plane), population zero during winter, then inhabited July through September by five fire lookouts perched like lightning rods on isolated vantage points. At night the lookouts find their only human conversation over the airwaves, their tiny voices crackling in static beneath black skies and swirls of clouds close enough to touch.

The Kerseys brought mummy bags, rain gear, and overnight packs, as well as a four-person tent, rain tarp, lightweight stove, and water filter. They weighed out nine days' worth of freeze-dried food. The Bob is one of the few places in the Lower 48 with a robust population of grizzly bears, so the Kerseys packed pepper spray and a 9 mm handgun. With no cell coverage, a minor injury like a sprained ankle or hypothermia could be serious.

And that's why it was strange when, on the fifth evening, shortly after setting up camp and heading off to collect wood, Vern and Trevor came across a man who looked simply unprepared. He wore army fatigues with a nylon poncho over his backpack. He knelt on the trail, filling a plastic milk jug where water trickled through the rocks, pouring it straight into his mouth. The men exchanged hellos. Vern sensed that the stranger wanted to be left alone, so he kept moving, but just to be safe, as the man entered the Kerseys' camp, where Donelle and Shelby were firing up the stove, Vern lingered on the rocks and listened.

"How you doing?" Donelle sang out. She was vivacious and fit, with a hint of country in her throaty voice.

The man smiled and made a motion to the holster on his hip. "Just to let you know, ma'am, I'm packin'."

Big man! Donelle thought to herself. Her own 9 mm lay on the log in plain view. But as she studied the man's face, he looked less dangerous than hungry, thin in the cheeks, maybe as young as her twenty-two-year-old son.

"How long you been on the trail?" she asked.

"Thirteen days."

"Wow!" she said. "Where did you start?"

He told her he'd walked from Hungry Horse, then spent three days at a lake. Hungry Horse was at least one hundred miles away, a tiny town on the northern edge of the wilderness. She asked the man where he was headed.

"I'm just going to follow the Wall," he said.

Donelle felt her maternal instinct kick in. This was not right. "There's no trail along the Wall," she said, showing him on her map where the trail diverged. "And once you get a little down the trail, there's no camping or fires allowed for four miles."

The man just nodded.

"There's plenty of good places around here," she said, making a welcoming gesture.

"I'm going to keep going."

"But it's almost dark."

"I'll just curl up under a tree," he said with a smile.

"We're going to cook dinner," Donelle said. "We brought way more food than we can eat."

"I'm fine."

"We really don't want to carry it all out with us."

"No, thank you, ma'am," he said.

The man bade them goodbye, and mother and daughter watched him disappear down the trail.

"What if he's some kind of psycho who's going to come back and kill us?" said Shelby.

"Nah," said Donelle. "He just has some things on his mind he's trying to work out."

The next morning a storm blew in, icy rain that soon turned to snow. The Kerseys broke camp and trudged out, chilled to the bone even in their new jackets and fleece. Vern built a fire at lunch. The next day the storm was worse, and the waterlogged family still hadn't reached the trailhead. They spent the seventh night shivering in the tent. Donelle hoped the stranger in his cotton fatigues and surplus poncho had found a place to stay dry.

On August 17, 2010, thirty-year-old veteran Noah Pippin arrived at his parents' home outside Traverse City in northern Michigan for a weeklong visit. Earlier that summer, after nearly three years as an officer with the Los Angeles police department, Noah had quit his job and told his parents, Michael and Rosalie, both sixty, that he planned to redeploy with the military. He said he was going to vacate his LA apartment, haul his possessions to Goodwill, and live out of his car at the National Guard Armory until he could transfer to a unit that was deploying to Afghanistan or Kosovo.

It was an abrupt decision, but not out of character. Noah was already a veteran of three fierce combat tours in Iraq as a Marine and had always seemed most at home among the strict regulations of military life. Many vets can't tolerate the tedium of a civilian existence, and servicemen routinely discard their possessions before tours, then buy new stuff when they return. Nor did it seem strange to Noah's parents that he planned to live out of his car. In 2007, after his honorable discharge, Noah had lived in his Buick sedan in a rest area on the freeway near Camp Pendleton, California, while he covered shifts at Lowe's and gathered letters of recommendation for jobs. No big deal. Rosalie and Mike were thrilled that they had convinced their eldest son to rent a truck and haul his belongings to their house near Lake Michigan. They were doubly thrilled when Noah arrived a day early. He and his dad and his brother Josiah, twenty-nine, unloaded the boxes into the basement. Then Noah announced that he would spend that night in a motel.

"It was just plain weird," said Rosalie, "the beginning of some weird things we did not understand." But like family often does, the Pippins found ways to explain their son's behavior. Noah Pippin had always lived by his own code—of duty, structure, and minimal possessions and attachments. He did not date and had never had a girlfriend or, for that matter, a boyfriend. Noah's father likened the code to that of a samurai warrior. And so it was on this visit. Noah's plan had been to arrive on August 18, and he meant to stick to it.

Despite the curious beginning, it was a wonderful week. The family took their fishing boat and puttered around the lake. (The youngest of the three brothers, Caleb, twenty-seven, lives in Texas and wasn't there.) Noah's weight had ballooned the previous year after a knee injury, and Rosalie was so pleased to see him back in good physical shape, smiling and basking in the northern summer sun. She forgave him for listening to his iPod instead of chatting. "Listen to this!" he said, placing the buds on his mother's ears. Wagner's Ring cycle, as usual.

Eight days after he arrived, Noah hoisted his backpack into a taxi. Mike and Rosalie had offered to drive him to the car-rental office, but he refused. The date was August 25, and he was due in San Diego for National Guard drill on September 10. He did not mention any plans for the drive home. His parents encouraged him to make a vacation of it. The cabdriver snapped a picture of the family, in which Noah looked intensely serene, his arms draped over the shoulders of his mother and brother. They hugged him goodbye and off he went. Minutes later Josiah found Noah's watch—an expensive Swiss Army model—and Rosalie called her son's cell. "Just give it to Josiah," he said.

For the next few weeks they heard nothing, but that wasn't unusual. On September 11, 2010—four days before the Kerseys encountered the stranger at the base of the Chinese Wall—the Pippins' phone rang. It was the sergeant from the California National Guard. Noah hadn't shown up for drill in San Diego. He was AWOL. Did they have any idea where he was?

The Pippins were alarmed. Given their son's strict adherence to his moral code, a scenario in which Noah had intentionally shirked his military duty was nearly inconceivable. After several calls to his phone went straight to voice mail, they began to investigate, discovering that they knew far less about their son than they had imagined.

From the car-rental agency, the Pippins learned that Noah had returned the vehicle just two days after his departure—not in San Diego but at the airport in Kalispell, Montana, more than 1,000 miles shy of his stated destination. Noah had never been to the state or even mentioned it. His phone records showed that on August 30 he had called a pizza parlor near Kalispell. The final call, placed on August 31 at 10:45 a.m., was to a different area code and had lasted four minutes. Mike dialed the number and explained to the man who answered that he was looking for his missing son.

"Dad," said the other voice. "This is your son Caleb."

Caleb's own phone bill confirmed that he had received the call—although his records indicated only two minutes. Caleb had no recollection of it. He sometimes works nights and sleeps during the day, and he remembered a call from Noah that woke him up, but he couldn't be sure it was on the day in question.

That fall, Mike Pippin flew to Kalispell, met with Flathead County detective Pat Walsh, and posted homemade signs around town featuring a color photocopy of a family photo with the handwritten words Missing Veteran and an arrow pointing to Noah. After the Kalispell news aired a story about the disappearance, a hunter named Bob Schall called in. He and his buddies had seen Pippin near the Chinese Wall on September 15 and offered him a cup of coffee, which he had accepted, and a hot meal, which he had declined. Pippin had walked into their camp late that afternoon, a few hours before he met the Kerseys. His bearing was military: "Yes, sir" and "No, sir." The men talked firearms. When Pippin revealed that he was carrying only a .38, a tiny five-shot revolver with a two-inch barrel, Bob Schall let out a hoot. "Well, son, if you come acrost a griz, you better save the last bullet for yourself!"

With Schall's help, Detective Walsh tracked down others who'd seen him. Earlier that same day, a backcountry ranger with the US Forest Service named Kraig Lange had been leading a string of horses up a set of switchbacks near the Wall, on a section of the Continental Divide Trail, which runs from Canada to Mexico, when he came across a man sleeping smack-dab in the rut of the trail. Lange asked him to move aside. "Yes, sir," said Pippin. "I'll take care of it right away, sir."

Surveying the small pack and spartan gear—Lange remembers Pippin wrapped in a poncho or bivy sack, perhaps without even a pad—the ranger asked if Pippin was a through-hiker.

"What's that?" said Noah.

"It was pretty weird," said Lange, who has worked twenty-nine years in the Bob. "I've never seen anyone sleep in the trail." Still, Lange felt no reason to be concerned. "He seemed to be very fit," Lange said. "Not malnourished or at the end of his rope." After they had passed, Lange and another ranger speculated that they'd just met some sort of "Special Forces kid."

The Pippins set up a Facebook page called Have You Seen Noah Pippin? A woman called from Missoula to report seeing a homeless man in fatigues who looked just like Noah. A Missoula cop questioned a look-alike on the sidewalk, but when the man stood up he was six foot three—three inches taller than Pippin. The case had gone cold.

The following summer, his photo appeared on the cover of the weekly newspaper in Missoula, where I live, eighty miles southwest of the Chinese Wall. I could not resist the mystery. I picked up the phone and called Mike Pippin.

Back in Traverse City, the Pippins had spent the long winter looking for clues at home. Noah was a methodical man, and in the wastebasket of the guest bedroom his parents found evidence of his planning: an instruction manual for a GPS unit, a package for a waterproof carrying case for the device, a sales tag for a gore-tex rain jacket, and a plastic bag from a new pair of Magnum-brand "Professional Boots for Tactical Operations."

Mike and Rosalie sifted through Noah's boxes in their basement. They discovered pamphlets about Montana hiking trails that had been mailed to his home in Los Angeles. In his notebook, printed in neat block letters, they found this:

SOUTH FROM HUNGRY HORSE ALONG THE
EASTERN EDGE OF THE FLATHEAD RESEVOIR
TO THE SPOTTED BEAR RIVER. THEN EAST
ON SPOTTED BEAR RIVER (TRAVELING ON
IT'S NORTHERN BANK) UNTIL BLUE LAKE(S) IS
REACHED.

Here was the first confirmation that Noah had not just wandered into the woods but had plotted his hike for weeks, possibly months. On the next page he had written:

WATCH
BINOS
X2 PONCHOS
GPS
COMPASS
X5 HONEY BOTTLES
WATER
BEEF JERKY
FLOTATION DEVICES

A serious wilderness expedition. But it raised questions. How long did Noah expect to survive the Bob Marshall in September on just jerky and honey? And what was he planning to do with flotation devices? Did he mean a personal flotation device—a life jacket? Why would he need more than one? More puzzling was his destination. Blue Lakes is a nondescript waypoint about twenty miles northwest of the Chinese Wall and would not present itself to someone browsing a guidebook or Googling "hike Bob Marshall" or "isolated wilderness Montana." Probably the only way Noah could have learned of the existence of Blue Lakes was if somebody had told him about it. But who?

Other discoveries were just as ambiguous. Another to-do list, scrawled on scratch paper in the wastebasket, included "Return vehicle to Toyota Financial." But Noah had not returned the 2002 Corolla that he still owed a couple thousand dollars on—and which he planned to live in. Instead, he had left it in the lot of an LA shopping mall, where it was promptly impounded and auctioned. The list also included "Close email account(s)." When he was in Iraq, Noah had regularly written his parents from his Yahoo account. If he had been planning to deploy again, why close it?

Months after his disappearance, the Pippins and Detective Walsh were asking the same two questions: Why had Noah walked into the Bob? And where was he now? The simplest explanation was that he had gone hiking, only to be overcome by the elements, a fall, a bear, freezing, or starving. But that didn't explain why he had concealed his plans from his family.

Suicide was a possibility—especially given Pippin's prior military service. While only 1 percent of Americans have served, studies have shown that vets account for 20 percent of the suicides in the United States. According to his parents, Noah had seemed preoccupied when they last saw him. He had canceled his accounts on Audible and iTunes and Steam (a video-game site) and given his mother his Kindle, with its eighty nonfiction books—ranging from de Tocqueville to Noam Chomsky, Naomi Klein to Nietzsche—saying, "I won't need this anymore." It had not struck Rosalie as strange; Noah often gave her his gadgets when he upgraded. But in retrospect his words were ominous. Still, his final known actions did not indicate suicide: Why would a man wanting to die buy all-new gear and plot a hundred-mile hike?

Maybe, then, Noah was still alive. Perhaps he had faked a disappearance and was living a new life, on the streets or in a different country or under a new identity, free of debt and military obligations or some other secret burden he could not share with his family. He was equipped to travel and had last been seen within walking distance of the Canadian border. The Pippins, like any family, clung to this hope, wondering if he had just decided to check out for a while and think things over. His brother Josiah imagined Noah alive and well, and told me, "It will be amusing to hear his reaction to all of this."

·+·

The Pippin home was once a café and boardinghouse for a railroad depot and village that were swept away by a tornado half a century ago. When I visited in October of 2011, fourteen months after their son's disappearance, a homemade sign on the lawn read EGGS $3 DOZ. With a hand-cranked coffee grinder and a woodstove, the house had that comforting smell of plank floors and the old-timey ticktock and hourly yodels of a cuckoo clock. Even with the computers and fax machine, the Pippin home resembled the 1800s as much as the twenty-first century.

In 1988, after stints in Memphis and Berkeley, the Pippins moved to northern Michigan, where Mike landed a job as a pension adviser. They are devout Christians, and Rosalie said the move was partly a retreat from the chaotic and corrupt world around them. "We wanted more control over our children's exposure to people," she told me. "When you see bad influences, you think: Let's not take them into our home." Both Mike and Rosalie had grown up with the television always on. They wanted their boys to be outdoors, climbing trees. They required Noah and his brothers to clean the chicken pens and collect the eggs.

The Pippins created a sheltered haven. Noah was a hardworking kid who tromped miles through the forest to the golf course where he was a groundskeeper. He never so much as sampled a joint. But for Noah, the pastoral idyll was mostly a proving ground for his real passion: the worlds he created in his imagination. With his brothers and friends, the woods became fantastic battlefields for ninjas, warriors, commandos, and space creatures. At night the boys played long games of cover and concealment, searching for one another with flashlights.

Soon enough, Noah discovered the dreaded television and video games. "I had everything at my place he wasn't allowed at his," remembers Patrick McDonnell, one of his closest childhood friends. "Cable TV, video games out the wazoo, freedom of expression, swear words. It was his escape into the world he'd often read about but wanted to experience. He'd spend all weekend at my house, glued to the television in my room, channel surfing and soaking everything in like a sponge."

A big kid, Noah played on the high school football team, but by then he was mining the experience for irony. While he liked the discipline and physical training, what he seemed to relish most—to boast about—was the fact that, in his two years on the squad, the team didn't win a single game.

In 1998, Noah went off to Central Michigan University, a three-hour drive from Traverse City. He changed his major from journalism to philosophy. Noah had chosen to be baptized when he was eighteen, but now, citing Nietzsche and Richard Dawkins, he declared first that God did not exist and then, putting a finer point on it, argued that because the existence of God could never be scientifically proven one way or the other, it wasn't worth debating. Unlike his Christian parents, who tried repeatedly to bring him back to God, Noah was a Man of Reason. After two years, he transferred to Michigan State University for prelaw, a move that his father now thinks was a mistake. "He just didn't fit in," said Mike Pippin. "Noah would like to go running—in a snowstorm—and then he'd come back to the dorms and everyone was sitting there smoking pot." Noah's grades declined, and in the summer of 2002 he left college without a degree.

Pippin was inducted into the Marine Corps on January 22, 2003, just as the nation was preparing for war in Iraq. He joined less for political or patriotic reasons than for the discipline, strength, and adventure it promised, and—above all—the honor. It was a word Noah used often, one he applied not just to his heroes from war memoirs and science fiction but also to the authors—Plato, Darwin, Adam Smith—whose strict adherence to truth had altered the course of civilization.

"In a very Aristotelian sense, he tried to have a good habit," said fellow Marine Aaron Nickols, who described Pippin as principled, deliberate, and intentional. Aristotle tells us that we are what we repeatedly do, and therefore excellence is not an act but a habit. "He never wavered from what he believed," said Nickols. "At all."

Noah shipped to Iraq in 2004. There, in the presence of his fellow Marines, he seemed embarrassed by his doting parents, letting their care packages sit unopened while his comrades jealously imagined the home-baked brownies and local dried fruits inside. In his two tours in Fallujah and one in Ramadi, Noah saw some of the worst fighting of the war, but he didn't speak much about it to his parents. During the thirty-day leave between his first and second tours, he didn't even visit home, choosing to remain in the barracks reading and gaming.

Although aloof, he could be tender with his mother, addressing her as Mutti and Madame Le Goose. From Fallujah he sent chatty emails about care packages ("I gobbled the cherries right up!"), about the family getting a new animal ("A FREAKING COW???!!! . . . LOL! Ohhhh man, I thought we had trouble with the chickens"), and about their mutual struggle to maintain their weight.

On September 29, 2006, during his final tour, Noah was almost killed. While he was manning the turret of a Humvee patrolling Fallujah, an SUV sped out of an alley. "Truck in convoy!" came the warning on the radio, but Noah and his team never even saw it. The SUV detonated, and the Humvee erupted in flame, lifted on two wheels, then somehow managed to land flat. The men were knocked unconscious but quickly came to and leaped from the burning wreckage. Noah was confined to the camp for medical observation but returned to work within twenty-four hours. "It was just a matter of time in my line of work," he wrote to his father. "I've made a full recovery except for my hearing which is pretty much shot. . . . Please don't tell mom cause I know she'll just make trouble for me!"

Mom learned soon enough. "Noah, God saved your life in this last blast and those of your buddies," she wrote. "For the last 4 years, your Dad and I have been asking Him to save your life until your surrender to him. Oh Noah, turn away from your life of self-will!"

But Noah did not surrender. His rejection of his parents' religion bordered on defiance. The dog tags he wore in combat were stamped just below his name and blood type with the word ATHEIST. During one visit home, he told his parents that he had employed the services of prostitutes. He also showed them photos of dozens of Iraqi corpses, the results of his efforts as a mortarman. One night his father told him how they had looked up at the moon above Michigan and realized that Noah had seen the same moon from Iraq, and they wondered what their son was thinking. "The only thing I thought about was that there are people out there who are trying to kill me," Noah laughed, dismissing the chance to confide any more.

"Ever since he was a teenager, he just never liked what we put out on the buffet," said Mike Pippin. "He did not accept our belief that Jesus is the Messiah. It just wasn't for him. I think it's obvious in retrospect that he is well suited to be a soldier or a policeman, and I wasn't that kind of person myself and I found it difficult to recognize."

When I visited the Pippins, they were beginning to accept the possibility that Noah was dead and were combing their memories of his last visit for clues about his emotional state and intentions. As a child he had been diagnosed with attention deficit hyperactivity disorder and medicated with Ritalin, and during his visit it had seemed to Rosalie that his symptoms were returning. As he sat at the dining room table, Rosalie mentioned a new book about the condition, which she suffered from as well. The author proposed that people with attention deficits were gifted in ways not always appreciated by society.

"Being this way is not an advantage," he snapped at her. "I'm defective."

"He was just so hard on himself," said Rosalie. Three days before his departure, at a party at Good Harbor Beach, she tried to spring Noah from his shell by introducing him to a family friend—also a Marine, also a vet. The men debated religion until Noah cut it short. Later he complained that discourse with the Marine had been like wrestling a beanbag. Any time Noah won a decisive point, the man rehashed the same emotional appeal. He inserted his headphones, oriented his lawn chair toward the sunset, and returned to his hardcover, *A House Built on Sand: Exposing Postmodernist Myths About Science.*

Noah simply hadn't been himself that week. "Normally, he would have laid on the couch and I would have scratched his back and he'd tell me the things deep in his heart," said Rosalie. "But this time we just never got to it. He just didn't open up."

Phone and credit card records subpoenaed by Detective Walsh reveal the activities of Noah Pippin's final week in civilization. After leaving his parents' house midmorning on August 25, Pippin ate the next day at a diner in Moorhead, Minnesota, nearly 800 miles away. Late that night, he called a motel in Hungry Horse. The following day he dropped off the car at the Kalispell airport, another 1,000 miles to the west. A taxi shuttled him from the airport to Hungry Horse, a settlement of 934 souls on the Flathead River.

For Walsh, a veteran detective whose father had once been Flathead County sheriff, the records presented as many questions as the clues at his parents' house did. Flanked by such jewels as Flathead Lake, Glacier National Park, and Whitefish resort, Hungry Horse is not a destination but a waypoint, offering little more than two gas stations, two diners, and two motels. Why, after such a deliberate drive west, did Pippin spend five days there? He took meals at the Huckleberry Patch, a tourist magnet that hawks huckleberry jams, pies, syrup, soaps, lotions, and saltwater taffy. He bought groceries—not expedition provisions but casual fare: sandwiches, apples, roast chicken, a couple of cans of Coke Zero. By all accounts Pippin hardly ever drank, yet in three days he bought a bottle of red wine, a bottle of white, a corkscrew, two cans of hard lemonade, and a premixed screwdriver. He placed calls to three credit card companies. Pippin purchased food in Hungry Horse each day between August 27 and 31, but he didn't check into the Mini Golden Inns until the 29th. Where had he spent the first two nights? Detective Walsh canvassed the other motels, with no luck.

On the morning of August 31, Pippin left without checking out, leaving behind three pairs of pants, a laptop case, a sheet of camouflage netting, and car chargers for his cell phone and laptop. His computer has not been found. From the menu at Elkhorn Grill, where the most expensive breakfast item is $9.95, he racked up a bill of $23.00. Was Noah with another person? Walsh couldn't find any waitresses who remembered him. At 10:45 a.m., Noah placed the lost call to his brother. And there the paper trail ends. After that, if what he told the Kerseys is true, he walked sixty-four miles on a dirt road to the Spotted Bear trailhead, then another thirty miles to the Chinese Wall, where he was last seen fifteen days later.

Through the long winter and into the spring of 2011, as authorities waited for snowmelt to allow a search, a few clues trickled in. Then, in August, a Boy Scout troop discovered a shirt stuffed into a tiny creek, just a few miles south of where Pippin was last seen. Three weeks later I boarded a Chinook helicopter at dawn, along with twenty members of the Lewis and Clark County search-and-rescue team, the sheriff himself, three deputies, one ranger, one TV reporter, and a cadaver dog. Rosalie Pippin had posted on Facebook, "The sheriff asked us to ask any praying people to pray for him and the team 4 things: wisdom, discernment, guidance, and for A MIRACLE!"

We flew low beneath the rain clouds, meandered between the forested flanks of Moose Creek, then topped over a grassy ridge and saw it—the Chinese Wall—cresting overhead like a tsunami. We found the shirt within an hour and called for the dog, who arrived with her handler, a man with a potbelly and a gray walrus mustache. Heavy snow was falling. The dog sniffed the fabric without interest and lapped water from the stream. "If sheeda got a scent of cadaver, sheeda lay down, or sat," the handler said mournfully. A deputy extracted the shirt. It could have been there for years, having grown a pelt of green moss. By now three inches of snow covered the forest floor, wildflowers bending beneath the load. "That's what the good Lord sent," said Sheriff Dutton, "so we can know what Noah went through."

The next morning was sunny, and we broke into teams and combed the forest and boulder fields. "Thousands of hidey-holes out there," said someone. If Pippin were injured or hypothermic or starved—or suicidal—he could have crawled into any one of them and died. Then again, if he'd walked fifteen days debating whether or not life was worth living, this place—if anything—might have convinced him that it was. I belly-crawled into a cave and probed its corners with my flashlight. Maybe he was sitting on a beach in Zihuatanejo.

The foul weather prevented the searchers from reaching the spot where the trail left the wall, and ultimately the shirt could not be identified as Pippin's. Bones pulled from caves were animal.

In October, a few weeks before the search team could launch a second mission, the Pippins dropped a bombshell.

"We've asked the searchers to stand down," Mike told me. "We can't for the moment tell you anything more about it, which is the same thing we told the deputies. We're going to investigate it ourselves and find out if it's actually credible. We've got information that Noah may be alive."

In April 2004, Noah Pippin and Charlie Company, First Battalion, Fifth Marines, arrived in Fallujah just days after insurgents ambushed four American contractors, mutilated and burned their bodies, and dangled them from the Euphrates Bridge. The Marines fought a month of intense urban warfare. "It was gruesome," said Major David Denial, Pippin's platoon commander. "You'd kill people, and the dogs would come eat them at night."

By all accounts, Noah Pippin was a good Marine. "He was very quiet and always could be relied on to get the job done," said Gunnery Sergeant Tracy Reddish, who years after retiring is still called Gunny Reddish by his men. Trying to piece together Pippin's life in Los Angeles and at Camp Pendleton, I'd flown to California to meet with Reddish and other members of his platoon. Whether charging an enemy position or scrubbing the toilet, Pippin never questioned an order. He was so averse to getting in trouble that when the men went out for beers in Oceanside in civvies, and were required to wear a flat-bottomed shirt or tuck their tails, Pippin did both.

Pippin's respect for rank approached meekness. One time a senior Marine throttled Pippin with a leghold until his face was bright pink, and as the others hollered for Pippin to fight back, he gasped that he wouldn't strike a corporal. His buddies determined that at 220 pounds he resembled a huge panda, and called him Man Panda. When Pippin revealed a fanatical love for Imperials, the cinnamon candies in MREs, his nickname evolved to Manda, the Elite Imperial Guard.

Although his gentleness invited teasing, it also won respect and affection. Adam Padavic joined the Corps when he was just nineteen, a kid from a small town in Illinois who wanted to be a cop, and he remembers Noah as one of the only senior Marines who didn't scream at the rookies or even raise his voice. "If you had a problem, you could go talk to him," said Andrew Chavez, another grunt from Charlie Company. "He treated us like a big brother, looking out for us. He'd notice if someone was getting upset, and he'd say, 'Calm down, it will be fine.'" Noah never drank, smoke, or chewed. In his free time at Pendleton, always struggling to maintain his weight, he would sometimes pack his gear and hike solo through the hills.

In February 2005, Pippin arrived for his second tour with Charlie One Five, in Ramadi, another insurgent stronghold seventy-seven miles west of Baghdad. The 215 men were housed in bunks at Camp Snake Pit, a long brown stucco barracks. Their mission was to drive convoys into the hostile city and capture or kill suspected terrorists. "Every house was considered unfriendly," said Reddish. "We went in with arms loaded, took over the house, made sure nobody was a threat, moved them all to one room, broke down as soon as possible, and got out of there."

Sometimes they found bad guys with guns and bombs, sometimes women and children huddled and wailing. Each day, Noah and his fellow Marines loaded into Humvees and trucks and motored toward town, knowing that at any second they could be blown sky-high. Charlie Company would eventually hit thirty-eight improvised explosive devices. "Ramadi was like the Wild, Wild West," said Reddish. "There was a shootout damn near every day." The Marines were required to haul the corpses of insurgents they had killed into vehicles for transport to a base, to be identified and then handed over to Iraqi authorities. "Noah was straight-faced," says Padavic. "He didn't share emotions. He didn't talk about killing or how many he'd killed."

The Marine whom Noah admired most was Matthew Trigo, who had proven himself an exceptional warrior in his first two tours. The letter of commendation for his Bronze Star reads like a Hollywood script. Trigo takes out three enemy vehicles with his Mk 19 automatic grenade launcher. Trigo rushes into gunfire and digs a position with his folding shovel, then decimates the enemy. Trigo loads a single round into his machine gun and from 750 yards kills the driver of a moving car. But Trigo takes no credit for running into gunfire to drag his brothers to safety.

"They were lifted by the Holy Spirit," he told me. "I was just an ambassador. Best case: I save you. Worst case: I'm with my Father in Heaven." A wall of muscle with a kind face and thin-rimmed eyeglasses, Trigo is a master of nine martial arts disciplines and was something like Charlie Company's resident mystic. When he learned that Noah was estranged from his Christian upbringing, Trigo tried to coax him back into the flock.

"Bring on your Nietzsche," Trigo told Pippin. "Give it your best shot. I'm just a Neanderthal Marine, but I've got truth and light on my side."

"You're my hero," Noah told Trigo. "I want to be like you."

"You can't be nice to me and then hard on yourself," said Trigo. Like Pippin's family, Trigo had noticed Noah's tendency to be self-critical. He told Noah, "I've lied, I've cheated. I kill men. I'm no better than you. Anything that's awesome about me is awesome about you."

Although most men in the platoon were not practicing Christians, Trigo led them in prayer. "Lord, unharden Noah's heart. No man can hear the prophecy and be unchanged. Intellect without love is educated barbarism."

When I asked if his brother Marines resented his preaching, Trigo seemed surprised.

"They love me," he said. "They love me."

Of all the war stories told by Pippin's fellow Marines, none was more devastating than what happened on June 16, 2005. It was about 115 degrees, and Adam Padavic climbed aboard his Humvee, lead vehicle, rear right seat, same as always. He had carved his initials on the steel bench with his pocketknife. Erik Heldt was up in the turret. As the engines roared, John Maloney opened the door. Maloney was Charlie Company's veteran captain, and the men loved him. "The best man I ever knew in my life," said Reddish. He was what Marines called a mustang—a grunt who'd risen to officer by proving himself. He wasn't some ROTC boy who had arrived in Iraq with a textbook, thinking he could tell combat vets what to do. "The best CO we ever had," Padavic told me one day at his apartment in Los Angeles. "He really loved us."

That morning, Maloney sent Padavic to another rig. "I'm riding here today," he said.

They made enemy contact at the first house they stopped at. They were out of the vehicles, up on a rooftop, taking fire, returning it. Then back to the convoy to pick up the Army engineers. On the way back to camp, there was an explosion. The men leaped from the vehicles and broke into a house, blasted through the windows, emptying their magazines into the streets, hot brass shells flying into their faces. "Fucking chaos," says Padavic. Suddenly Gunny Reddish appeared: "Where are the body bags?" Padavic didn't understand. Why did they need body bags for these guys? "It's not for them. Maloney's been hit." An IED had ripped open the fuel tank, the Humvee exploding and flipping in a storm of flame. When the fighting subsided, Reddish ordered his men away and brought in another platoon to hoist up the wreckage to find Heldt. He wanted his men to remember their brothers as they were in life.

As Padavic told me this story, he asked if I minded stepping outside with him so he could smoke. "I get kind of emotional," he said. We stood beneath the eucalyptus trees and hazy LA sunshine. He stubbed out his cigarette and tossed the butt. "Cap Maloney was a big guy," he said, his voice cracking. He held his hands apart as if he were measuring a fish. "His body bag was only this big."

That afternoon, Camp Snake Pit was miserable. Maloney and Heldt were dead, and three others were critically burned. Gunny Reddish remembers Pippin and Padavic sitting on the porch, a look of shock and grief on their faces. Reddish didn't see the good in sitting around and moaning about it all day. What was done was done. They needed to take their minds off it. "Get your gear," he ordered. "We're going after the bad guys."

Noah Pippin was the first man on the truck.

As I waited to hear from the Pippins about the mysterious development, I traveled around Montana tracing Noah's known whereabouts. Those who had seen him last were struck with a similar impression that he was saddled with a great emotional burden. I spoke with Bob Schall, who arrived at my Missoula home in jeans, a snap-button dress shirt, and a weathered Stetson. He recalled that after Pippin drained his coffee and walked off, Schall said to his friend, "That boy's got some problems." A few hours later, as the embers burned red, his friend turned to him and said, "You're right."

Schall figured the Marine had been through a divorce or something like that and was wandering the woods to clear his head. "That's what I did after my divorces," said Schall. "All of them!"

I drove to Hungry Horse from Missoula. It was a crisp fall day, cottonwoods bursting yellow on the banks of the river. At the Mini Golden Inns, Noah's last stop, the proprietor, Kodye VanSickle, showed me Room 59, where the aquamarine carpets and blond furnishings and framed watercolors delivered on the marquee's promise of Squeaky Clean Rooms. VanSickle was a delicate woman with gray hair, glasses, and sparkling eyes.

"He looked like he was carrying way too much," she told me. "His exterior being was silent, like he could not express it to anyone."

"What was on the interior?" I said.

"He was suffering," she said. "The kind you have to do alone. He was searching for that connection that feels whole. I saw a dark shadow over his being."

"Do you think he's alive?"

She paused as if communicating with the ether.

"I'm not feeling that at all." She cupped her breast. "I have a prayer heart—he's in there. He's one I wish hadn't gotten away."

She looked me in the eyes. "You were meant to be here, too." Ms. VanSickle placed a medallion in my palm. Saint Jude. "The saint of impossible causes," she told me. "You're going to need this."

From Hungry Horse I crossed the Rockies to Great Falls and looked up the Kerseys. "Not a day goes by when I don't think about him," Donelle told me as we sat in their living room more than a year after their encounter. "If I would have known that I was the last person to see him, maybe I could have convinced him to stay." Vern Kersey has had a recurring dream in which he is searching for Noah in the woods. Finally he comes upon a tiny ramshackle cabin. He pushes open the door. Hunched over a rickety table, eyes hollow and face drawn with emaciation, like a ghost, is Noah Pippin.

It wasn't until late October that Noah's parents filled me in about their new development. They had received a phone call from a man named Miguel who told them he had read about Noah's disappearance online. He said he had a niece who tended bar at the Loco Gringo in Tijuana. She had a boyfriend, a big American with a shaved head who looked just like the pictures Miguel had seen of Noah. Miguel said he had a friend named Carlos from the National Guard who had helped buy the man a fake passport. Miguel wanted to know if it could be Noah, and if so, was it safe for his niece to be dating this man. Was he a killer? Rosalie said that her son was not dangerous. Miguel said he would call back.

A month later, a credit card company called looking for Noah. Rosalie explained that he had been missing for more than a year. The agent said, "Well, someone's been using this card." The account had been opened at a department store in Iowa on August 15, 2010, two days before Noah had arrived at his parents' house in Michigan. Someone had been making purchases with the card—and paying it off—as recently as March 2011. The Pippins asked to see the statements but, maddeningly, were told that only Noah himself could request information about his account.

The Pippins were cautious but elated. Regaining hope that Noah was alive, the family was determined to respect his privacy, which was why they decided to investigate the lead themselves instead of going to the police. Mike Pippin canceled his upcoming trip to canvass small towns in Montana and planned a visit to San Diego instead. For the first time in a year, the Pippins believed they were within reach of finding their son.

·+·

Noah Pippin returned from Iraq in 2007 to a nation that was largely indifferent. "America is not at war," said Gunny Reddish. "America is at the mall." When the war began in 2003, 74 percent of Americans believed it was worth fighting. By the time Noah returned, that number had dropped to 33 percent, where it has remained ever since. An Iraq vet can surmise that two of three people he encounters don't consider his sacrifice worth the trouble.

"You come back to this oblivion," says Reddish, "and people don't even care that you're in a bad way, that your friends had to be identified from a dog tag in their boots. They say, 'You did a great job. Now, how much money do you owe me this month?'"

A few weeks before his discharge, in March 2007, Noah visited home, and his parents threw him a twenty-seventh birthday party. Noah "has learned that he is more anxious than most in social situations and has a tendency toward paranoia and obsessive thinking," Rosalie wrote to a friend at the time. "Yesterday he described to Josiah that his 'demons' are beginning to come back (i.e. depression, anger, anxiety, etc.) and he lightly told Josiah it's time for him to leave."

"He looked war-weary, subdued, and overall just tired, like many vets I've seen since," wrote his friend Patrick McDonnell, who was preparing to deploy to Afghanistan. "It may have been a combination of his experiences overseas and the amount of growing up since we last saw one another, but I could tell at least a little part of my childhood friend wasn't there in his eyes anymore."

When Noah returned to Pendleton, his closest buddies had been discharged. "The Marines are allowing him to stay in the barracks until April 21 but he does not know what he's going to do after that date," Rosalie wrote to a military support group. "Does anyone in your group have experience with how to help a son transition to civilian life?"

Noah left the Marine Corps with very little savings. After living in his car for six months, he was hired by the LAPD. His training salary didn't cover all the gear and uniforms, and the California National Guard was offering a hefty incentive. For a Marine, the National Guard was a step down, but he needed the money. "I ended up joining the army (lol)," he wrote to Marine Andrew Chavez, "and they gave me a $20,000 dollar bonus in '07 for going into the National Guard (lol) as an infantryman."

While he waited for the payment, Noah lived in his car in the alleys near the police training center. With his military background, he was made a squad leader. But the honor only caused more anxiety: it was stressful enough to arrive an hour early to use the shower. The cadets teased him because sometimes he smelled like a homeless man; they didn't realize he actually was one.

Eventually, Noah rented a single bedroom in the back of an old house on the southern fringe of Koreatown, on a barred-window stretch of Crenshaw Boulevard, one of the city's busiest arteries. The landlord lived in front and spoke no English. Noah shared a bathroom and kitchen down the hall with some other cops. He furnished his room with an air mattress, a single chair, a television, and a small table for his laptop. There was no closet, and his few possessions were scattered in boxes on the floor. For the first year or so he ate out or ordered in, until his parents shipped him a Crock-Pot from the Sears catalog.

As a probationary officer, Noah was assigned to the crime-ridden Southeast District. Figueroa Street is dotted with storefront churches, payday-loan merchants, places to send money south of the border, and ratty motels. At night it's populated by streetwalkers and crack dealers.

Noah felt like he was arresting people for the same misdemeanors day in and day out, only to see them resurface a few days later. Instead of fixing a busted system, he was enabling it. Noah complained that some of the officers who trained him were lazy. They would respond to a call at the end of their shift, and if the senior officer didn't want to do the paperwork, he would tell the citizen to file it in person at the station. "Noah is a black-and-white guy," said his father, "but the LAPD was gray."

Although he expressed his unease to his family, Pippin's code of honor prevented him from publicly speaking ill of his fellow officers. "In Noah's background and way of thinking, he still owed loyalty to his peers no matter what they did wrong or how those things affected him," said his brother Caleb. "That's an idea and pressure that was placed on him mostly due to his military background."

Just a few months into his rookie year, Noah was called up by the National Guard to deploy to Kosovo, but he tore his ACL during a training exercise. After surgery, the Army paid for a physical rehabilitation program in Los Angeles and gave him a desk job in a downtown skyscraper, in the security office of the Army Corps of Engineers. His boss, Jeffrey Koontz, is an avuncular, bald-headed man who patrols his windowless cubicle in combat fatigues and fields phone calls by punching the speaker button and hollering, "Sergeant Major!" When Pippin arrived for his first day on the job—also bald, also in fatigues—everyone joked that Sergeant Major had hired his own son.

"I'd be proud to have Noah as a son," said Koontz. He remembers Pippin as quiet, earnest, and unfailingly polite. "We had some great conversations," says Koontz. "He was a really deep thinker, very analytical, not a typical cop."

Noah commuted in camo in his Corolla, up Crenshaw and across Wilshire. By parking in the five-story garage, it was possible for him to spend a day at work without ever going outside, or for that matter looking out a window. He arrived with his PT bag and worked out in the building's gym. Sergeant Major often invited Pippin to lunch, but Noah declined, typically eating from a brown bag by himself in the break room. He never talked about the war;

Koontz never even knew he'd been in Iraq. A woman in the office found the stoic GI dreamy and would alter her route to linger at his desk, but he never so much as asked for her phone number.

Near the end of 2009, when Noah left the skyscraper, Sergeant Major offered him a permanent job. For several months he left follow-up messages, but Pippin never called back.

·+·

Noah Pippin never sought treatment for, nor was he diagnosed with, post-traumatic stress disorder. He once told his parents that he was worried that any sort of medical treatment—even for the hearing loss he suffered— might rule out future jobs in the military or law enforcement. Nonetheless, Pippin's behavior after returning from Iraq appears to fit the symptoms, which often include the reexperiencing of combat, avoiding intimacy, and withdrawing from friends and family. Once during training for night-combat operations with the LAPD, in which he and his fellow cadets had to identify paper pop-ups as either threats (a man with a gun) or civilians (a woman with a baby), Pippin screamed "Contact front!" and in a barrage of cursing emptied his magazine at the target. In an exercise where cadets practiced arresting one another, Pippin discovered a gun on his "suspect" and knocked the handcuffed man face-first onto the ground. He was reprimanded but deemed fit to continue his training. I asked an LAPD spokesman if Officer Pippin had ever been evaluated for mental health issues, and he told me that such personnel records were confidential. Pippin's commander at the National Guard said that Pippin and all guardsmen were regularly evaluated for physical and mental health.

Diagnosed or not, the war has taken its toll on the men of Charlie One Five. During my visit with Gunny Reddish, he told me that seven years after Ramadi he still gets phone calls, sometimes in the middle of the night, from young men—scared, drunk, about to do something stupid. He starts out gently, telling them to put down the bottle, take a deep breath, calm down. If that doesn't work, he reverts to drill sergeant, tells them to shut the fuck up right now or he's driving halfway up the state of California to put his boot in their ass.

Pippin never made such calls to Reddish or any of his other Marines. Indeed, several living in the LA area had not even known that he was close by.

Pippin told his mother that some of his Marine buddies would get together, but because he'd gained so much weight after his injury, he was embarrassed to meet them. He became isolated. Noah did not keep in touch with his classmates from the academy, nor did he become close to officers from the Southeast Precinct.

When Pippin wasn't at work or the gym, he was at home, reading books, playing video games, and sinking deeper into his own mind. When I learned from his brother Josiah that Noah used the online moniker "benx6444," I searched and found a long record of his writings and activities—perhaps the most revealing history of a man who kept largely to himself. He logged hundreds of hours gaming, his favorites being Warhammer 40,000: Dawn of War (106 hours), Command and Conquer (89 hours), and Jagged Alliance (68 hours).

The site he apparently visited most was the Skeptics Guide to the Universe, a forum dedicated to "the paranormal, fringe science, and controversial claims from a scientific point of view." In the year leading up to his disappearance, Noah posted there 2,774 times. He indulged his passion for speculation and history and philosophy: "You wake up on a stretch of beach outside of Rome [in 10 BC]. How do you earn your living? What could you contribute? Build? Manufacture? What would be the easiest profession to take on/make to become rich?"

On a site dedicated to the Austrian economist Ludwig von Mises, Noah split the sort of hairs generally reserved for graduate seminars:

> Is there really a contradiction here between what Mises says about the impossibility of planning an economy due, in large part, to the unpredictable nature of human action and Mises's seeming implicit assertion that he has, according to the reviewer, "a tool for distinguishing one event from another, and for judging when they are the same."

In the Skeptics' forum, Noah showed increasing cynicism toward his profession. He quipped, "Cops = glorified janitors." In a thread offering the glib career advice "ROTC > Full Scholarship > Job > $$$$ > Live somewhere else > Shoot people," benx amended the final line to "Order other people to shoot people." To a young man seeking advice on love, benx replied, "It doesn't exist."

Pippin's online writings reveal a man slipping into the rabbit hole of his own mind. Instead of tackling the big questions, Pippin wove ever more complicated defenses of the smallest points. On GameSpot.com, he employed his rhetorical gifts to savage a review of a video game:

> Joe Dobson's whiny review of 'Army of Two' isn't so
> much about the game as it is about his POLITICAL
> VIEWS on a subject and how he feels the game treats his
> political views. . . . Dobson can't handle someone else's
> perspective, or an interesting dialogue about the effec-
> tiveness of State Militarys vs Private ones. He's already
> made up his mind, and anyone attempting to even talk
> about this issue without his stamp of approval, or who
> isn't in lockstep with him gets their game shutdown.
> What a clown.

In November 2009, Pippin bought an expensive hunting rifle. Taking it to a shooting range was one of the few activities he remained passionate about. "It's so freakin' cool!" he wrote. "It's not like ordering a burger at McDonalds or buying furniture. When you walk into a firing range, you suddenly become aware that your fellow Man is there with you. It's kinda scary until you look left and right and see that . . . it's cool, ya know? You can trust each other."

He wrote that after mastering his rifle at the range, he might like to try hunting big game like bear, elk, and deer. Another poster mentioned that hunting black bear was illegal in Montana. Sometime thereafter, Pippin requested the hiking pamphlets for Yellowstone and the adjacent Gallatin National Forest. This was the closest link I found between Pippin and the Bob Marshall. But as for the rifle, instead of carrying it into the woods, Pippin left it in the basement of his parents' house.

·+·

Miguel called again in October. He told the Pippins that Carlos's cousin, who was living in the country illegally, and Noah were holed up at a cheap motel in El Cajon, a San Diego suburb. He said that Noah was holding a job in the

States, crossing the border to see his girlfriend. Miguel said that one day, while Carlos's cousin was at work, Noah invited his buddies over for a party. When the cousin returned, everything had been stolen. Since he was living illegally, he couldn't call the police. He was a real hardworking guy, said Miguel, just trying to get ahead, to support his family back in Mexico, and it was a real shame that because of Noah he'd lost everything.

The Pippins grew suspicious and asked Miguel for his phone number, but he declined. They asked if he had a Facebook page, and he said yes. They saw that it had been created that same day. The photo of Miguel was one easily available online. Feeling like they were in over their heads, the Pippins finally revealed their conversations to Detective Walsh, who told them without hesitation that the calls were part of a common scam used to shake down families of missing persons. "I see this kind of thing every day," he said. The phone calls from Miguel ceased.

Walsh also subpoenaed the credit card records. He didn't give much credence to the theory that Pippin was alive and shopping. More likely, someone had found Noah's wallet and had been using the card. As it turned out, the hope offered by the credit card agent was false; what appeared to be recent activity was actually just paperwork blips caused by the transfer of Noah's account from one bank to another.

Then, just as the case seemed to turn cold once again, another witness came forward. In October, Steven Pierce was driving near his home in Kalispell when he heard the story on the radio about the missing Marine. By then, a year had passed since his hunting trip in the Bob. Noah—that biblical name—rang a bell. Pierce called Detective Walsh.

On the evening of September 12, 2010, three days before Noah had last been seen by the Kerseys, Pierce had hauled his trailer along the sixty-four miles of dirt road from Hungry Horse to the campground at Beaver Creek on the Spotted Bear River. He led the horses off the trailer and fed them some hay. He noticed the man at the adjacent site with no vehicle and said hello.

Pierce remembers the stranger as none too friendly. Pippin kept his back turned when Pierce started asking questions and said curtly that he'd hiked in from Hungry Horse. Seeing the fatigues, Pierce asked if he was military, and Noah told him he was a vet.

"You been over in Iraq?"

"Got back a little while ago."

"I was in Vietnam," said Pierce, hoping to break the ice. "Navy."

Noah didn't answer.

"If you're going hiking in these parts, you need a gun," said Pierce. "Do you have one?"

"Yes, sir," he said. "Just a .38."

"That ain't much to stuff in the face of a grizzly when he's chewing on your foot."

"It's all I got."

"Where you from?"

"Southern California."

Pierce surveyed Noah's camp: a one-man bivy tent, a lightweight sleeping bag, a hunting knife, a small backpack, a plastic jug. It appeared to be all his worldly possessions. No provisions that Pierce could see.

"You're obviously not a hunter," said Pierce. "What are you doing out here, anyway?"

Pippin admitted that he'd had some financial problems. The only way to get out from under them, he said, had been to join the National Guard for the signing bonus—which he'd already spent—and now he was locked into more duty. He told the hunter he didn't want to go back to Iraq or Afghanistan. He was adamant about it.

This was a drastic break from what he had told everyone else. Like so much in the case of Noah Pippin, it just doesn't add up. If his financial problems were paramount, his parents, who had often encouraged him to finish college with the GI Bill, would have helped him make the transition. If his chief concern was avoiding a fourth tour, simply remaining in his Guard unit would have afforded him more than a year to figure out a solution. Maybe he felt that he had checkmated himself: by quitting his job, he had no choice but to redeploy, but now twelve days alone in the woods had brought the fatal clarity that he couldn't go back to combat, and neither could he face the shame of having failed to report.

Two things are clear. First, the date was September 12, a full two days after he was legally required to report for drill—a fact that surely weighed heavily on a Marine who valued honor above all. The man who found sanctuary in the rules had, for the first time, broken them. Raised in black and white, saved or damned, he could not help but consider himself one of the defective. Second, as he grappled with these life-and-death decisions, he did so without the parents, brothers, and Marines who loved him.

The two war veterans regarded one another at that campground picnic table.

"Are you AWOL right now?" said Pierce.

Noah wouldn't face him.

Pierce asked again.

"Yes, I'm AWOL."

"That's not good, son," said Pierce. "Marines don't do that shit. We don't cop out on our country."

Noah turned his back and said, "I'm going to bed now."

"There's bad weather coming," said Pierce. "You gonna be all right?"

"Yes, sir."

"You know the trails out here?"

"Yes, sir."

Pierce returned to his truck and brought Noah a couple of granola bars and an old map. When he set out on the trail in the morning, he didn't notice whether or not Pippin was still there.

·+·

Where is Saint Jude when we need him? Kodye VanSickle at the Mini Golden Inns prays the novena to the patron saint of lost causes, of cases despaired of. In the winter of 2012, Pippin's whereabouts were still a mystery. Beset by nightmares, Vern Kersey volunteered himself for the next search mission, sure he could lead them to the right spot. Detective Walsh retired before solving the case, but during his final month as a police officer he went hunting, and of all the grounds he could have chosen, he picked the Spotted Bear River, where he retraced Noah's path; he saw a couple of bucks but didn't take a shot. Gunny Reddish retired too, and when he fielded those midnight phone calls from his men, he was glad he spared them the horror of what lay beneath that incinerated wreck in Ramadi, a vision he was never able to shake. When I left the Pippins in November, they prayed with me, asking for an end to this, hoping that if Noah was alive he might contact them. The war is officially over now, but it wanders our woods, haunts our dreams, and occupies our prayers.

On a Sunday afternoon in Los Angeles, I got a call from Matthew Trigo. I drove north three hours through the high desert and found him in a spacious home with a green lawn, kids on bikes, and afternoon sunshine on the streets. While we talked in his backyard, the distant sun dropping slowly as the hours eased by, his three children crawled onto his lap and he twirled them with his Popeye arms as if they were kittens. Trigo told me he is on disability for his wounds, has trouble holding a job, and doesn't use the phone much. "I'm a believer in being completely present in the moment," he said. If a call distracts him from his children, he ignores it.

"I wish I was still there," he told me. "When you hear another friend is dead, you think: I should be there." I asked how he reconciled the demands of war with the tenets of his faith: Thou shall not kill, and Turn the other cheek. He spoke of the Old Testament warriors, of David slaying Goliath, of Samson destroying a thousand enemies with the jawbone of a donkey. "I'm a hypocrite and a sinner," said Trigo. "But we are redeemed by the blood of Christ."

Across this landscape of believers, Pippin's knell rings in biblical tones. His Father created a Garden, but Noah Pippin walked out of it, then found the fallen world impossible. While Trigo was able to navigate the jagged terrain between Camp Snake Pit and here, Pippin had not found his way home. Trigo told me that the last he had heard from Noah was a few years back, when Trigo agreed to serve as a reference for the police job. He and Noah were messaging, Trigo's wife doing the actual typing, and Noah tapped in the same lines he had used in Iraq. "You're my hero," Noah wrote. "I want to be like you."

"He was searching for peace," Trigo speculated, "and couldn't find it, so he went to wilderness, where there is nothing to rebel against. You can't rebel against nature."

I asked Trigo if the police department had ever called him.

"No, they did not," he told me. "I was waiting for them. I had a lot of good things to say about him."

The Cave Dreamer

When friends from cities come to visit, when they want to know why I've spent my adult life in the Utah desert instead of a sensible town with possibilities for advancement, I no longer send them to the national parks or the famous wilderness. I take them ten miles down the highway to the 50,000 cubic-foot cave that Albert Christensen blasted in the sandstone.

You can't miss it. They've painted the name on the sandstone cliff in glaring white letters the size of cars. HOLE N" THE ROCK, it shouts, and for four dollars you can take a tour. There you'll learn that Albert Christensen and his wife Gladys opened Hole N" The Rock as a diner in 1945, and that he was a "famous artist, sculptor, and taxidermist." She collected dolls and rocks and practiced lapidary. They had a son. They believed in God and lived in a cave.

I moved in 1993 to Moab, a tiny island of trailer parks and junk cars in the unending desert. I had not meant to arrive in Utah as much as I had meant to escape from America, and I came to love Moab for what it lacked. There was no shopping mall or strip of factory outlets, or even a shoe store. It was fifty miles to a movie theater.

But America was following me, boiling over from the cities and spilling into the desert. First motels and fast food, then coffee houses and a movie theater. And over the years, Hole N" The Rock gained a sort of integrity for refusing to budge. Then, a New York luxury travel company unveiled blueprints for "Cloudrock," a thousand-dollar-a-night resort lodge, with hundreds of condos behind a locked gate and a village of trophy homes in the style of the Hopi. My home was about to be seized by the people I'd escaped from, and all they wanted from the place was the scenery. I knew there was something more profound that draws us to the desert, and it was in my attempt to articulate it that I began my long and curious investigation into the home and the lives of Albert and Gladys Christensen.

·+·

If the desert is on the brink of gentrification, nobody said so to the folks at the World Famous Hole N" The Rock House. Oblivious to the cappuccino shacks and time-shares blossoming on the sage flats, the owners offer the same ten-minute cave tour as they did in 1958. Based on the kitschy exterior and the sixteen-year-old girl serving as your guide, you expect something light—fun house mirrors and trapdoors. But right away your guide sets a somber tone, announcing that the home is nothing less than a "memorial to its creators."

"Albert passed away in 1957," she says, as if he were a war hero, "and Gladys in 1974." The first exhibit in the dimly lit cavern is Albert's oil paintings of stagecoaches, Franklin Delano Roosevelt, and a portrait of Jesus called "Sermon on the Mount" that your guide says Albert painted as a gift for his wife. There he is: the savior, with sunlight flooding across his distorted features. "It's Albert Christensen's most famous work," she says. If this is a famous painting, you know of a whole batch of certified masterpieces down at Goodwill. An old man in a US Navy cap lets out an approving grunt.

And then there's the stuffed donkey. It wears a flower between its ears and is coming unstitched in the mouth. It's ugly. "This is Harry," says your guide, "Albert's pet donkey and his first attempt at taxidermy work. Harry helped take out the rock as it was blasted."

Your guide doesn't laugh, or smile, or smirk. She doesn't see anything funny about the stuffed donkey. She has memorized the script and speaks in the bored monotone of a stewardess demonstrating the oxygen masks.

"To my right is a full-grown wild mustang," she continues. "To my left is a mustang colt."

The horses are locked in positions of agonized spasms. Someone behind you stifles a giggle. Then you are led to a collection of dolls, laid out on the bed like little orphans with pleading faces and outstretched hands. "This was Gladys's bedroom, after Albert passed away. It is just as she left it."

It feels like death in there, like snooping around your grandmother's bedroom the day of the funeral, with her figurines and porcelain thimbles still perfectly arranged on the bookshelf, her Bible and *Reader's Digests* stacked on the nightstand. And to make matters more peculiar, this tour guide—is she perhaps the Christensens' granddaughter?—has not only let a bunch of strangers into Grandma's house, she is also reciting a script about the bathtub carved in the rock. "Gladys called it her own private little swimming pool. Please follow me this way."

Why is someone charging four dollars to see this junk? Who were these people? Why did they blast this giant cave in the middle of the desert? Why did they think car tourists would pay to see their dolls and their donkey? Then someone asks the guide the question you were afraid to ask:

"Are you like: *related* to these people?"

"I just work here," she snaps, with a look that says she gets that question all the time and if she hears it again she might just walk off this dumb job. Then she warns you to watch your head on the way out, suggests the sixteen-postcard booklet for sale in the gift shop, and gives directions to Gladys and Albert's graves, just out the front door past the porta-potties.

·+·

"It takes a special person to buy a cave home," realtor Julie Bierschild told the *Salt Lake Tribune* after Erik Jensen did just that. In 2000, Jensen spent most of his life savings to purchase the World Famous Hole N" The Rock House from Gladys Christensen's son, Hub Davis, who inherited the land and business in 1974. When I arrived one day at the cave home, Jensen was wearing shorts and tennis shoes, pushing a wheelbarrow of wet concrete. A cigarette drooped beneath a thick mustache. I'd called ahead and told him I was a writer. Jensen set down the wheelbarrow and escorted me around the grounds, showing me the improvements that were planned, underway, or already completed.

"What we have here is a mining theme," Erik said. "Or Old West. Next week I'm bringing in a stagecoach. And maybe a teepee. I want to give people something to look at, somewhere to walk around and enjoy their experience."

For starters, he'd raised a big American flag and a big Utah flag from the sandstone above the home. The old snack bar building, which housed exactly one soda machine and one ice-cream sandwich machine, was being remodeled and stuccoed "Spanish-style" into a full-service hot dog stand. In the meantime, Jensen had hauled in a Coca-Cola trailer to sell drinks and snacks. He had unrolled a lawn of green sod, installed two fountains, and littered the premises with old mining equipment, iron tools, and horse tack. Later in the day he was driving to Moab to pick up an old mining cart he'd bought at a pawn shop.

"Do you remember how much fun it was the first time you drove a car?" he asked me. "That's how I feel now."

Jensen's voice was gravelly and his skin weathered. He told me he was born in Denmark (he pronounces his name YEN-sen) and moved to Utah as a boy when his mother married a Mormon missionary. Once he turned eighteen, he became an American citizen and served in Vietnam. Since then, he's made a living as a painting contractor.

Jensen thought the place had been somewhat neglected when he bought it. The bathrooms were filthy. Tumbleweeds blew back and forth. So now he was giving it a total makeover. While the new toilets in the new snack bar were under construction, a row of aquamarine porta-potties had been placed in the cactus garden, en route to the gravesite. A few miles up the highway, a new billboard would proclaim, "Tours! Refreshments! Statuary!" Erik's business partner owns a foundry in Salt Lake City where he manufactures concrete lawn statues and furniture; their partnership began when Jensen ordered a pet gravestone for his backyard. As a result, the cliff home has become southern Utah's only outlet for life-size gnomes, gargoyles, and Virgin Marys.

"The car tourists won't buy something real big, like this frog, because it's so heavy," said Jensen, "but they might take home one of the smaller ones, like the turtle. And I think as soon as people in Moab, and in Monticello, find out about this—as soon as the word gets around that we have statues—a lot of people will come down. I mean, you can't get this stuff in Moab. Those lions would look great in a front yard."

The lions lay there wisely, paws crossed before them.

"Look at this table: It took four people to carry it."

Jensen lit another cigarette and told me of his plans for something he called a Shadowbox, a wooden case filled with text and old pictures that would overlook the parking lot.

"I see people pull in, slow down, then leave. That pisses me off. Even if this Shadowbox could save one customer a day, I'd be happy."

And before I knew it he had hired me—I was a writer, after all— to compose the text for the soon-to-be-built Shadowbox. He needed someone who could make the words "properly scripted."

"There will be some money in it for you," he said. "It won't make you rich, but it'll be some cash."

We shook hands on the deal and looked out across the garden of prospectors and angels and the Loch Ness Monster.

"This stuff will last forever," said Erik Jensen.

·+·

When Jensen bought Hole N" The Rock, the sale included everything inside. He invited me into the mobile home next to the cave where he and his family were staying for the summer, and I spent an afternoon sifting through an old trunk of handwritten notes, news clippings, letters from visitors, advertisements, and tour scripts. Before long I had separated the memorabilia into three stacks.

I called the first stack Innocence, and it contained nostalgic evidence of a happy bygone era. There was a photo of Albert with his horn-rimmed glasses and pencil moustache grinning beside an old road sign that read, "Bonafide home of Ol' Moki Al, the Cliff Dweller." In boots and khakis he could have been an archaeologist looking for King Tut's tomb. Another photo showed the girls of Grand County High School's class of 1950 on their senior ditch day, and a hand-typed menu advertised the specials from the summer of '47.

CREAMED—CHICKEN—ALA—KING—ON—
TOAST
LITTLE—PIG—SAUAGE'S—WITH—
CREAMED—GRAVY
CANNIED—SWEET—POTATOES
LAYOR—CAKE
TAILOR—MADE
BY—THE—CLIFF—DWELLER
YOURS—TRULY
A. L. CHRISTENSEN
"JUST—GOOD—FOOD—THAT'S—ALL"

I called the second stack Ambition. Here I found the origins of that reverence that I'd heard on the tour. Hole N" The Rock stationary from the 1950s touted "America's most unique dining room"; Albert was a "Sculptor, Artist, Creator and Engineer" and Gladys an "Artist and Decorator." I found this autobiographical profile scribbled in Albert's handwriting:

> America's most outstanding sculptor . . . the one and
> only artist of his kind, being an accomplished sculptor
> with international acclaim in marble, rock, sand stone,
> or quartzite, any type of stone.

On a pamphlet written by Gladys in 1958—the year after Albert's death—she had scribbled out the word "Diner" on the letterhead and replaced it with "Memorial of A. L. Christensen."

> This marvelous structure was created by the hands of one
> man, A. L. Christensen, my husband. He devoted much
> of his life to the creation of this breathtaking colosal cave,
> our home, and to the art, which occupies its interior . . .
>   The power which the artist possessed is prevelnt in
> all his works. People feel this inspiration of power in an
> instant when they step into this masterpiece of work-
> manship and engineering.

I left the third stack for later and wandered out into the sunshine. I was sensing that the myth of Albert and Gladys as great creators was not just second-rate, but actually untrue. To set the story straight, Erik Jensen suggested I meet Ilene Christensen, the widow of Albert's brother, who still lived just up the dirt road. I phoned her from the office, and asked if she'd answer some questions.

"I don't think they'd want to hear what I have to say," she said, but invited me up anyway.

I plodded up the dirt road and knocked on the front door of a singlewide trailer. A young woman answered and I asked if she was Mrs. Christensen.

"No, that's my mother. She's in the next one up."

Ilene Christensen's mobile home sits in a large dry valley rimmed in by stunning sandstone cliffs that contain Hole N" The Rock. It was a hot summer day, the temperature above one hundred, and when I finally found her, I was happy to be invited in where the air was cool and the swamp cooler hummed. Mrs. Christensen looked to be about seventy years old, and wore a cotton gown and slippers. She smiled without showing her teeth, and her eyes flashed. We sat down at a little kitchen table where a portrait of a Native American hung on the wall. She began by telling me that she had moved to Hole N" The Rock in 1945, when she married Albert's younger brother Leo, who had just returned from the war.

"Leo came out here in 1934 and homesteaded this land. After the war he got a GI loan and opened the diner. Albert helped some, and he was a great cook, but it was Leo's property."

"When did Albert begin blasting the cave?"

"Didn't."

"Excuse me?"

"Leo did all the work," she said. "Albert was just a layabout."

"So what do you think of the story that they tell over there to the tourists?"

Mrs. Christensen paused and twisted her lips, looking for the right word.

"It's bullshit," she announced. "That bathtub that they claim is carved into the rock: it's metal. I saw them build it, then cover it with plaster to make it look like rock."

The story was quickly becoming more complicated than just a man with a dream. Mrs. Christensen told me that in 1945, Leo and Albert came to Hole N" The Rock with their wives, Ilene and her sister Rita. Blasting a single room in the cliff, the brothers opened a roadside diner. While Leo saw to the excavation and the finances, Albert cooked, painted, and sculpted. He also drank. Ilene remembered Albert, during one of his binges, stabbing himself in the throat. By 1949, Rita was fed up, and packed up her children (from a previous marriage) and divorced Albert. Albert then disappeared, leaving Leo to run the business. Ilene could not tell me where Albert was in those years; she didn't see him until 1953 when she and Leo were moving to Moab to enroll their children in school. That was when Albert arrived to take over the diner with his new wife, Gladys Davis.

"He was charming," Mrs. Christensen said of her brother-in-law. "But he was crooked."

She told me that her husband had once owned all eighty acres here, but that when Albert got into financial troubles, her husband deeded him four acres to get a loan. Albert never paid his brother for the land, and in his will left it to Gladys.

"So how did Albert come to own the Hole N" The Rock?" I asked.

"That sits on four acres. The other seventy-six belong to me, and my children and grandchildren. As soon as Albert and Gladys took over, they got into some money trouble. I think he borrowed some money and couldn't pay it back. He was going to lose the business, so my husband deeded him the four acres. Albert was supposed to pay him fifteen thousand dollars for it, but he died."

"And then what happened?"

"Albert willed it to Gladys."

"And Gladys willed it to their son?"

"*Her* son. Albert didn't have any children."

She smiled while my brain gears spun. I recalled that Gladys's son had just sold Hole N" The Rock for three-quarters a million dollars.

"So Albert lost the family land."

She nodded. Her voice dropped to a whisper. "When he and Gladys first met, he drove her and her husband out to California. The three of them went together. Well, the husband died out there. Acute alcoholism is what they called it. They brought the body home, and pretty soon they got married."

I sat there waiting for more.

"Albert was in Leavenworth."

She let that remark hang a while. I suspected she was enjoying this.

"What for?"

"My husband never said." She shrugged. "I heard that he killed a man."

·+·

As much as the memorial tour insisted that life at Hole N" The Rock was all family and God and taxidermy, my research disagreed. Squinting at microfilm in the public library, I found a 1955 story of a prostitution bust in a trailer parked just down the road from Hole N" The Rock. I mailed off a letter to the Federal Bureau of Prisons to see what I could find out about Albert. And I returned to the trunk, where the third stack of memorabilia—the one I called Disillusion—was dwarfing the other two.

In 1952 Albert surfaced in Montrose, Colorado, where Gladys Davis and her husband Hubert owned a motel and a taxi company. On August 20, 1952, with $64.82, Albert founded the Alcoholics Rehabilitation Center of the Southwestern Colorado Rockies. It was a live-in home where men could pay three dollars per night to sober up. A sign out front read, "Your credit is good because if you really want AA you won't be broke long."

Albert named himself President and General Manager; the secretary was Gladys Davis. Just months later, Albert and the Davises took the trip to California that Ilene Christensen had told me about. A letter from Albert's mother, dated November 2, 1952, offers condolences for the "tragedy," and says, "You did as much as you could to get that poor soul on the right track." The trip was meant to dry out Mr. Davis, as Albert fancied himself a sobriety expert. But instead of cured, Mr. Davis found himself dead.

Albert's rehab center quickly ran out of money. He scrawled a rambling ten-page resignation to the city council, then eloped with Gladys to Utah, where they converted to Mormonism. Before bolting from town, he scooped up the thousand dollars in the bank account of his nonprofit corporation, justifying in his letter of resignation: "I may need it some day very bad, even worse than I do now, and believe me folks I am pretty broke because not only my money, but six (6) months time has gone into this work."

In March of 1953, the newlywed Christensens arrived at Hole N" The Rock, where they would spend the remainder of their lives.

·+·

Above all, Albert Christensen thought of himself as an artist. In 1941, before embarking on the blasting of Hole N" The Rock, he set out to create a sculpture of Mount Rushmore proportions in a nearby natural stone amphitheater, which he believed could hold 100,000 spectators. The Unity Monument was to feature the faces of Franklin D. Roosevelt and his opponent in the 1940 presidential election, Senator Wendell Willkie, joined by the forty-foot wingspan of a bald eagle. This would be the reformed convict's tribute to his country. Albert carved an eight-foot scale version of the monument, apparently a model for the larger work. But within weeks of completion of the small sculpture, agents from the Department of the Interior blasted his work into pebbles and dust.

"I believe the eagle was facing the wrong way," was the only explanation offered by Mr. N. F. Waddell of the US Division of Investigation in the wake of the incident. "We have certain rules. We don't give out much information."

Albert never returned to the Unity Monument. Years later, Gladys Christensen wrote that its creation was the beginning of his decline in health, as he had worked on it in twenty-four-hour stretches with only one meal and no breaks. "When they obliterated it, it almost took the very heart out of my husband."

But he pressed on. One of his scribbles read:

> I have a service to render, a service to mankind.
> I am an artist.
> Ladies and Gentlemen, I see beauty in everything. There
> is beauty in every face I look upon—I see some of the
> most beautiful thing that was ever created by God—and
> that is Mankind.

A news clipping from 1955 reported that the grand re-opening of Hole N" The Rock as a gallery of Albert's art was delayed by his hospitalization. He scrawled an article about himself which reported:

> X-Convict A. L. Christensen of Moab, Utah, was found
> in a critical condition Monday of this week, suffering
> from a heart attack dew to over exertion and improper
> diet and the lack of money to buy the prescribed heart
> medications for the thromboses condition from which
> he suffers.

The imaginary narrator, someone named "Buck," continues:

I have only known "Ol Chris a few months but during those few months I can truthfully say I never met a more hospitable person, with menny menny capabilities—always a word for the other fellow. One day he said to me, "Buck, this world is full of kindness and it seems to me a shame these wars and rumors of wars are destructive, and fantastic disillusions [are] fraught about as a result of poor thinking, poor raising, excessive drinking among those who have the whip in the aggressive nations. From my reading I am convinced that those boys doing the fighting, whether Russians, Germans, Chinese, Japanese and definitely our American boys would rather be home raising a pinto bean, a carrot, or what have you, for the sum total of nothing than to be fighting for his life with another human soul.

"It's hell to be an X-Convict because there is always some who are ready to bring the thing to life. I have paid that bill to society. I was told menny times I was an asset to the Institution—but there are a good menny times out in the world that I get knocked to my knees."

In his writings, Christensen emerges less as a builder of pyramids than as a pusher of heavy rocks. Blasting a hole in the rock was the only thing left after his other dreams had failed. When the letter finally arrived from the Federal Bureau of Prisons, I was disappointed that Albert had not been a murderer or bank robber. That might have given him the immortality he wanted. Instead, he had been convicted twice in the early 1930s for violating the Dyer Act: transporting stolen vehicles across state lines. He spent a year in Leavenworth, was released, then broke parole. The next time he served eighteen months. He was hardly even successful as a criminal.

The last item I discovered in his trunk was a heartbreaking 1957 list of his revised ambitions: first, to recover from his "illness," second, to pay his debts, and third, to build fifty deluxe cabins at Hole N" The Rock to keep the business afloat. Weeks later, Albert Christensen died of a heart attack at age fifty-three.

When I returned to Hole N" The Rock to submit my text for Erik Jensen's Shadowbox, the soda trailer was gone. The snack shop had failed after a five-day run, and Jensen had had to scrap the word "Refreshments" from the "Tours! Refreshments! Statuary!" billboard. "We didn't even make enough money to pay wages," he said.

Instead of soft drinks, there were now emus. Jensen brought down a pair of the huge birds from his emu ranch upstate. When I arrived, he was just finishing work on the corral, a rustic fence of thick logs. He thought the animals would give visitors another interesting thing to look at. He read what I'd written for the Shadowbox, approved, and asked if I'd write another blurb about the emus. When I told him I didn't know much about the subject, he dropped a ten-pound copy of *The Ratite Encyclopedia* in my arms.

"Be sure to put in there that we have emu eggs for sale in the gift shop."

Jensen had other new ideas for improvement. He wanted to have the state declare the place a Point of Interest and put up one of those brass historical markers that you see on the highways. When I told them it was probably a long process to get the state to build such a thing, he contemplated, then said, "Maybe I could just have one made myself."

Jensen had new plans for the Spanish-style snack bar building, in whose roof was now installed a mission bell. He knew that the existing gift shop, which sells such items as a Hole N" The Rock shot glass in the shape of a boot, a Deerslayer boomerang, and a do-it-yourself model of a cavalry fort, would not appeal to the new type of tourist coming to Moab, the wealthy people who might stay at Cloudrock.

"These people aren't going to want a twenty-dollar clock for their mansions," he said. The snack bar would instead house an Indian trading post, with high-end jewelry, pottery, and rugs, and would draw a more upscale shopper.

"I've got to raise the bottom line," he said. "As soon as we took over: boom, I upped the price from three dollars to four. Nobody flinched."

As I followed Jensen into the house to get paid, I asked him why he had bought Hole N" The Rock in the first place. He told me that he and his son were driving to Texas to paint an apartment complex when they stopped in Moab for sodas and cigarettes. The town was hopping with spring break bikers and jeepers. "I called my wife and said: Honey, get on the Internet and book us a trip to Moab. It's in our own backyard, and we've never been." A few weeks later, Jensen and his wife and children came to Moab and took a jeep tour and a river float. Then, while drinking beer by the motel pool, he opened the local newspaper and saw an ad for a "Once in a Lifetime Business Opportunity." He dialed the number on his cell phone, and a realtor arrived poolside with a packet of materials.

"The next thing I knew," said Jensen: "Well, here I am."

Jensen wrote me a check and tore it from the ledger. One hundred dollars. Then he said there was one more thing he'd like me to write. He'd noticed that the tour script was a bit outdated. Corny. People sometimes laughed when they weren't supposed to. He asked if I could lighten it up, make it a bit funnier *on purpose*. I told him I'd do it if I could find the time, but already I knew I wouldn't. I couldn't change the script. I liked it too much the way it was.

Jensen's modular home was empty. With summer ending, his family had moved back home to Salt Lake City for school. He told me he was going to stay down all winter to oversee Hole N" The Rock.

"I've put just about all the money I've earned in my life into this," said Erik Jensen. "It better fly."

·+·

Albert Christensen's Unity Monument hides in a sandstone cove, a short drive followed by a short walk from his home. I drove out there at dusk. Thin red clouds stretched out on the horizon. Cars were quiet on the highway. The rock was golden. This was where the reformed convict banged his hammer against chisel, paying tribute to his country, imagining the citizens gathered below to honor their leaders.

More than fifty years later, Albert's artifacts still littered the sandstone slope. A ladder of piñon logs tied with bailing wire lay naked beneath a tree. Short iron bars poked from the ground, remains of the stairs that Albert had climbed, hauling his tools to the cliff.

The faces of Roosevelt and Willkie were gone now, chipped away to featureless blobs. Only Senator Willkie's left ear somehow survived the hatchet. While we hope history will remember our triumphs and wash away our failures, Albert's disappointment had not begun to erode. Sheltered from wind and water, the chisel cuts looked fresh, arranged in a crude outline of the eagle's wings. I reached up and ran my fingers over the cuts, preserved as perfectly as a statue in a museum. A truck rolled silently up the distant highway. The desert was empty and nobody was looking.

The Man Who Would Be Jack London

I

I parked at the visitor's center of Jack London State Park, awaiting the arrival of America's—and the world's—preeminent Jack London impersonator. We'd been telephoning and exchanging emails for six months, and I'd finally flown to San Francisco, rented a car, and driven up to Sonoma County, site of London's Beauty Ranch and the place where in 1916 the author succumbed to a life of smoking, drinking, and hard living—and died at age forty. When a slick pickup glided into the lot, I saw a frame around the license plate that said *Mike Wilson as Jack London*. I knew I had my man.

The Call of the Wild was one of the first books I owned. It sat on the shelf beside four-legged weepers like *Old Yeller*, *The Incredible Journey*, and *Where the Red Fern Grows*. Informal polling among friends who consider themselves well-read confirmed that while just about everyone could identify London as an author of dog books for boys, only the rarest few had, since puberty, read any of his fifty books. Even fewer knew that the bulk of London's work has nothing to do with dogs, or wolves, or any other creature. Jack London churned out novels and essays—at the unwavering rate of one thousand words a day—delving into the turn-of-the-century's most contentious debates: poverty and class injustice; the threat of authoritarianism and the specter of a workers' revolution; Darwinism and eugenics; prohibition and the plague of alcoholism; and the place of that American archetype—the freedom-seeking individualist—in an increasingly industrial and interdependent nation. He was the most successful writer of his era, his handsome mug so widely published in the nascent age of photography that some historians call him America's first celebrity. And while his name remains nearly as iconic as canon standards like Mark Twain or Ernest Hemingway, in my ten years of studying literature I was never assigned a single London book.

In the months preceding my trip to Sonoma's Valley of the Moon, I'd been gulping up his books—most of which, I'd learned, were not regularly stocked at the local bookstore. In them I was finding the origins of three strands of twentieth-century writing. In his stylization of action and pitiless depictions of death and violence, I heard the quintessentially American voice that would come to be called Hemingwayesque, and that a century later echoes in the novels of Cormac McCarthy. London's pugnacious political essays and gloomy futuristic fables seem the blueprint for anti-totalitarian works like *1984*, *Brave New World*, and *It Can't Happen Here*. And his loose tales of countrywide rambling, freight-hopping, and bohemian freedom surely inspired the Beats, who would come fifty years later.

Writing in the *New York Times Book Review*, E. L. Doctorow pronounced London "the most-widely read American author in the world." More than Twain or Hemingway or Melville. Something of a literary footnote in his own country, Jack London is considered an emblematic American author in Japan, Russia, Eastern Europe, and elsewhere. *The Call of the Wild* has been translated into eighty languages, more than any other American work. An Albanian anthology of American literature pictures Jack London along with Mark Twain on its cover. A collection of London stories in Russian sold 200,000 copies in the first printing. On his deathbed, Lenin asked his wife to read him a Jack London story.

But here in America, in lieu of literary acclaim, London gets his picture on a postage stamp and a mall named after him in his hometown of Oakland, California. Once a decrepit port, Oakland's Jack London Square is now, according to its publicity squad, "a dynamic destination buzzing with restaurants, shops, hotels, entertainment, recreation, outdoor markets and special events." For $300, patrons can sponsor a "Wolf Track," a bronze marker laid down in the stone plaza embossed with a personal message—a sort of earthy, Northern California answer to the Hollywood Walk of Fame. (My visit to Jack London Square yielded rows of brightly-painted but vacant shops, the husk of a defunct TGI Fridays, and a scant few Wolf Tracks inscribed with epitaphs like: *Peanut / A giant of a dog / Love Eddie*.) A high school and a youth soccer league also bear London's name, and each year Kenwood Vineyards bottles a "Jack London Series," sporting the author's signature and a drawing of a wolf. The grapes are grown in Valley of the Moon, on the former site of London's ranch.

Shunned by the elites, Jack London's legacy has been left to a ragtag army of hobbyists, autodidacts, marketeers, middle-tier academics, the self-published, and fanatics. Which pretty much explains what I was doing in a Sonoma parking lot waiting for a fifty-six-year-old Jack London impersonator, original composer of Jack London-related songs, author and publisher of a book called *Jack London's Klondike Adventures*, and not least of all, the 2005 Jack London Man of the Year, as decreed by the Glen Ellen, California-based Jack London Foundation. When I'd written to see if I could catch one of his shows, he replied: "No, unfortunately, at least as of this time, there are no Jack London performances scheduled for either of those dates; that is why I am available. So, if you don't mind, I will come as Mike Wilson."

I guessed I was lucky to get any time with him at all. Nonetheless, when Wilson stepped out of the truck as his mere self, I felt a pang of disappointment. Instead of the trademark costume—riding boots, white suit, a Stetson—he wore jeans, a tie-dye t-shirt, and the kind of glasses that get darker under bright light. It was September, a sunny and dry California morning, the grasses brown and the trees not yet turning. I'd flown out from Brooklyn where I was hustling to make it as a freelancer. Wilson pumped my hand, called me buddy, and said it looked like I'd worn the right kind of shoes for the hike.

"Betcha don't see anything like this where *you* live," he said with a chuckle. Then he pointed up at a eucalyptus grove on a hill where we were headed, and said, "Unlike Jack, I actually knew what the country out here was all about. You know why Jack ended up here, don't you? It was a woman, buddy. Shit, isn't it always?"

Mike Wilson has been impersonating Jack London at schools, Masonic lodges, and historical festivals for eighteen years. He once performed for 1,500 children in a single day, and he was hired by Disney to consult on a movie version of *White Fang*. I asked when his next show was, and he said he didn't have any confirmed just yet. This struck me as odd, considering the busy schedule he'd alluded to. Wilson seemed to sense my apprehension.

"Because of the Jack London thing, I've become a really serious writer," he told me, throwing back the last of his coffee and setting the travel mug in his truck. "I used to just write articles, probably like you do, to make money. But in '94 I stopped doing hackwork."

He asked if I was in good shape, and when I nodded, we started out along the asphalt, the last patches of dew vaporizing as the morning shadows receded. "Now I write what I want," he said. "That's why I keep up a job as a hardware store manager."

2

After twenty-five years without reading Jack London, my interest was sparked not by his own books, but by *Sailor on Horseback*, Irving Stone's lurid 1938 biography. As Stone tells it, London's life was as romantic and ruggedly American as any novel ever written. He was born poor in San Francisco in 1876 to an unwed spiritualist. His father was most likely an itinerant astrologist who never fessed up to paternity. Jack grew up in the crushing poverty of the Oakland slums, quitting school to work in a cannery at age thirteen. By fifteen he was a regular at the waterfront saloons, had bought a sloop called the *Razzle Dazzle*, and was cruising the bay as an oyster pirate. London shipped out to Japan on a seal-hunting ship at seventeen, worked in a jute mill and as a coal shoveler, then at eighteen traversed the country on freight trains, serving a month in a prison camp in upstate New York for vagrancy. Convinced that hard labor would kill him, London completed high school in a single year, and then enrolled at the University of California at Berkeley. He was proclaimed the "Boy Socialist" for his soapbox oratory at Oakland City Hall Park. But Jack had already outgrown the college campus: "The life there was healthful and athletic, but too juvenile," he would later write. "I had bucked with big men. I knew mysterious and violent things." After running out of money during his second semester, Jack quit college and steamed north to prospect for gold, returned home empty-handed, now determined to become a writer. In 1903, at the age of twenty-seven, he wrote *The Call of the Wild*, for which he was paid a total of $2,000; the book brought immediate worldwide fame and over the next century would sell millions of copies.

In the span of the next fifteen years, London wrote fifty books and hundreds of magazine pieces. He lived undercover in the East End of London to write *People of the Abyss*, a study of poverty and a critique of industrial capitalism. He covered wars in Japan and Mexico, and the San Francisco earthquake of 1906. Twice he turned down offers from Eugene Debs to run as vice president on the Socialist ticket. He divorced his first wife and married a free-spirited older woman named Charmian Kittredge whom he called "Mate-Woman."

Disenchanted by his own success, in 1907 London attempted to quit the limelight. He designed and built a boat, the *Snark*, for which he planned a seven-year voyage around the world. The crew he'd enlisted turned out to be incompetent, so Jack taught himself to navigate along the Mexican coast before raising the sail for Hawaii. The *Snark* got as far as Australia before Jack came down with a rare tropical illness and had to cut the trip short.

Back in California, London continued to write his daily thousand words while pursuing his grandest plan yet: an agrarian utopia, applying sustainable and organic techniques to raise grapes, hogs, and other crops. The unemployed were welcome to hammer or plow in exchange for room and board. Around a grand dining table of writers, artists, statesmen, sailors and hobos, London led fiery debates on philosophy and agriculture and art and politics. He began construction of Wolf House, a mansion built of local volcanic stone and redwood timbers, which he predicted would stand for a thousand years. But after three years of building, on the eve of completion, Wolf House burned to the ground. Scientists would later blame the spontaneous combustion of turpentine-soaked rags, but at the time London suspected sabotage by a political enemy or an ungrateful worker.

Jack was heartbroken. His drinking worsened. His muscled body sagged. He could not kick the kidney disease he'd acquired in the South Pacific. In 1916, Jack London died of uremic poisoning—kidney failure—at the Beauty Ranch. In *Sailor on Horseback*, Stone describes the death as suicide: "On the floor of the room [the doctor] found two empty vials labeled morphine sulfate and atropine sulfate; on the night table he found a pad of paper with some figures on it which represented a calculation of the lethal dose of the drug." Stone's version seemed to be foretold in the novel *Martin Eden*, in which Jack's autobiographical hero, so disgusted with the bourgeois world that has accepted him, flings himself from a ship cabin window and sinks to the ocean bottom. In his memoir of a life of drinking, *John Barleycorn*, London obsesses over death in hallucinatory chats with "the noseless one."

But modern-day London aficionados are quick to point out that Irving Stone was a liar. His book was so riddled with error and exaggeration that after its first printing the publisher changed its classification from Biography to "Biographical Novel." Still, the debate over Jack's death fuels the cottage industry of Jack London hagiography.

The epicenter is Sonoma County, home of the State Park and headquarters of the Jack London Foundation. The group was founded in 1974 by Russ Kingman: advertising executive, proprietor of the World of Jack London Bookstore and Research Center, and a man acknowledged in his lifetime as "the foremost collector of Jack London books and artifacts." In his self-published 1979 *A Pictorial Biography of Jack London*, Kingman debunked Irving Stone's suicide theory:

> Jack had taken morphine as any patient would who
> had renal colic. It was highly possible that in the throes
> of his terrible suffering he had taken extra doses of the
> morphine . . . It was possible that the extra morphine
> was a contributory factor, but the coma was induced by
> retention of bodily poisons his inoperable kidneys could
> no longer release.

(Although widely regarded as the most accurate biography, the book is currently in print only through a publisher in the Czech Republic.)

In the decade since Kingman's death, his protégés have carried the torch. In a post on the Foundation's website called, "A Comparative Study: How Jack London's Death Was Depicted by Various Biographers," the author reasons: "I do not believe it is necessary to calculate an overdose. The easiest action would be to take a large amount. I believe that without any hard evidence presented by any biographer that no one should claim to know that Jack London committed suicide." Joining the chorus is Jack London International, a bilingual website whose hosts describe themselves as "a group of German Jack London aficionados and experts, along with direct descendants of Jack London and other members of Jack London's family." An essay by Reinhold

Wissdorf called "Suicide? Nope!" recounts the author's pilgrimage to Beauty Ranch, where he wept at Jack's grave, and after viewing London's death certificate, determined that the biographies he'd read were lies. And then there's the impersonator Mike Wilson, who runs his own Londonalia site. "His death certificate states that he died of uremic poisoning," Wilson writes bluntly. The word suicide is not mentioned.

3

"A lot of people who don't know any better consider this one of Jack's great follies," said Mike Wilson, as we passed into the shade of a eucalyptus grove that London planted a century earlier. "Actually it was common sense. They say that if you're going to grow trees for lumber you shouldn't plant them so close together. Jack *knew that*, but the people who criticize him don't."

Wilson explained that the trees were grown not for lumber but for pier pylons, and he went on to differentiate between the two camps of Jack London readers: the "academians" who just want to put Jack on a couch and analyze him and his books to death, and then the guys like Mike Wilson, "brass tacks kind of guys," the "blue-collar scholars" who really appreciate Jack the person.

"I consider my strong suit to be that I know his *life* better than anybody else I've heard of, or run into. There are people who *think* they know better, but they just don't know shit. I'm the workingman's Jack London expert."

Wilson is quick to note the similarities between himself and Jack. Both are from the working class and shunned college; both married middle-class college girls; both dabbled in ranching and farming in Sonoma County; both struggled between writing hackwork and writing literature. Wilson told me that there were two basic facts to understanding Jack London: first, that he was America's first successful blue-collar writer, and second, that he was a socialist.

"If you look up the word socialist in Webster's dictionary it will tell you it's a form of communism," Mike said. "Well, that dictionary was bought and paid for, just like Webster, by capitalists. Jack defined socialist as anyone who endeavors to improve the society in which he lives. Mike Wilson's definition is easier than that. Either you're a socialist or an anti-socialist. Either you care about people—or you don't."

Mike Wilson's definition of "impersonator" is equally fixed. Despite his own re-creations of the author, he believes there is a limit to the bodily empathy a living human can experience with the dead author. "I can't tell you how many people I've met who've declared to me, straight-faced, that they're the reincarnation of Jack London. The first thing I do is bust up. They get offended. But neither Jack nor I believe in reincarnation in that sense."

As we walked past the old pig pens and the grain silo toward the cottage where Jack died, Mike told me that he'd first become interested in London when he came to San Francisco during 1967's Summer of Love. "Summer of *Sex* would have been a lot more accurate. But let me tell you a secret, buddy: it's *always* the Summer of Love, if you're in the mood." Wilson discovered Lawrence Ferlinghetti's City Lights bookstore, where he was turned on to literature and first began hearing what he considered a lot of slander about Jack London—that he was a drunk, a homo, a lothario, a suicide. Years later, when Wilson had composed a folk-rock song about the author, he was invited to Russ Kingman's bookstore in Glen Ellen. There, in the legendary smoky backroom among London diehards, he began to discover the real truth.

"He wasn't really a womanizer, like a lot of people like to carry on," Mike assured me. "The ladies liked him because he was a gentleman."

Citing the eloquence and compassion with which Jack wrote about women, Mike discredited rumors in academia that Jack was gay. Wilson scoffed at the suicide theories, noting that anyone who understood Jack's personality would know that he was not a quitter. And as for Jack's professed atheism, Mike rattled off a direct quotation: "'My house will be standing, act of God permitting, for a thousand years.' Now does that sound like the words of an atheist? Not really. Not if you look up the definition. There's one that Webster got right."

Alcoholism is another touchy subject. In *John Barleycorn*, London recounts a life ravaged by suicidal benders, drinking alone, and hitting the bottle first thing in the morning—all the while insisting that he is not an alcoholic. Wilson agrees. "There's a whole lot of hooey and nonsense about Jack London the alcoholic. Don't buy a bit of it, OK? Jack London was not an alcoholic, not if you know what an alcoholic is. He's a fellow who drank. But there's a hell of a difference between a guy who drinks and an alcoholic."

Wilson had a couple of anecdotes that sealed his case. For one, Jack once carried a bottle of whiskey all the way across the Yukon, and then instead of drinking it, gave it to one of the fellows for anesthesia before amputation. But perhaps the most ridiculous lie Mike Wilson has ever heard is that Jack used to ride a white horse from the ranch down to the saloon in Glen Ellen, where he'd drink himself into a stupor and amuse the townspeople by falling off that same white horse.

"*Jack never even owned a white horse!*" Wilson declared triumphantly. "His favorite horse was a *sorrel*! And Jack had a full bar up here! Why the hell would he ride down there? It's not like he was aching for company."

"Isn't it possible—" I faltered, sensing some cracks in this reasoning, "that he just rode down on a different-colored horse, and that was the memory that was mistaken, but that actually the rest of the story is true?"

Wilson looked at me as if I were a half-wit.

"*Any*thing's possible," he said gently. "'Cause I wasn't really there, OK? And that's one of the things that's humbling about history: unless you were *with* Alexander, you're not really sure what happened."

Humbled by history, we pressed on toward the ruins of Wolf House. I wanted to ask who Alexander was but felt too scolded already. We walked past vineyards, still active and maintained by a distant relative of London, heavy with grapes in the autumn sun. But the bucolic scene did not soothe Wilson's irritation.

"Here's the thing that guys like me who have to work for a living in a hardware store really resent," he said, his voice rising. "If I want money from the National Endowment for the Humanities, you can just kiss it goodbye, because I'm not in academia and I don't have a professor standing beside me saying, 'This is my boy. Make sure you take care of him.' The only people who get those endowments are associated with universities. It's that simple. You and me—Mr. John Q. Public paying taxes—we're never going to see that money, because we're not set up with tenure in a university. What really bugs me, what should bug you—sixty thousand dollars a year to be a professor over there at that university—OK, and then you get a leave of absence, with pay, and the National Endowment for the Humanities gives you money to write the book, and you still own it. Such a deal! I think it sucks."

Academians are a perpetual thorn in Wilson's side. He cut back his hours at the hardware store to devote more time to his two major works: one, a biography of London, and the other, a full-length musical. But when I asked him the titles of the works, he wouldn't tell me.

"I've been ripped off for more titles than any writer I know," he said "It's not that I don't like you. But one of the titles has already been ripped off for at least two academic papers. Those two fools used it just for their damn theses. But since they were living in academia they didn't get what it really meant."

As we climbed a hill, Mike turned and walked backward. He invited me to try it, too, and told me that the technique allowed you to keep your breath better. "You see? It's a whole different set of muscles."

I nodded, paying close attention to the muscles that make my lungs contract. Maybe he was right: maybe it *did* feel different.

"This hill always reminds me of Chilkoot Pass," he said, invoking the famous trail to the Yukon where London and all gold rushers began their trek.

"Have you been there?" I said.

"I wanted to go up there for the Centennial. But I couldn't find anyone to sponsor me. I was making seven dollars an hour at the time. I've got a wife and two kids. Just couldn't do it."

4

The keeping of the Jack London flame has not been wholly relegated to renegade non-academians. Jeanne Kingman Reese, a professor at the University of Texas, San Antonio, heads the Jack London Society, a coalition of dogged academics who publish a newsletter titled "The Call" and sponsor a biennial conference on Londonalia. But the undisputed godfather—the "big gorilla of academia," according to Wilson—is Dr. Earle Labor, who for more than three decades has taught American literature at the Centenary College of Louisiana, a Methodist school of about nine hundred students. Labor first read a twenty-five-cent paperback copy of *Martin Eden* while in boot camp in the early '50s. He decided right then to get a PhD and write a dissertation on London. But when he arrived at the University of Wisconsin, the American lit specialist, Frederick Hoffman, declined to direct the dissertation, saying, "Jack London really isn't a twentieth-century author—and besides, I don't know that much about him." Professor Hoffman, in his book *The Modern Novel in America*, had already dismissed London as "an interesting sideshow in the Naturalist carnival." Earle forged ahead, and in 1974 he published a biographical study of London. "His status as a great writer or as a major American author is yet to be established," Earle wrote, noting that such an honor "must be won by fair election at the critical polls. My primary aim is to place London's name on the ballot."

Thirty years later, it would seem that Jack London has landed on the ballot. In 1976, one hundred years after London's birth, Andrew Sinclair's biography *Jack* became a bestseller. In 1982, the Library of America delivered two 1000-page plus collections. In 1988, Stanford University, with Dr. Labor as editor, published the three-volume *Letters of Jack London*. Five years later Stanford followed with another three-volume set: the *Complete Short Stories*, all 197 of them, at a whopping 2,629 pages. In 1994, Viking trotted out *The Portable Jack London*, putting him in the company of Whitman, Mark Twain, and other canon staples. Since 1998, eight of his books have been reissued as Modern Library Classics. A new biography by Alex Kershaw was published in 1997 by St. Martin's.

When I reached Dr. Labor by telephone, he was on summer break, trying to finish a biography that its publisher, Farrar, Straus and Giroux, has trumpeted as definitive. "I've been out in academia fifty years and I'm trying to write an honest book about Jack," he told me. "Right now I'm ten years late on the contract, but I'm hoping to finish up this summer." Labor has contempt for the biographers who have come before him. Irving Stone is "the ultimate sleaze. Everyone thinks he's an asshole." Andrew Sinclair's book is "a facile, misleading account of London's life and personality, with obsessive emphasis upon his medical problems." Alex Kershaw "didn't want to tell the truth. He wanted to sell the book."

"They've been worse than inadequate, but misleading, with everyone trying to make a buck off of Jack," Dr. Earle told me. "His life is exciting enough you don't have to distort."

Fighting sensationalism on one flank, Labor has spent his career fighting snobbery on the other. "In the '40s and '50s, with the New Criticism, they were elitist. They liked T. S. Eliot and Henry James," he said. But Labor's work seems to have cracked the barrier. "Stanford was wary because London had been an untouchable for so long in the establishment, so that was a breakthrough." And adding Jack to the Viking series was no easy feat. "It took me thirty years to include London in that series, because the market wasn't ready, but now they're doing a second printing."

Approaching his eightieth birthday, Dr. Labor still teaches undergraduate literature classes, and has hosted four Jack London seminars sponsored by the National Endowment for the Humanities, with students from all over the world. He tells of one young man, born fatherless into an African village, who moved to the city and learned French, and who credits his will to survive with his discovery of *The Call of The Wild*. And while he still won't call London the greatest American author, he thinks London's influence worldwide may be greater than any of his countrymen, so he's come up with a slightly different accolade: Jack London, America's Greatest *World* Novelist. With a hint of pride, he told me that Susan Sontag's obituaries noted that it was *Martin Eden* that had inspired her to become a writer.

"Before you ring off," he said, pausing, as if suddenly struck by the most important thing. "You gotta know that he did not commit suicide. There's no evidence whatsoever."

5

I had some concerns about Mike Wilson as Jack London. For one: Mike is fifty-six, and Jack died at forty. But when I asked Mike about this discrepancy, he indicated that the communion he felt with Jack was deeper than I'd guessed. "We are brothers in an understanding that transcends time and space," he said. "Jack's a good friend of mine. I understand him, and he would understand me. You see?"

We were down at the ruins of Wolf House, a haunting and sprawling foundation of lava-stone blocks. After the fire, London lacked the heart to rebuild. So the stones remain, two stories high in some places, hemmed in by the encroaching redwoods that each year refuse a little more sunlight. Wilson told me that when he does his tours with schoolchildren, Wolf House is their favorite place.

"Dressing up like Jack is like being Santa Claus, man. Kids have this weird thing where they automatically tune in to you. They love the fantasy. The first time I walked out there, it took me probably five minutes to get hooked."

Mike Wilson said he never asked for accolades. "There's a whole lot of people in the world of Jack London that are beauty contestants. I'm not putting them down. Everyone has something they want to be. But I never set out to be recognized for Jack London."

But what, then, drives him to keep doing it? Surely the small fees and acclaim of second-graders is not enough. I was beginning to see that for Mike Wilson, impersonation was no parlor game.

"Sometimes I'll be doing this stuff and I become so choked up with emotion that I just come apart. Afterwards I am exhausted. I have to struggle to drive home, and then I collapse. I give it every ounce I've got. Even my wife says: *Oh my god, it's my husband—but you're Jack London.*"

It was more akin to the channeling of a spirit. Yet something was gnawing at me. A few years back, when the local newspaper teamed up with the park for a gala celebration, instead of Wilson they chose a younger man, a professional actor from San Francisco. "He was better connected than me," Wilson told me. "He was on the inside track with the park people, while I'm just a guerilla out in the weeds."

What's more, I had asked two separate park rangers to recommend an impersonator. Both, apologetically, and asking that I not use their names, advised me to go with the other guy. And I was struck with a terrible fear for Mike Wilson: what if, despite his years of devotion and his depth of feeling—what if he's not even very good at it?

And so, dreading what I might learn, I decided there was only one way to find out. I sensed that this warm afternoon in the redwood shade of Wolf House might be my only chance to feel the soul of Jack London channeled into the present. So I asked Wilson if he'd recite a couple lines from his act. Now was the time.

I held out the tape recorder, pleadingly.

6

In early 2005, the town of El Segundo, a middle-class suburb of Los Angeles, expanded its public library with two new reading rooms. The librarians proposed to name each room after an author, and chose Agatha Christie and Jack London. Expected to rubber-stamp the choice, the City Council instead reared up in defiance.

"I'm also a great fan of Jack London. I read all his books as a kid," said Councilman John Gaines, joining with Mayor Kelly McDowell to vote down the proposal. "But quite frankly, he was a world-renowned communist."

"From the modern-day perspective, Jack London's political views would not be seen as mainstream, certainly not in my community," Mayor McDowell told the *Los Angeles Times*. "This is a conservative city with traditional values."

While Dr. Labor may be correct that London is rejected by the elites who keep the canon, it's also true that London gets no quarter from anyone. Yes, aesthetes still deny him because he lacks the artistry of James or Faulkner: in a new introduction to *John Barleycorn*, Pete Hamill writes, "Hemingway was a great literary artist and London was not." But those seeking didactic tracts are equally put off, not by London's sometimes clumsy style, but by his politics. While his life epitomized the rags-to-riches fable of American social mobility that might appease the Babbitts squawking for traditional values in their library books, London's writings condemned that very myth. It's hard to imagine a librarian at a Jack London Reading Room counseling a twelve-year-old on what exactly London meant when, in *The Iron Heel*, the swashbuckling and heroic Ernest Everhard tells the daughter of a capitalist:

> The gown you wear is stained with blood. The food you
> eat is a bloody stew. The blood of little children and of
> strong men is dripping from your very roof-beams. I can
> close my eyes, now, and hear it drip, drop, drip, drop, all
> about me.

And those on the left who might teach his vision of class struggle are stymied, too, vexed to explain to freshmen London's worship of "blond beasts" or Martin Eden's opinion of a "clever Jew" who represents

> the whole miserable mass of weaklings and inefficients
> who perished according to biological law on the ragged
> confines of life. They were the unfit. In spite of their
> cunning proclivities for cooperation, Nature rejected
> them for the exceptional man.

London's political tracts have the uncanny ability to offend just about everyone. And once we exclude them, we're left pretty much with the dog and sailor stories. In a letter just after London's death, H. L. Mencken assessed him with a clarity that eludes many modern-day admirers:

> I have often argued that he was one of the few American authors who really knew how to write. The difficulty with him was that he was an ignorant and credulous man. His lack of culture caused him to embrace all sorts of socialistic bosh, and whenever he put it into his stories, he ruined them. But when he set out to tell a simple tale, he always told it superbly.

Turns out that these superb, simple tales hit a nerve that still tingles a century later.

But for the true believers, the best way to reconcile Jack's contradictions is to ignore them. Consider this poetic passage etched on signs in Jack London State Park:

> I ride out over my beautiful ranch. Between my legs is a beautiful horse. The air is wine . . . I have everything to make me glad I am alive. I am filled with dreams and mysteries. I am all sun and air and sparkle.

These lines from *John Barleycorn* are taken wildly out of context. They are culled from a brooding chapter which begins, "I am oppressed by the cosmic sadness that has always been the heritage of man," and pivots quickly toward morbidity:

> And yet, with jaundiced eye I gaze upon all the beauty and wonder about me, and with jaundiced brain consider the pitiful figure I cut in this world that endured so long without me and that will endure again without me.

Many of those interested in remembering Jack London at all prefer to remember him in a certain way. They want an optimist, imbued with that homegrown individualism that many Americans cherish and claim as their heritage. They want an up-from-the-bootstraps success story, a fatherless wharf rat who, without a college education, transformed himself into the richest author of his time. They don't want him fraught with doubt and mired in half-baked philosophies. To admit that our hero despaired, was addicted, that he abandoned his wife and children, or that he may have taken his own life, is simply too much for the romantic image to bear.

The longing for a noble Jack London is a longing for youth: not just our own youth, but our country's youth—that bustling, innocent era before the first World War, when America was a budding tree, an agrarian democracy with a booming industrial economy, before adulthood had required the sacrifices of the World Wars, before our adventures in Vietnam and Iraq undermined the righteousness of the American experiment. Of course, Black and Indigenous people who suffered enslavement and genocide at the hands of white America never believed this version of innocence, but white Americans believed in their own virtue the way a young man does. They believed that all their fights were for their own survival. No surprise that a century later it's mostly white men who are clinging to the noble Jack. The Jack London of myth embodied that adolescent and robust America, and he died just as that America shipped its boys to Europe and began its century of adulthood, no longer a carefree provincial Eden but now a superpower, with all the requisite moral compromises.

We believe in Jack London out on the trail—frostbitten in the whipping wind, driving the dogs toward adventure—with the same fervor that we believe that George Washington stood bravely on the bow as he crossed the Delaware. We don't want him disillusioned and drunk, hunched over a typewriter, despairing the fate of modern man and powerless to mend it.

But to idealize London's youth and to ignore his suffering is to lapse into nostalgia, and to miss the point—and the power—of his best work. My favorite Jack London scene is in *The Call of the Wild* when Buck, the dog-hero who has been stolen from California and enslaved on a Yukon sled team, is rescued by a stranger. Buck's current masters are a trio of tenderfoots whose sled is packed with unnecessary luxuries. "The wonderful patience of the trail which comes to men who toil hard and suffer sore, and remain sweet of speech and kindly, did not come to these two men and women." Their frivolous load weakens their dogs and delays their arrival at a frozen river crossing where John Thornton, whittling an axe-handle, warns them that the ice is beginning to thaw. The driver ignores him, but as he whips the dogs, they won't budge. Thornton continues to whittle. "It was idle, he knew, to get between a fool and his folly; while two or three fools more or less would not alter the scheme of things." But as the driver keeps whipping helpless Buck, Thornton leaps up in animal rage. "'If you strike that dog again, I'll kill you,' he at last managed to say in a choking voice." Thornton thumps someone with the axe handle, cuts the dog free, and in six lovely lines, the fate of the sled party is settled.

> Mercedes's scream came to their ears. They saw Charles
> turn and make one step to run back, and then a whole
> section of ice give way and disappear. A yawning hole
> was all that was to be seen. The bottom had dropped out
> of the trail.
> John Thornton and Buck looked at each other.
> "You poor devil," said John Thornton, and Buck
> licked his hand.

Fate is administered, not by God or government, but by an indifferent natural order.

The prospectors are not punished for their hubris; rather, they reap the natural consequences of their actions. Buck's life is saved, not by man's charitable intentions or his own pluck, but by the spontaneous, irrational, and violent spasm of a stranger. Stripping away myths of justice, salvation, charity, and self-determination, London insists that nonetheless our decisions matter profoundly. They are all that we have. In London's world, even those who sink, hardly noticed, to their deaths are afforded a certain dignity, and I've come to believe that this respect for his characters—this love, even—is what keeps his books alive in the hearts of those unaware that such earnestness has fallen from literary fashion, that inspires some African villager to toil rather than despair, and that has brought me on this pilgrimage to a dusty ruin with an aging hardware man for whom dressing up like Jack London is a transcendent act of communion. Free from the judgments he can't resist in his political work, London grants his characters the freedom toward which all people, real and imagined, eventually strive: the freedom to love and dream, to fight and suffer, and the freedom to die.

7

"I don't know how visionary you are," Mike Wilson told me, "but I'm extremely visionary." We were sitting on a shady bench not far from Jack's grave, and Mike was telling me about the original stage musical he was writing.

My attempt to coax Mike Wilson into Jack London had not succeeded. He had smiled awkwardly, and said that he could not just slip into the role at the drop of a hat. It required preparation. Later I realized that my request had been callow, as unrealistic as encountering a swami in an airport and asking if he wouldn't levitate for me, just for a sec. It's not that Mike Wilson wasn't up to the task; it was I who was somehow inadequate as an audience.

Instead, Wilson was told how he was endeavoring to tell the story of Jack's generation through song. So far, the draft was well over a hundred pages, with two acts and eighteen original songs. Most of the music came to him in a series of dreams which he described as "biblical." He recounted the first scene he had ever dreamt, in which a young man and woman emerge on the deck of a sloop. They whisper to each other and then embrace, and kiss, and start dancing.

"They dance around the deck," Wilson said. "They dance up and down the mast, and they dance out on the edge of the sail. It's this beautiful waltz." Wilson took off his glasses and quietly sang the melody that arrived in his dream. "La-da, da-da-da, la-da, da-da-da. They're singing. It's so beautiful, and my wife wakes me up and says, *Honey, are you OK*, and I've got tears running down my cheek."

Wilson slid his glasses back onto his face. From where we sat in the eucalyptus shade, we could see the September sun beating down on the brown hills. With that we headed back up the slope toward Jack and Charmian's graves, where we would finish our tour. I wanted to know how he did it. How did Mike Wilson maintain the inspiration after all these years? While his hero had self-destructed through a brutal life of indulging all appetites, Mike Wilson seemed to be aging mellowly. Unlike Jack, he'd curbed his drinking. Unlike Jack, he'd kept a marriage and family together for three decades.

"The thing that I have, that Jack never really allowed himself to have," Mike told me, "was a complete surrender to the fact that God is running the universe. He didn't have the personal hope that a man of faith has. Because he never really believed. Jack understood every iota of it—just like my wife does. I'm a Baptist deacon. I've told her about it a dozen times to the point where she said: *Shut up, I don't want to hear about it anymore.*

"I'm sure Jack had come to that same point with friends of his who were ministers. And they really wanted in their worst way to save their friend Jack, who was a great guy, but who couldn't seem to make that reach. And you're trying for all you're worth, with all your heart to get him to, to say: *Jack, make the reach.* But he wouldn't do it."

I would never learn how well Mike Wilson could impersonate Jack London. Maybe he was brilliant. Maybe not. In his own peculiar way, he was plodding one step at a time toward Chilkoot Pass with the frozen wind in his face. Year after year, school group after school group, Mike Wilson, man of faith, reached deep inside himself to channel this drunken atheist.

"I focus my mind," Wilson said. "I say a prayer to the Almighty, because He is a good friend of mine. And I say: Hey, let me portray my brother well. He's never let me down. And I come up with stuff that I amaze myself. When I actually put on the costume and am there with all the young faces, I'm Jack London. And I don't pull any punches."

A Buick Toward the Apocalypse

John Weisheit wanted to stop the war. It hadn't yet started, so there was still time. He and his friend Owen decided to drive 2,000 miles from Utah, across the January blizzard, to march on the Washington mall. One problem: Owen Lammers was legally blind. John needed a second driver, someone without a job or responsibilities. He called me.

"In which car?" I said. I knew John drove a pickup with only a bench seat.

"A Honda Accord." He was borrowing it.

"Does it have a good stereo?"

"Sure."

"CD player?"

"Now you're being silly."

John said that we had a free place to stay in DC, and that he and Owen would pay for gas. Weisheit and Lammers constituted two-thirds of the staff of Living Rivers, an organization whose mission was to decommission dams, beginning with, but not limited to, the Glen Canyon Dam on the Colorado River, some 300 miles downstream from Moab, Utah, where we all lived. John has also been a river guide on the Colorado for twenty years. He had been invited to testify before the National Park Service headquarters in DC on the issue of prohibiting motorboats from the Grand Canyon, a ban he supported. Forty-eight years old, he had never been further east than Denver.

When they arrived at my door, there was no new Honda. Instead, they sat in a sagging 1984 Buick Century with paint peeling off the roof, 170,000 miles on the odometer. An orange light said SERVICE ENGINE SOON as we topped a rise on the way out of town. I asked if this thing was going to make it.

"I have no idea," said John. He was clean-shaven with rimless glasses, dressed as usual in a plaid shirt and jeans and work boots. "But then: You never do know if you're going to make it."

"It's the Browermobile," said Owen. "Of course it'll make it."

"We used to drive David Brower around in this car when he came to town."

"Drive him where?"

David Brower was an environmental hero, the head of the Sierra Club back in the '60s when the group blocked plans to dam the Grand Canyon and the Green River. He had recently died.

"The airport. To restaurants. To demonstrations."

It began snowing just east of Grand Junction, Colorado, a condition which would persist for the next forty-two hours until the sun rose in eastern Maryland. Owen read the map and announced that we had about 2,000 miles to DC. He wore a shock of white hair and coke-bottle glasses and held the map so close that it touched his nose. The Browermobile rattled, groaned, and trembled. I would later learn that John had acquired the vehicle as a donation to Living Rivers—a gift from his wife's parents. There was no tape player, and the radio crackled through a single muffled speaker. The driver's side door could only be opened from the outside. Most importantly, each time a semi-truck roared past and buried us in snow and grit, the windshield wipers didn't work. I tried to put it into perspective: we were, after all, stopping a war.

Coasting down into Denver from the Rockies, I asked how far west he'd been.

"The Santa Monica pier."

"Ever been to any other countries?"

"Mexico," he said, then after some thought added, "Twice."

In addition to stopping the war and banning motors in the Grand Canyon, John Weisheit had two other goals for his first transnational car trip: to see the Mississippi River and to eat his first Krispy Kreme doughnut.

I'd first met John eight years earlier when we guided a river trip down Desolation Canyon in Utah. I was twenty-three, he was forty. He was the trip leader. Our clients were three families with small children. One afternoon I ended up with the kids on my boat and fell behind the rest of the boats. I looked up and realized the other boats were out of sight. I decided to fire up the outboard motor to catch up. But I didn't really know how to use the motor. I flipped some switches and pulled the cord. No luck. I pumped the fuel line and switched it out of neutral into forward. I pulled the cord again. The motor revved into a roar and the boat shot forward. The propeller whacked a rock and kicked up out of the water. The motor was broken. When I arrived at camp two hours later, sore and strained from rowing against the afternoon squalls, I reported to John with terrible shame that I'd wrecked the motor.

"That's all right," he said. "I break motors all the time. You shouldn't feel bad until you do the big one."

"The big one?"

"That's when you *lose* the motor. I once lost a motor, then borrowed one from another guide, then lost that one, too. On the same day."

Halfway through Kansas, with the midnight snow collecting across the dark flats, John revealed something else I'd never known: before becoming a river guide he'd been a Jehovah's Witness, for ten years. He'd converted at age twenty, then married a member of the church.

"You went door to door and all that?" I said.

"Of all Christians," he said, "Jehovah's Witnesses are the most like early Christians, the way they teach the scripture. I admire that. But eventually I stopped believing it. Sometimes I feel bad for all those people I converted."

"What's with all the end-of-the-world stuff?" I asked.

John explained how the prophecies of the Book of Genesis had been halfway fulfilled by the coming of Jesus, and that the Witnesses were waiting for the second half—the apocalypse—to come true, also. As we sped through the featureless prairie he was citing verse that linked Armageddon with Adam's original sin. After about ten minutes he said, "You probably shouldn't get me started on scripture. I could talk about this all the way to DC."

But, he said, he'd been a bit of a doomsayer as long as he could remember. He recalls telling his dad when he was twelve years old: "This world is so screwed up. It's all going to end someday. It can't go on like this."

John was born in Southern California in 1954. Growing up near Los Angeles, his family often took trips to the Pacific Ocean to the west and the Colorado River to the east. In the late 1960s his parents fled the crowds and pollution and moved to Phoenix, Arizona, which at that time was a modest desert town of about 500,000 people. The family took a guided raft trip down the Grand Canyon, and after that were hooked. They bought a rubber raft and began taking their own trips. After high school, John enrolled at a local community college where he lasted three weeks. "One day I just walked out in the middle of a math class. That was it. I never went back." In 1972 he received his draft notification, and went to the board to begin the process of becoming a Conscientious Objector. But the woman at the board told him not to bother: his lottery number was 300 out of 365. He wouldn't be called to Vietnam. Weisheit worked two years on a cotton farm, then took a job remodeling houses in Phoenix, and soon after converted to the Jehovah's Witnesses and married a girl from the church. Starting his own construction business, he spent a decade making good money on the Phoenix construction explosion, running rivers, converting people to his religion, and drinking heavily.

In 1982, he and his wife volunteered as swampers with the legendary Grand Canyon river guide, Georgie White. They soon realized that they could make a living taking people down the river. In the span of two years, John sold his company, divorced his wife, stopped drinking, and moved to Moab and became a river guide. When I asked him why he had never guided on the Grand Canyon he said, "I just hated the dam. I hated the crowds." So instead he worked upriver in Cataract, Desolation, and Westwater Canyons, in the process logging more than 250 trips through Cataract Canyon, which at high water has the largest rapids in North America.

John's introduction to political activism was not exactly voluntary. In 1996, a Salt Lake City physician founded the Glen Canyon Institute, dedicated to restoring the stretch of the river submerged in 1964 with the building of Glen Canyon Dam. Cataract Canyon river-runners are famously hostile toward the dam, and toward the reservoir called Lake Powell that floods the last thirty miles of the canyon. Instead of floating the river, boaters are required to bring a motor and buzz across the flat blue lake populated by houseboats and jet-skis. And for many environmentalists, the Glen Canyon Dam is the holy grail of the movement: the ultimate example of a senseless and short-sighted bureaucracy destroying nature for the benefit of power and water consortiums. Around that time, no fewer than five new books had been published about the plight of Glen Canyon, adding to the novels by Edward Abbey and Jim Harrison about pissed-off dreamers scheming to blow the thing to bits.

When the Grand Canyon Institute was seeking board members, Weisheit's name came up. "I was known as someone who really, really hated the dam," he told me. One of the other board members was David Brower, the octogenarian former director of the Sierra Club. Many regard Brower as the twentieth century's most important and effective environmentalist, and credit him with not only transforming the Sierra Club from an outing club to a political lobbying force, but in the process blocking the government from building dams that would have flooded Grand Canyon and Dinosaur National Parks. Meeting Brower was cathartic for Weisheit. He recalls complaining to Brower that the movement, particularly the Sierra Club, had veered from its grass-roots origins to a money-thirsty, top-heavy bureaucracy.

"So why don't you do something about it?" Brower asked him.

Weisheit and Lammers, another board member, left GCI and founded their own organization. The express purpose of the Glen Canyon Action Network was direct political action toward decommissioning of the dam. They opened shop in Moab, renting a Main Street building that used to house an ice-cream parlor. They kept the ice-cream business, partially to pay the rent and partially to indoctrinate unsuspecting tourists to their cause. Passersby seeking a cool milkshake wandered into the ice-cream store painted like the lost sandstone alcoves of Glen Canyon, and with their double scoop got a pamphlet on dam decommissioning and as long a lecture as they were willing to endure.

Over the years, GCAN and the ice-cream parlor evolved into Living Rivers, an advocacy group with a wider scope, tackling dam projects on other rivers. Weisheit has been known to attend Bureau of Reclamation meetings dressed as a fish—to be precise, as a humpback chub, a tiny, homely species of bottom-feeder that has been driven to the brink of extinction by dams. In 2000, Weisheit ran for Utah Legislature as a member of the Green Party, gaining 17 percent of the vote against the Republican incumbent. (There was no Democrat in the race.) In Grand County, where Moab sits, he won 40 percent.

John and a group of local environmentalists organized a local chapter of the Sierra Club, calling themselves the "Glen Canyon Group," an overtly political name, as Glen Canyon technically no longer exists. (It's now called Lake Powell.) Despite an attempt by the Utah chapter to block the name, the Moab group eventually won out.

Weisheit's most notable political act came in the winter of 2002, when the Sierra Club's national board issued a statement opposing "weapons of mass destruction," but not explicitly opposing an American invasion of Iraq.

Weisheit was disgusted that a liberal organization could implicitly condone warfare, and his first inclination was to resign from the executive committee. But remembering David Brower's lesson that *someone* had to change things, John and the three other leaders of the Glen Canyon Group publicly condemned the war resolution, and the club's leadership in general. "We believe the vast majority of Club members oppose the Bush administration policy, including the plan to escalate the war with Iraq," said the letter of the "Glen Canyon Four." "By adopting these shameful resolutions instead, the Board betrayed Club members and breached its leadership trust."

The story was picked up by the *New York Times*, the *Los Angeles Times*, and Pacifica Radio. Sierra Club chat rooms flickered with excitement as members from around the nation logged in to support or attack the dissenters. There was talk that they would be stripped of their leadership positions by the national board. There were threats and intimations that the Glen Canyon Four would be relieved of their posts for publicly disputing the national leadership, followed by shrill accusations of "gag rules" and McCarthyism against the Club. In the following months, without an official change of position, the national Sierra Club quietly lent its name to the Win Without War movement.

All of which brought John Weisheit, two months later, to be piloting his twenty-year-old Buick through the land of Waffle House and Flying J, braving 2,000 miles of blizzard to stop a war. The Browermobile got terrible gas mileage, causing us to fill up every four hours or so, and thus requiring hundreds of gallons of the stuff to protest a war for oil. We pulled into a truck stop at four in the morning in Missouri so that he could take a driving shift and I could sleep. John filled his thermos with coffee and, getting back into the car, proudly displayed a bag of Krispy Kreme doughnuts. He filled his coffee cup and as we returned to I-70, he took his first bite, and declared it delicious, just like the doughnuts he used to eat as a kid.

He flipped on the radio, and found a talk show on the AM band. The callers and the host were blaming the war in Iraq on the "enviro whackos" who were blocking oil drilling in Alaska.

"Well," said John, sipping his coffee. "That's us."

As the long winter night continued, he looked up from the steering wheel and said, "Albuquerque."

A truck roared past.

"That's the first city they'll abandon. They've already run out of water."

His visions are of righteous Mother Nature, in the form of a hundred-year drought or a five-hundred-year flood, wreaking its vengeance on the sinful water wasters of Phoenix, spilling over its man-made levees and taking out riverfront real estate development and carrying it along where it would knock over bridges and freeways. Later, as I was drifting to sleep, he called back to me: "Do you know how many fucking golf courses there are in municipal Phoenix?"

"One hundred?" I guessed, rubbing my eyes.

"Seven hundred and fifty-eight."

The windshield wiper situation was worsening. Every ten minutes John rolled down the window and, with one hand on the wheel, reached the other hand out the window and splashed water on the windshield. Soon another semi-truck barreled past and caked the glass with ice and dirt. The process splashed cold water on the driver and the sleeper. The Midwestern sky was graying in the east as we passed a three-story roadside cross, built of smooth concrete and bathed in milky electric light.

"Christians," said Weisheit. "They claim to believe in the Christ, but they sure don't live like him. Change is going to have to come from the grass roots. This top-down bullshit just doesn't work. Look at Martin Luther King. Gandhi. Look what Jesus did with just twelve followers."

Later that day we crossed the Mississippi River in St. Louis. It was a moment I had wanted to witness—the riverman getting his first glimpse of the river—but instead I was sleeping in back. When I awoke I found myself in Illinois. I asked John what he'd thought of the Mississippi.

"Very, very low," he said. "Channels and sandbars was all you could see."

We arrived in Washington Friday morning at rush hour, some forty-two hours after our departure from Moab, and drove directly to the Bureau of the Interior for John's meeting with the Park Service. We met in a dark wood-paneled suite with men in suits and some in the olive green ranger uniforms. When called to speak, John spoke slowly and plainly, and did not veer into policy or law. He told what a peaceful and beautiful place the Grand Canyon is, how he'd spent years of his life on its river, and how it was all ruined by the loud buzz of motors. He spoke uninterrupted for about five minutes, did not ask for questions or provide follow-up, and then stood and walked out of the meeting.

After checking into the townhouse where we were staying—it belonged to an old friend of Owen's—we bundled up in parkas and gloves and made for the Capitol. We had an afternoon to be tourists. The cars parked on the narrow streets of Capitol Hill were covered with two inches of snow. We visited the office of our congressman, Scott Matheson, and secured gallery passes, then took the tour of the capitol. In the atrium we viewed the historical dioramas while the guide delivered a peculiar sanitized narrative of the founding of America (warm friendship from Indians, no mention of slaves). "This is so gaudy," said John of our nation's capital. "It's all so fake to me. I mean: did they think this was Rome?" John found most of the DC public architecture similarly garish and ostentatious, except for the main lobby at Union Station, which he liked.

The House of Representatives had the day off, but we were able to watch the Senate in action: two senators droning on about a contract to build cruise ships. The other ninety-eight members were nowhere to be seen. But the gallery was warm, and we were allowed to sit, so we took quick naps before venturing back out into the cold.

The next morning, as we walked out onto the mall for the march, the frozen blades of grass were brittle beneath our feet. Thousands of people marched: smatterings of teenaged anarchists, but mostly adults: Veterans for Peace, Jews Against the Occupation, and lots of gray-haired Christian church groups. Owen had a large banner of Moab's Delicate Arch with a peace sign superimposed on it, and John held a forest green flag of the Sierra Club. I asked if he thought he'd get into further trouble for "representing" the Club without its consent, and he shrugged.

"They're going to kick me out anyway," he said. "What else can they do?"

"This whole industrial revolution is a mistake," John said, as we inched along in the rush hour gridlock. Another big storm was predicted, and we'd decided to take I-40 through the southern states rather than backtrack through the frozen north. John was driving the first shift to Virginia. "What we need to get back to is a hunter-gatherer system."

"I'd love to see Lake Powell drained," I said. "But I don't want to be a hunter-gatherer. And let's assume that you had the power to take this country back to pre-industrial revolution times. What percentage of the people do you think would want to go with you?"

"Okay, so maybe not to hunter-gatherers. But I'd like to see it illegal to throw away cans and bottles. And I'd ban paper cups. There's no need to use things just once then throw them away. I'd dissolve all corporations with more than fifteen employees. And we'd go totally solar."

I drove a shift until two AM, just inside the Tennessee border, and then we switched again. The Browermobile was trembling worse than usual, coughing and oozing engine oil at an alarming rate in addition to the usual drip of transmission fluid. I fell asleep in the back seat and when I awoke we were exiting the highway. It was dark out.

"Where are we?" I said.

"A motel," said John. "It's on me."

It was five AM and we were in Nashville, Tennessee.

Later that morning we found ourselves at CarMax, a slick car lot beside a freeway, a national franchise, sort of the Home Depot of used cars. Our salesman was stout and strapping and handsome. His name was David, and if not for the word CarMax embroidered on his golf shirt he might have looked like he'd just stepped off the porch of the Sigma Chi house. John was interested in a Toyota Camry—something that got good gas mileage. On our second test-drive David told us that he'd just moved there from Atlanta, where he'd been going to school.

"School for what?" said Owen. "To learn how to sell cars?"

"Actually this is just a bridge job," he said.

"A bridge to what?"

"I've got a degree in electrical engineering," he said. "I've applied to work at the nuclear plant for the Tennessee Valley Authority."

"NUCLEAR?" Owen shouted. "You could choose anything, and you choose nuclear power? Well, God help you."

"It's got a lot of pep," said John, accelerating the sedan up the on-ramp of the freeway.

"Well, I took the TVA test and that's what I qualified for."

"I thought all you needed to work for the TVA was freshman algebra."

Owen proceeded to deliver a short but thorough lecture on the Tennessee Valley Authority: that it is an incompetent, subsidized bureaucracy that steals from the taxpayers with one hand while paying dividends to its investors with its others.

"Handles well, too," said John.

"It's a good car," said our salesman.

I then explained to our salesman that the occupation of his current clients was trying to take down dams. David considered this for a moment while we glided off the freeway off-ramp.

"Well, how do you propose we get our energy?"

"Use less," said John.

The car was listed for $7,995, and John was all set to buy it. But when we returned to the showroom we noticed a trail of smoke sneaking out from under the hood. We popped the trunk and found oil leaking from the engine and frying on the catalytic converter. The engine seal seemed to be filled with silicon, indicating that a mechanic had been inside there, fixing who knows what.

"Forget about this one," said John.

"Well," said David. "I'm glad we found that now, rather than later."

"You were about to sell us a lemon!" declared Owen.

The only other Camry was $10,995. It was newer, fancier, and had fewer miles.

"Shall we go out to the lot and find it?" suggested David.

"You go out and find it," said Owen. "We'll wait inside for you."

The Camry in which David returned was noticeably nicer than the one we'd just driven.

"This one has a sunroof," said David.

John wrinkled his nose. "One more thing to break. And it'll probably leak."

"And a CD player."

"I don't have any CDs."

The test drive of the final Camry was successful. John decided to buy it. Of course, he didn't have any money, so he'd have to set up some credit.

"How much you think you can give us for the Browermobile?" I asked our salesman.

David was hesitant. "We'd have to have our appraisers inspect it."

"We'd let it go for four grand," I said with a straight face.

He watched me carefully, then decided I was joking and laughed.

"That was a joke, right?"

"No."

His eyes widened. "Really?"

"I was actually thinking four hundred was about right," said John.

John retreated to David's cubicle to do the paperwork. Owen and I drank hot cocoa in the lobby and watched Fox News on television. Rumsfeld was fielding questions from reporters, explaining the reasons for war. We tried to change the channel, but it seemed locked on Fox. Finally I got up and sat in on the financing meeting.

The estimate of the Browermobile had returned at $500. CarMax would retain one hundred of that for a mysterious "sales fee." That $400 was all that was required for a down payment on the $11,000 car. John would sign some papers and we'd drive away, simple as that.

"Have you ever financed a car before?" David asked him.

"Twenty-one years ago," said John.

"That probably doesn't count. Do you own a home?"

"Yes."

"How much are your payments?"

"It's paid off. I built it myself."

"Well, congratulations," said David.

"Thank you."

"I built a house, too," said David. "In Atlanta."

John and David drifted off the topic of car finance and talked about post-and-beam construction, forced-air furnaces, and molded wooden paneling. David said he'd had to sell the house he built in order to move to Nashville, to be closer to his wife's parents. He pointed to a photo on his desk: they'd just had their first baby, a son.

"I didn't want my wife to have to work," he said. "That's why I took this job."

While we waited for the credit check, David had us bring the Browermobile into the garage and unload it. Out came the river bags and sleeping bags and tool boxes. Out came a big poster with a picture of an Iraqi child and the slogan *No Blood for Oil.*

"So long to the Browermobile," said Owen.

"David Brower used to drive in this car," I told David.

The salesman gave us a blank look. He hefted a duffel bag out of the trunk and set it in the heap with the rest.

"David Brower is the greatest environmentalist of the century," John told him. "Without him we'd have dams in the Grand Canyon, dams in Dinosaur National Park."

Our luggage looked ragged and puny, piled there in the car dealership beside the bags of road salt. I handed David a pamphlet we'd acquired in DC. It was called "Bush at Midterm: A Chronicle of Environmental Devastation."

"Take this," I said. "Maybe we'll convert you."

"Probably not. My dad was a lieutenant colonel in the military," he said. "Special forces. Green beret."

"So you probably don't want an anti-war poster?"

"Nah. I hope that's not going to make you change your mind on the car."

"Of course not," said John. He laid one hand on David's shoulder in a manner that seemed fatherly. Then he opened his wallet and gave David a business card. "When you come to Moab, come by the shop for an ice cream. And we'll take you down the river. Then you'll see why we care so much about this stuff."

We emptied the Browermobile of everything. John requested a moment alone with the car to "say goodbye," and then a mechanic drove it away. It died after ten feet, and the mechanic restarted it and babied it across the lot.

John's credit checked out, and we packed our bags into the new-used Camry. Later that night in Memphis we would stop for dinner and Owen would buy CDs for the new stereo. John, having never bought a CD, was so galled by the prices that he instead bought three Bob Dylan cassettes for ten dollars. Luckily, the Camry played tapes, too.

David the salesman walked alongside the car as John idled out of the lot. John thanked him again, and repeated his offer to take David and his family down the river.

"I hope we weren't too much of a pain in the ass," said Owen.

David considered the point.

"I think it's good to get to know people from other cultures."

And with that we eased onto the freeway, westbound. Ten days later the president would announce that Iraq was acquiring uranium, and that if war was forced upon us, we would fight with the full force and might of the United States military, and we would prevail. The new car drove fast and smooth, thirty miles to the gallon, and we had only half the country left to cross.

The Dropout in Your Inbox

Before I changed American politics forever, I was a dropout. I lived in a town of five thousand in the middle of the desert. I worked summers as a backcountry guide, and in the winters I traveled and wrote. I held a master's degree and had finished a book, but sales were small, and getting published hadn't brought fame or acclaim. But no matter: Living was cheap. I paid $300 to rent a trailer on an acre of tumbleweeds, and I had learned that by eating only beans, tortillas, tea, and honey, I could subsist on five dollars per week. Between the light workload, good weather, and swimming in the river, I was almost content.

And besides, I was taking a moral stand. Casting aside riches and ambition to dwell in the desert, I was protesting the excesses of the Clinton years. People had too much stuff. They were spoiled and pampered, the sort of weak-willed citizens who might one day let our sacred democracy drift into dictatorship. I was looking forward to a stock-market crash that would sweep the moneylenders from the temple.

Then came the 2000 election. It had been easy to ignore politics in the '90s, especially since I didn't have television or read a newspaper (I considered my ignorance preferable to the propaganda peddled by networks and publishers who were, after all, puppets for bad corporations). As far as I was concerned, both parties were corrupted by some nebulous source of evil that I called Big Money, and because Utah's five electoral votes were guaranteed to go Republican, I cast my protest vote for Ralph Nader. It never occurred to me that George W. Bush might actually become president.

On Election Night I watched the returns with my best friend in Moab, Mathew Gross, also a published author, also a dropout. He had an encyclopedic knowledge of politics and a master's degree in environmental studies, but worked as a waiter. Since neither of us had Internet service, we gathered at a friend's house and clicked refresh on a news site. When the Drudge Report announced that Gore had won Florida, we got in the truck and drove downtown to celebrate at the bar.

Somewhere in that five-minute drive across the autumn streets of Moab, Bush took the election. Matt and I drank glumly at the bar until it closed. We had been robbed by Big Money. We wanted a fight.

But who could we fight? The next election was four years away. And besides, we were slackers in a windblown tourist trap. We had no political power, no connection to power, and we knew of no mechanism in the national process by which people like us could access power. Democracy didn't work. We were shut out. Something had to be done.

About that time, a New York company announced plans to build a thousand-dollar-per-night luxury hotel on a mesa just outside of Moab. The developers were allied with rich investors and with the state of Utah, and they arrived in town with a team of powerful lawyers. They proposed million-dollar "pueblo-style villas" here in a town where the average income was about $30,000, and the dominant architectural form was doublewides. They would have day spas and five-star restaurants and drought-inducing golf courses. It was to be called Cloudrock, a name that dripped with fake Native spirituality and back-to-the-earth opulence. Here was Big Money incarnate.

But this foe was not as insurmountable as the president of the United States, the Florida secretary of state, or a partisan Supreme Court. If we couldn't keep the bastards out of Washington, well, at least we'd keep them off of the mesa. All the anger and powerlessness Matt and I felt about the election, we channeled against Cloudrock. And so began the curious odyssey that would eventually land me startlingly close to the control panel of the first insurgent political event in a generation: the presidential campaign of Howard Dean.

In a small town like Moab, Utah, the levers of power are within the grasp of just about anyone willing to reach for them. Matt and I got ourselves appointed to something called the County Board of Adjustments. No one seemed to know what the board did; it hadn't met in years. But upon close reading of the code, Matt discovered that the Board of Adjustments existed to hear appeals of land-use code decisions. For instance: the Cloudrock decision.

We formed the Moab Citizens Alliance. We held meetings and hung fliers. We wrote letters to the editor. At the height of the MCA's prominence, there were only about twenty actual members, but that didn't matter. I discovered a talent. I could write political tracts quickly—in a single draft. Holed up in the office of Matt's tiny duplex, we wrote fiery populist manifestos. My copy was bold. "Are we going to let a New York City real estate developer hike up the cost of living so that regular working people like you and me can't afford to live here anymore?" went one of my salvos. "These developers are trying to hitch a horse to the Ritz-Carlton and call it a dude ranch."

We were a team. Matt had the ideas, and I had the words. Our press releases were picked up by papers in Salt Lake City and Colorado. Cloudrock was mentioned unfavorably in the *New York Times*. Matt was interviewed on the local news. We had an audience. My vanity, wounded by the tiny readership of my book, sprang to life. We fancied ourselves like Robert Kennedy or Cesar Chavez, standing up for the little guy, staring power in the face and giving it the finger. Grinning like young Napoleons, we locked ourselves in that office, convinced that the ideas we incubated would seed a grassroots movement and influence the minds of millions.

But the town elders did not applaud our civic enthusiasm. The Moab Citizens Alliance was roundly denounced. The editorial page of the only weekly paper called us elitist, radical, obstructionist, anti-growth, and a threat to the American way. When Matt rallied a crowd of hundreds with a rousing speech at a public meeting, the county council did not share their enthusiasm. Instead, the chairwoman gave Matt a personal scolding, and the council voted to approve Cloudrock.

We were defeated.

.+.

The placid '90s had ended. The electorate was divided. America had been attacked. We were at war in Afghanistan, and rumbling toward Iraq. The stock market had collapsed. President Bush was dismantling decades of environmental protection.

Our defeat in Moab was mirrored nationally. Instead of fighting, Democrats were capitulating. On election night in 2002, Matt and I sat at the same bar, drinking the same beer, watching the same results. Too timid to either embrace or oppose the looming war, the Democrats lost seats in both the House and the Senate. I had worried that the Clinton years had made Americans too complacent to protect their democracy, and now my fears seemed to be realized.

Matt quickly moved past our Cloudrock bruises. When his term on the Board of Adjustments expired, he was not reappointed. He finally got dial-up Internet, and his political passion found a new outlet: websites where political junkies stayed up all night debating. Blogs, he called them. This was the dumbest thing I had ever heard about.

"It's about the memes," he said.

I could think of no response.

"*Memes*," he repeated. Here was a way that anyone, anywhere—people like us—could gain power, and not in some two-bit local boondoggle like Cloudrock, but in politics on a national scale. "One blogger frames a political debate, and he influences the other bloggers, who in turn influence the press, who in turn influence the masses!"

"Whatever," I said. "No one will ever read those things."

Even if our Cloudrock fight was lost, I wasn't willing to quit. When someone appealed the approval to the Board of Adjustments, I was in a position to vote. I knew I couldn't overcome the other four members, but winning wasn't the point. I wanted to go down swinging.

The hearing arrived. I sat, for the first time, on the other side of the chamber. Now I was the one who could vote, and I relished looking down at my opponents in the gallery whose only recourse was to approach the board and try to sway me. My bias was evident, and again I was denounced. Lawyers from Cloudrock and the state of Utah demanded that I recuse myself. A member of the planning commission presented a legal affidavit accusing me of conspiring with the plaintiffs. And then another board member turned to me and asked savagely:

"Are you now, or have you ever been, a member of the Moab Citizens Alliance?"

I refused to answer. I was not on trial here. My grip on power was tenuous, but I had come this far and I would be damned if I would let it go.

I cast my vote to overturn a one-man minority, and once again Big Money steamrolled over me.

·+·

In early 2003, the blogosphere—that's what Matt insisted on calling it—was buzzing about an unknown former governor from Vermont who had the audacity to run for president. One day Matt called me to his computer and, utilizing the day's most cutting-edge technology, showed me a one-inch screen, in streaming video, of this stiff, pugilistic Yankee giving a speech.

"What I want to know is what in the world so many Democrats are doing supporting the president's unilateral intervention in Iraq," he snarled. He shook his fist. By the end, his face was red and he was shouting: "I want my country back! I'm tired of being divided. I don't want to listen to the fundamentalist preachers anymore!"

This was the first politician I had ever seen who was as pissed off as I was, and who was willing to say it. He was a fighter. I sensed two things. First, there was something to this Internet, after all. It let me bypass the media and get a straight dose of politics. And second, that little man on that little screen, who didn't even have his own website: he could alter history.

Matt was even more moved than I was. He drove to Vermont, borrowed his dad's suit and tie, and showed up at Dean headquarters in Burlington. After a few days stuffing envelopes, he proposed to campaign manager Joe Trippi that Dean launch a blog. The rest is sort of history. Hundreds of thousands of people began reading Blog for America, the first such website by a political candidate. Using email and online fund-raising, the Dean campaign raised $819,000 in a single day, a record. Dean shot up in the polls, ahead of such establishment warhorses as John Kerry and Joe Lieberman.

I caught the bug, too. I was up in Alaska that summer, guiding a wilderness trip with teenagers. I did not sleep in a bed for two months. But whenever I got near a computer I logged on to see what Matt was up to. I even clicked the button and entered my credit card digits and, with my twenty dollars, made my first-ever political contribution.

Trippi made Matt Director of Internet Communications. Matt was working a hundred hours a week. He was mentioned in *Time* magazine, featured on television. Teresa Heinz Kerry singled out "that young man from Utah" as an example of why Dean was besting her husband in the polls. Matt wrote the blog posts and the emails that were raking in millions of dollars, but he also supervised a small staff on the web team, and as the campaign heated up, he needed help. That's when I got the call.

"Come out to Vermont and be my writer."

It was closest I've ever come to being in an episode of *Mission Impossible*. I got on a plane in Anchorage and moved in to an apartment in Burlington with Matt and his wife. I showed up at headquarters with a full beard, a flannel shirt, and cowboy boots. They looked at me askance. This was the guy that Mathew Gross had brought in to write the magic emails? To be the online voice of the first-ever online presidential campaign?

We on the web team were the darlings of the campaign. Our average age was twenty-seven—none of us had worked on a campaign before. But instead of the veteran operatives in Political, Finance, Field, Research, it was us rookies that Trippi sequestered in the cubicles around his office. We answered only to him. We kept odd hours, coming and going in the middle of the night, sometimes working from home, but always logging at least sixteen hours a day, seven days a week.

It was one in the morning, and the office was empty except for the web team's lair, where we gazed at blinking screens beneath towers of pizza boxes. Trippi looked over the shoulders of Matt and me, sucking on Diet Pepsi and cherry-flavored Skoal, moaning at the progress of an email we were composing. He had set a staggering goal of $15 million to raise in the third quarter, far more than any Democrat had ever raised. Now with just days to go, we were more than $2 million short. Trippi's eyes were puffy. His shirt was untucked. His belly was bulging.

"That's terrible," he said. "Is that the best you can do?"

Trippi had worked for seven presidential campaigns, from George McGovern to Ted Kennedy to Dick Gephardt. He'd never won: now he'd come out of retirement for this final hurrah. Trippi was Fagin; we were the ragged band of orphans and pickpockets. Or maybe more like it: we were the Bad News Bears. He looked over our shoulders and rubbed his eyes. No one spoke, for fear of getting yelled at.

"You guys just don't get it," Trippi said finally, and sulked back toward his office. "I swear to god one of these days you're gonna make me stroke out."

"What was he so pissed about?" someone said.

"No freakin' clue."

"Keep your head low so it doesn't get chopped off."

Five minutes later Trippi bellowed from his office: "Gross! Get in here!" Matt rushed in with a pad and pen. Listening at the door, the rest of us could hear Trippi howling like a wounded beast. Finally Matt emerged with a page of scribbles and translated it to me.

"I'll have it first thing in the morning," I said.

Matt jerked his thumb toward Trippi's cave.

"You'll have it in fifteen minutes."

I flipped open my laptop and started writing. I believed that what we were doing was sacred. We were cutting Big Money out of politics. Instead of two-thousand-dollar-per-plate fund-raisers, or bundled corporate donations for hundreds of thousands of dollars, we were out-raising the others twenty dollars at a time. But in order to rid politics of Big Money, my job was to always—*always*—ask for money. Never could I write an email that simply outlined a position. Howard Dean's idealism was grand, but it didn't put the scare on Kerry and Lieberman and Karl Rove. Trippi had drilled it into us: without our fund-raising, we were Dennis Kucinich. So as I wrote, the only way supporters could prove their commitment to the cause was with cash. They weren't *donating*. That word was stricken from my vocabulary. Instead, each time they clicked on that precious contribution link, they were joining a movement. In fifteen minutes I forwarded a draft to Matt.

Dear Friend,

You are on the verge of making history. Through telephone, mail, and Internet you have brought $12.5 million to Howard Dean's campaign to bring the people back into presidential politics. Three days from the end of the quarter, you are poised to reach the goal of $15 million.

Ever since March, when this campaign began with seven devoted workers in a three-room office, the Washington insiders have marshaled their forces to stop you from taking your country back. Sure, they want your vote—but they won't give you a decisive role in determining the next president of the

United States. Your energy, enthusiasm, and contributions over the last six months have ignited a new faith in the power of the grassroots and shaken the foundations of establishment politics in both parties.

Click here to reclaim your democracy.

Now is the time to send an even stronger message to the DC insiders: the grass roots are deep—and permanent. We won't be pulled out by the politics of the past, by the name-calling and infighting of career Washington insiders. You have already demonstrated that the people can hoist a rural governor from underdog to frontrunner. Now let's send a message that the next election will not be decided by insiders, back room deals, big money, and special interests—it will be decided by you, the people.

You are unstoppable.

Click here to send a message.

And sure enough, we ended the third quarter with more cash raised than any other Democrat in history. Thousands of Americans—people like me who'd never before given a cent to the corrupt political process—were coughing up what they could afford. Hundreds sent emails, thanking us for what we were doing, sure that we were changing America for the better. A handwritten note and a hundred-dollar check arrived from a Wyoming grandmother who said she was the only liberal in her town. "Run with it," she wrote.

During the months leading up to the Iowa caucus, I slept with my laptop beside my pillow. I woke in the middle of the night and scrolled through the blog's comments. Matt and I would start posting first thing in the morning, before going to the office, before taking a shower, before having breakfast.

My fantasy had come true: holed up in a tiny apartment, we were wielding what felt like actual power, and influencing the masses. By this time my second book had come out, picked up a few good reviews, and sold a couple thousand copies. A couple thousand? Nuts. That many people were reading my blog posts in the first minute! We wrote them so fast to such a hungry audience that within seconds of posting we'd have dozens of comments, cheers, corrections. Every week, Dean climbed in the polls and the web traffic surged, and the tech teams raced to expand the servers and build the system. We had more readers than most national newspapers. And what's more, the press corps was reading our blog and emails. We knew it because sometimes they'd quote us directly, and other times they'd just repeat the meme we'd planted the day before. Here we were at the breakfast table, me and Matt from Moab, Utah, guiding national political discourse in our pajamas.

.+.

The campaign was taking a personal toll. Matt's wife had gotten sick, but Matt couldn't take time off from the campaign to take care of her, so she went to stay with her parents in North Carolina. My problems were less dire but more humiliating. I had a bad case of carpal tunnel in my wrist—the one I moused with. I was taking 2,400 milligrams of ibuprofen per day, and, just six months after climbing Alaskan peaks, I was reduced to wearing one of those reinforced medical wrist guards.

But we couldn't rest now. The establishment was running scared. As soon as we won Iowa, the rest of the states would fall like dominoes toward the convention. One night, Matt and I discussed whether, after the campaign, we'd return to our spartan lives in the desert, or if we'd move to Washington to take jobs with the Dean administration.

But then came Iowa. We didn't just lose. We got creamed. A distant third after Kerry and Edwards. That night we went to bed proud in our defeat, and by the next morning we were the laughingstock of the nation. Every TV channel and radio station was playing Howard Dean's concession speech. Over and over. You know the one: where he screams the names of all the states, trembling like Mussolini, then finally lets out what could only be called a yawp.

"All my work here," Matt predicted, "will be eclipsed in history by this one speech."

But there was still New Hampshire. Never mind the naysayers, I was dispatched to New Hampshire to report on the insuppressible momentum for Governor Dean. I blogged from rallies in Nashua and Plymouth:

> The cameras are clicking from a wall of press and TV reporters, but the real excitement here is much simpler—it's a community. A roomful of ordinary Americans, tired of being divided, tired of feeling powerless, coming together to restore our republic—to participate in our own government.

> If more than a thousand New Hampshirites come out on a subzero Sunday
> night to stand up with Howard Dean, imagine what we'll do when we all stand up.

I ended with an exhortation to click here and take back your country. The money kept flowing. That momentum I was reporting—it was real!

But we didn't win New Hampshire. The dominoes were falling in the wrong direction. And now the campaign collapsed. Trippi quit. Or maybe he was fired. It was never explained. The day after New Hampshire he said goodbye with tears in his eyes, ran a gauntlet of reporters outside the office, and drove home to Maryland. The political director quit. And then Matt gave notice on our apartment. He got in his truck and drove down to North Carolina to tend to his wife. The ship was without its captains.

·+·

Headquarters was in chaos. Desks were empty in the middle of the day. Howard Dean himself gathered us into a conference room, and tersely explained that there would be no paychecks this month. But the new campaign manager, someone none of us knew, arrived with the good news that we could still pull this one out. We'd win the next state. But we didn't win South Carolina, or Arizona, or New Mexico, or Oklahoma, or Michigan, or Maine.

Fine. We would win Wisconsin, and after that the states would fall like dominoes.

Our supporters were turning on us. The blog inbox filled with personal and vicious accusations of incompetence, of stupidity, of betrayal. They demanded their money back. At first I responded to each email with gentle optimism—we'll win in Wisconsin!—but finally they were too demoralizing. They hurt my wrist. I deleted them unopened.

Then I was called in to the office of the higher-ups. I'd never been called here before. Yes, they explained, we'd raised nearly $40 million, shattering political records. But we'd spent it all. In fact we'd spent more. We were in the hole. We didn't have enough money for doughnuts and coffee on Election Day in Wisconsin.

"We need to raise $700,000 by Friday," someone told me. "And you're the only one who knows how to write those magic emails."

This one wasn't to be signed by one of the higher-ups, but by Governor Dean himself. This was his final rallying cry.

"Can you get us a draft in thirty minutes?"

I drove home, where I could concentrate. There were two problems. First, the whole thing was unethical. I'd badgered our supporters for months because I believed their contributions would restore our democracy. Now I knew they were just throwing their dollars at a lost cause. Yet if we didn't ask for money, the press and the other candidates would know that we'd given up. And then we'd lose Wisconsin without a fight.

And here was the bigger problem: I had no idea what to say. Trippi was gone. Matt was gone. I only knew how to follow instructions.

I spent about six minutes thinking. Now I had twenty-four to write the draft. I couldn't go on like this, telling them that the first domino was about to fall. What we needed was an ultimatum.

"The entire race has come down to this," I began. "We must win Wisconsin."

I omitted the flourishes and cut straight to the ask: give us fifty dollars. "All that you have worked for these past months is on the line on a single day, in a single state." Anything less than a victory in Wisconsin, my letter threatened, "will put us out of the race."

But by the time I returned to the office with my draft, I couldn't find any higher-ups to approve it. It was eight o'clock. People had gone to dinner or gone home. I didn't want to spend the whole night nursing this letter through all the appropriate channels. I wanted to go to sleep. I forwarded the draft to the tech guys.

"Make sure someone approves this before you send it out."

·+·

My phone woke me up at 6:00 a.m. "Who approved your email?" someone said.

"I don't know," I said. "Why?"

"Look at the *New York Times*."

I opened my computer and my belly seized up. Headline: DEAN SAYS HE'LL QUIT IF HE DOESN'T WIN WISCONSIN. Lead: In an email addressed to his supporters, Howard Dean said last night, etc., etc. It had a finality and recklessness that you don't hear in politics. It was something only an amateur would say.

My unedited email had been blasted out just after midnight, and the *Times* reporter had filed the story before most anyone else had read it. And here was the snag: among those who were not familiar with the email's ultimatum was its ostensible author, Howard Dean himself.

Campaigning in Wisconsin, Dean was startled to learn from the *New York Times* that he was on the verge of quitting the race. On a conference call with HQ first thing in the morning, no one could locate anyone associated with the email. The best they could tell, some of those kids from the web team had written the thing from whole cloth and taken it upon themselves to launch it to the multitudes.

The blog was in mutiny. "Please reconsider this," wrote one of the diehards. "I have worked my a** off for this campaign. Don't I deserve the opportunity to vote for the candidate I have poured untold hours of effort into?"

"People, save your money," wrote someone else. "Invest it, instead of throwing it away on a finished campaign."

I drove to the office like a man to the gallows. I had sunk the cause on which the hopes of millions rested. I tried to assume an attitude of penitence for the imminent violence. But I didn't feel guilty. Instead, I was pleased with myself.

I wish I could report that my pleasure came from having done what was right. Maybe, I rationalized, I had done Howard Dean a favor. Everyone besides him knew he was finished, and maybe my email was a necessary nudge toward reality. Surely I'd done right by those true believers who would have continued to pony up once a week between now and the convention, sure that if they could just believe harder and sacrifice more, eventually we could reclaim our country and the principles upon which it was founded.

No, that wasn't the cause of this thrilling pride.

However unintentionally, I had dipped my finger in the flow of history, and watched it divert. I had tasted power. It was not power democratically earned and justly administered, that ideal in whose service I had come to Vermont. Instead it was the sheer egoism of having my will manifested simply because I said so. It was the seed of tyranny, the very thing I was fighting to defeat.

When I reached headquarters that morning, I learned that the new campaign manager had, in fact, approved my email. Any blame for its wrongness lay with him, not me. The waters of history that I thought I'd diverted—they quickly returned to their channel. In a week, Howard Dean would lose Wisconsin and quit the race, finalizing a fate that, since the Iowa debacle, had been apparent to all but the most blindly faithful.

Meanwhile, I was a hero. My email drew the required $700,000 in the first day—the second-biggest fund-raising day of the campaign—and eventually doubled its goal. I didn't tell anyone at headquarters about my thrilling taste of power. I strapped on my wrist guard and returned to my cubicle, where we still had another week to save our republic, with me at the keyboard, sounding the bugle and rallying the troops.

Too Much Fun for Just One State

From where I'm standing on the old Wendover Air Base, the brightest thing in the sky is the State Line Casino. It's a square concrete castle bathed in white light. A marquee blinks and flashes. The giant neon-light cowboy is waving at me from just that side of the Nevada border. Come on in, he seems to be saying. It's a cold October night. As for me, I'm over here in Utah.

In the foreground, a line of sedans is crawling single file onto the air base. The headlights jiggle as they bump over the potholes. They cruise past the abandoned barracks, empty lots of tumbleweeds, dangerous-looking heaps of rusted machinery. The only life on the air base is at the old officers' club, a two-story wood plank building with peeling paint and boards on the windows. One hundred cars are parked outside; lights blink from behind the boarded-up windows. I can hear the bounding oom-pah-pah of a Mexican ranchera band.

Suddenly, in unison, blue and red lights begin to spin on the roofs of the sedans. It's the state police. There are a lot of them; I stop counting at thirteen. They surround the dance hall, and before long the music quits and people stream out into the night. The men wear white cowboy hats. They load into cars with their wives and sisters and children, and drive away through the corridor of police cars. State troopers in brown uniforms wave flashlights and holler at everyone to hurry it up. They're not much older than the Mexican teenagers in baggy pants and snakeskin boots who curse the cops under their breath and slink off in a pack across the air base. The taco truck drives away.

Within half an hour everyone is gone except the police. They are conducting a search of the premises. Later, they will arrest the operator of the dance hall and take him one hundred miles to the Tooele County jail.

Meanwhile, the State Line Casino is still shining like a full moon from Nevada. Wendover Will the mechanical cowboy waves his stiff electric arm, back and forth, back and forth. He's been waving it all along.

Lisa Willcox is on stage dressed as Gloria Estefan. She wears skintight pants made of a shimmering purple-pink material that could either be vinyl or rubber. A complementary halter top reveals a firm abdomen that seems a result of rigorous tummy exercising. Before this she was Shania Twain, dressed in a similarly revealing leopard-skin bodysuit.

A spotlight follows Lisa as she spins across the stage with complicated Latin footwork and a flower tucked above her ear. Her cheeks are red and her teeth, white. The music issuing from the band is impressive. The sound of a brass section blares from the synthesizer. Lisa Willcox beats a timbal with a single drumstick, does a spin. A disco ball turns on the ceiling and the backlighting of the stage fades from tangerine to lavender to turquoise. Then she takes a bow, bids adios to the crowd, and whirls offstage.

There are six people in the audience.

Based on this performance, I make the following guesses: Lisa Willcox comes from a small town in the middle of America; she was the prettiest girl in her high school; and she spent her teen years dancing in front of the mirror singing Madonna into the hair dryer.

"Ladies and Gentlemen," booms an unseen announcer, "give a big hand for Michael Jackson's stepfather!"

Now here comes Lisa's husband, Pete, as Elvis Presley. He wears the requisite white leather bodysuit with fringe and rhinestones. He shakes his hips. He looks just like him.

Pete and Lisa Willcox make up "It Takes Two," their self-owned and -managed cabaret revue, which includes her impressions of Estefan, Twain, Madonna, and Cher, and his take on Elvis, Buddy Holly, John Lennon, and the Rat Pack, to name just a few. They've been married four years and performing as It Takes Two for eighteen months. Before that he did Elvis and she did Madonna as part of big Las Vegas revues.

"It was very limiting," Pete Willcox tells me in between shows. "You can only go as far as the producer wants you to go. His show, his deal. But with this show, we can go as far as we can go."

I am sitting with Pete and Lisa at a small bar table at the State Line Casino. Pete wears a plaid sport coat and a black turtleneck; Lisa wears a sparkly silver dress and has long bleach-blonde hair. Both hold styrofoam cups of tea and milk. A John Denver song plays from somewhere, peppered with the casino sounds of computerized bells and whistles, and coins clanking out of slot machines.

"I don't want to be as presumptuous as to say the Sonny and Cher of the Millennium," says Pete, sipping his tea through a stir-straw, "but let's go ahead and say that, for the fun of it."

Lisa gets up to find some more honey. She brings back two packets and squeezes them into her drink. The first of my guesses about her proves to be true; she was born in 1970 in Taylor, Michigan, a town which has "a lot of hicks." After a year of college, she began singing in a rock band and moved to Florida to make it big. The band didn't do too well, so she found an agent who placed her in an all-guy band, who soon decided they didn't want a female in their group. Finally, she passed an audition to be one of three singers in a "girl group" called Maiden America, with whom she toured for two years. Now she laughs, recalling that the music was mostly sequenced, and that she and her partners faked playing their instruments.

"It was good for me," she says. "It taught me how to front a group, how to work a stage, and things like that. We'd go to a new place every two weeks."

One place they played was Las Vegas, at the Flamingo Hilton. She recounts this all with a slight musical lilt in her voice, either a leftover from her small-town childhood, or a byproduct of professionally imitating Shania Twain. It is charming in either case. She tells me that it was in Las Vegas where she met Pete Willcox, the Elvis impersonator.

"I talked her into doing Madonna," says Pete. "I thought if she'd sit down and do Madonna, she could save money and record original material."

Before coming to Vegas, Pete Willcox had lived in Los Angeles for twenty years, working the steakhouse circuit—chains like Reuben's and Charley Brown's. He'd perform by himself with a drum machine, singing songs by Neil Diamond and James Taylor and the like. He speaks with a soft country drawl, muffled as if he'd had a tooth pulled the day before. I guess that after a lifetime of being Elvis, one invariably starts to talk like Elvis.

"Even up to now, that was my favorite form of entertainment," he says. "At least half of the night was original music. You have to play somebody else's songs to make them listen to yours."

But with the advent of disco, the steakhouse scene started to deteriorate. By the late '80s, Pete packed up and moved to Vegas because it catered to the type of show he did.

"Los Angeles is very trendy, very hip," he says. "It's dreadful trying to make a living. They want the latest alternative group, that's it."

Lisa also spent a short time in Los Angeles, playing the clubs and trying to get a record deal to record original music.

"Most alternative music is so negative," she tells me. "There's so much negativity in everyday life. I didn't want it in the music, too."

"We don't want to present negative sides of life," agrees Pete, "unless to show that it can be overcome."

They met at a Vegas revue that included Maiden America and Pete's Elvis act, and began dating. Both dreamed of one day recording albums of original music.

"I was really trying to nudge Lisa toward sitting in town and letting her career bloom."

So the two settled in Las Vegas and got regular jobs at the big revues, Lisa as Madonna and Pete as Elvis. The money was good. Working two ten-minute slots, an impersonator makes over $1,000 a night. They also worked cruise ships.

"There's a lot better money in impressions than in regular bands," says Lisa. "A lot stronger money. Our thing is that if you have to sing other people's music anyway, to make a living, you might as well make the most money you can until you move on."

"You might as well dress up like them," says Pete.

In the meantime, both are writing original songs and recording demo tapes that may someday land them a contract. Now, it's five minutes till ten. They have to leave for their second show. They set down their foam cups.

"Impersonation's a weird business," says Lisa.

It's 9:45 a.m. and Ramiro Ascencio has just eaten the better part of a grilled chicken sandwich. He left the curly fries pretty much alone. We are sitting at a booth in the Rainbow Cafe at the Rainbow Casino, beneath a trellis of speckled ivy leaves. Looking out the tableside windows, I do not see the dusty crags of the Wendover desert, but a pink pastel sky above a quaint cottage, opening onto a tidy vineyard. In order to give the customer the sense of having his petit-déjeuner in Bordeaux, the provincial French countryside has been painted on the wall. The ivy turns out to be polyester.

Ramiro Ascencio is the director of food services here. He also owns the Salon Vaquero nightclub that was raided by state police. He spent a night in jail. He wears a pressed white shirt and a tie that includes the colors purple, turquoise, and mango, the tones that apparently dominated the artist's palette when he set out to paint the Rainbow. The carpet in the casino room depicts stars, planets, meteors, and rainbows in these colors. The ceiling is mirrored. The Rainforest Room, home to the Rainforest Buffet, is filled with life-size fake palm trees and stuffed tropical birds. That carpet, along with the buffet staff's shirts, is a vivid diorama of jungle life, complete with banana leaves and bird-of-paradise flowers. It's sort of the same pattern that's on Ramiro's tie, and I note that it looks a bit out of place here in the south of France.

Despite the cartoonish surroundings, Ramiro Ascencio is all business. He is a stocky man with blow-dried hair and a trimmed mustache. He is the first employee I've seen this morning who does not wear a name tag, so I assume his job is of high rank. He is telling me the story of how the "Espanish" came to make up 75 percent of Wendover's 7,000 residents. While he tells me this, an occasional wave of discomfort rises from his chest to his mouth, and he must press his lips together to diffuse an enormous belch. It's the grilled chicken, I presume.

Ramiro tells me that a long time ago, maybe in the '60s, a man from Murguia, in the Mexican state of Zacatecas, was taking a train across the American West. He got off in Wendover and found work at the State Line, the only casino at the time. The pay was good, and he called home to tell his friends. In time, more Zacatecans moved north to work in the casinos. In the 1980s, when gambling took off, they flooded in. Many are transient, more still have settled in Wendover and bought homes. He crumples his paper napkin and lays it on the curly fries.

"Now the Espanish in Wendover," says Ascencio, "It's like one family."

Ascencio himself is not Zacatecan. He was born in Michoacan, in the south of Mexico, and crossed the border to California at age fifteen. He has worked in restaurants all his life. Four years ago he moved his family from Orange County to Wendover to take the management job at the Rainbow Casino, where Saturn and Neptune adorn the carpet. He and his wife bought a house on the Nevada side, and their three children were all born in America. He owns two small businesses: a small shop called Novedades Ascencio that stocks Mexican magazines, compact discs, and clothing, and Promociones Ascencio, that holds dances and concerts at the Salon Vaquero. He also rents out the hall for weddings and quinceañeras. Ramiro applied for citizenship three years ago, but his request has still not gone through.

I ask him if a lot of Mexican babies were born in Wendover as American citizens, and he says not in Wendover, but in the Salt Lake hospitals, or at least on the way there.

"Last week my cousin's wife have a baby on the side of the road," he said. "They have to pull over the trailer by Tooele."

What's foremost in Ramiro's mind this morning is that somebody ratted on him. He has run his nightclub for two years without any problems from the city, and now he gets raided by the state liquor agency from Salt Lake City. He had just checked out with the city the day before, and got the green light, so he was sure they hadn't blown the whistle. That meant that someone else had tipped off the state. He has an idea of who it was, but he's not sure yet. Someone caused him to spend the night in jail. Now he has to go to court next week, and he has to hire a lawyer.

"It's boll-shit," he says. "I am hard worker. I get all the forms, all the papers."

I ask him why someone would report him to the state, and he shrugs.

"Maybe they don't like it for the Espanish to succeed. To make money. I don't do nothing wrong."

I ask him if he thinks there is a lot of discrimination here and he shrugs. He tells me that no Hispanic has ever been elected to political office in Wendover, Utah, or in West Wendover, Nevada.

"It's the next step," he says. "Maybe I'm not the one, but someone is."

Hi, I just wanted to talk about our local fast-food industry. I was always hoping that someday we should get a McDonald's, and by golly we finally did. My kids were real happy about that. I was pleasantly surprised when I read that we were getting an Arby's. We've gone to McDonald's several times and so I thought I would take the kids to Arby's this week.

After pulling into the drive-thru the wrong way, I was so embarrassed that we just left, but I'm sure the food was great, at least it smelled good.

We'll try again.

C. M.
West Wendover

—a letter to the *Wendover Times*

On a Sunday night I am at Wendover Cinema and Video. There are three small screens here which acquire movies that were not popular even when they first came out. I once saw a midweek matinee here; there were four people in the audience.

You can also rent videocassettes in the lobby. Typically one employee runs both the box office and the rental counter. I've seen three or four different women do this job. The owner is a fat man who has a small office whose door sits between the Dramas and the New Releases. The local kids know him by name and he sometimes comes out of his office to chat with them around the Sega Genesis shelf. Once, I heard he and an employee having a loud, vicious argument from behind the office door. Both were cursing. It ended with the woman storming out of the office in tears, announcing that she'd quit, and rushing out the front door.

Wendover Cinema sits on a desert shelf overlooking the interstate in a newly developed neighborhood optimistically called Bonneville Heights. There is a complex of low-income apartments and condominiums built on this large flat spot, with some larger "custom homes" on the hillside. Next to the movie theater is a Mexican carnicería and a hair salon.

With little evidence to support myself, I have bestowed some dignity on this dusty outcropping of suburbia. Mostly it's because the people living and working here have ignored the prevailing wisdom to set up shop in Nevada, and have done so in Utah instead.

The disadvantages are numerous. The most obvious is that Nevadans don't pay state income tax; Utahns do. But the contrast runs deeper. West Wendover is a town on the make. Just incorporated in 1991, its coffers are rich from casinos, fast-food chains, and a supermarket. There are brand-new schools and a public library, and wide streets of smooth asphalt. The city's slick promotional booklet proclaims West Wendover "a jewel of promise in the high desert that surrounds it . . . a community that offers business and employment opportunities, an excellent quality of life, education, recreation—all the advantages civilization brings without the disadvantages of crowded urban living." Glossy color pictures depict neat tract houses, the new high school, and the Toana Vista golf course. Giving scant mention to the casinos which employ the majority of townspeople, the booklet depicts these employees as upstanding, well-groomed, and phenomenally content with their unending hours of leisure, filled up primarily with tennis, little league, and horseback riding. The actual work of the gambling and service industry—washing dishes, dealing cards, making beds, serving cocktails, mopping floors, ejecting drunks—is conspicuously absent from "Come Grow With Us!", but the literature is convincing evidence nonetheless of the town's prosperity.

Across the border, it's a different story. The city of Wendover, Utah, declared bankruptcy. Its Main Street business consists of pawn shops and creaky-mattress motor lodges. Its civic election campaigns include one candidate publicly offering a "fist full of knuckles" to his opponent. Once elected, city officials are so notoriously incompetent—even the simplest proposals to repair potted roads or crumbling sidewalks are killed by infighting and debate—that the editor at the West Wendover newspaper told me that he'd come up with a new policy concerning Wendover, Utah, politics: "I don't cover it, because no one would believe me. When I try to report a story that the council has fired their garbage collector in order to do it themselves, at an increase of twenty dollars per barrel, people think I'm making it up."

In short, Wendover is the collision of Utah and Nevada. The east side is an outpost of Deseret, legislated by the communitarian morality that remains from the day of Brigham Young's oligarchy. West Wendover is all about freedom, economic and moral, a satellite of Las Vegas's sin-and-money laissez faire, which in the 1990s has rendered itself the picture of middle-class decorum.

Together, the dissimilar towns form something known as Wendover, USA, a place touted on highway billboards as containing "too much excitement for just one state." The Wendover Area Chamber of Commerce and Tourism prints up a smart little business directory, whose eight pages boast of shops, hotels, and restaurants, and of such wholesome attractions as the Bonneville Salt Flats speedway and the Donner Party Trail. It's a strange publication, perhaps indicative of the difficulty of reconciling Utah's old-fashioned uprightness with Nevada's profitable debauchery. On one page you'll see a list of churches and schools; on the next an advertisement screams, "UNEDITED Adult Movies and Magazines: The Kind You Can't Buy in Utah, just across the border in West Wendover, Nevada." A full three-quarters of the directory's underwriters represent the gambling and pornography industries.

But for some reason, there is development popping up at Bonneville Heights, Utah, at the video counter where I find myself. Maybe there is some sort of allegiance to Utah. Maybe there are some Mormons involved; despite the influx of gambling sinners and Mexican Catholics, the Latter-day Saints still maintain a ward in Wendover. At any rate, Utah lucked out and got the only movie theater in town.

Tonight, a pale, pretty girl is working the counter. I have assumed that she is the daughter of the owner, maybe because she's allowed to bring her two-year-old son to work. Presently the child is at her feet. A man renting a video is wearing sweatpants, construction boots, and a motorcycle helmet. The helmet covers the entire face and chin, with a tinted windscreen across the eyes.

"Two forty-one," says the girl.

"Two forty what?" says the man from within the big black helmet. The muffled voice has a recognizable hillbilly drawl, like Elvis. It's unmistakably Pete Willcox.

"Two forty-one," repeats the girl, taking his money and making change.

"These are due back on Tuesday," she says.

Pete flips up his windscreen. "What's that?"

"Tuesday," she says, a bit louder.

"Right," says Pete. He buries the videotape in his fanny pack and leaves. I hear the roar of his motorcycle.

I bring my selection to the desk and ask the cashier why she thinks that man wouldn't take off his helmet.

She has no idea. "He comes in here all the time."

"Does he always wear his helmet?" I say.

She shakes her head and rings up my rental. "He's the entertainer who does the Elvis show at the casino," she says helpfully, as if to explain that, while she herself certainly does not endorse indoor helmet-wearing by Elvis impersonators, it is simply one of the many breaches of civility that a person must tolerate if she is to make her home in Wendover, Utah.

I thank her and am about to leave when she adds, as a conciliatory afterthought, "My son didn't like it."

"The show?"

"The helmet. It scared him."

> *When in April the sweet showers fall*
> . . . .
> *When also Zephyrus with his sweet breath*
> *Exhales an air in every grove and heath*
> . . . .
> *Then people long to go on pilgrimages*
> *And palmers long to seek the stranger strands*
> *Of far-off saints, hallowed in sundry lands.*
>
> —Chaucer, *Canterbury Tales*

It has been a long time since the train stopped in Wendover to deliver the man from Murguia who laid the first seed for the community of Mexicans and Mexican-Americans. Nowadays the train blasts right through. Not only does it not stop, it doesn't even slow down.

The California Zephyr made its first voyage from Chicago to places west in March of 1949. The stainless-steel diesel streamliner was christened after Zephyrus, the Roman god of the West Wind, and terminated at the Pacific Ocean at San Francisco. Along the way, passengers were served fine food and beverages by a coterie of neatly dressed stewardesses called Zephyrettes. The train was the finest piece of technology that post-war America could offer its citizens. Each train was equipped with the famous "Vista-Dome," a lounge car covered with a glass canopy, and it was from these Pacer X-style chambers that a generation of train travelers got their first panoramic view of the Rockies, the Sierras, and the Great Salt Flats.

In the days of inexpensive jet travel, Amtrak's California Zephyr is a novelty, and its selling power is the nostalgia of a train trip. The conductors still call "All Aboard!" at each stop, but the words ring slightly false to the modern traveler in the way that the words "Prepare for Blastoff!" might sound on an astronaut-themed roller coaster. And indeed, the Zephyr milks the sightseeing element of its itinerary. Lounge cars still have domed glass in the ceilings, and all chairs point outward, so that passengers can sip up the scenery with their Cabernet Sauvignon. The train spends its daylight hours in the jewels of the American West: the Rockies and the Sierra Nevada. Coming from San Francisco, darkness falls just past Winnemucca, and the sun rises near Price, Utah.

What gets blacked out—the scenery not worth seeing—is the majority of the Great Basin and the Salt Flats. There is a six-hour stretch between Elko, Nevada, and Salt Lake City, where the train doesn't stop at all.

The Zephyr roars through Wendover just after midnight, passengers sleeping soundly.

It's been said in Nevada that going to a casino for the music is like going to a whorehouse for a hamburger. The difference is that you have to pay for the hamburger. And though I cannot testify to the quality of brothel chuck, I am witnessing one of the finer free concerts I can remember.

I am watching the band R.E.T. perform in the State Line Casino. They are not on the showroom stage where Pete and Lisa Willcox play, but crammed onto a small stage above the bar in the casino proper. There are six Black men on stage, and when they dance in unison they must tuck in their elbows to keep from knocking into one another. The bass player swings his instrument back and forth to the beat, narrowly missing an electric piano on the left and a microphone on the right. I would say that the average age of the performers is forty, though the main singer, clad in black silk and gold chains, looks about twenty-five. His head is shaved and polished; he's beating a tambourine against his thigh. The band is playing "What's Going On" by Marvin Gaye, and the crowd is bouncing. I count eleven Black people in the audience, which is more than I've seen in a month in Wendover. A 300-pound man is shimmying on his bar stool. People are dancing. People are actually paying attention to the music—watching and singing along and tapping their feet—enough so that nobody is playing the slot machines.

During the set break, I sit down with the bandleader as he gulps down a whiskey and Coke. His name is Raymond Hatcher and he's been a professional musician for more than twenty years; as a teenager in Sacramento, he and his five siblings formed a family act called Black Nature. He wears a backward Kangol with his wet curls streaming out the back. The waitress sets another drink on the table.

"That's what I like about Wendover," says Raymond Hatcher, sipping the straw to get the last out from the ice cubes. "They're pretty laid back."

He tells me that in most casinos, musicians aren't allowed to drink. Once on a riverboat casino in Mississippi, his singer, D Money—"that dude with the bald head"—had a glass of beer an hour before show time. The manager saw it, and D Money was eighty-sixed for life. Then Ray, who manages the band, had to write a letter of apology to the casino, assuring the casino that D Money had been fired. It was not really a problem, though, because R.E.T. has rotating members, so the next time they went to the steamboat, he simply brought a different singer. Ray told me that he currently has twelve band members; sometimes he has R.E.T. playing simultaneously in two different places. Six in Nevada, six in Mississippi. Members come and go all the time.

"We used to have a guitar player," says Ray, "but he turned out to have diabetes, and the traveling was too much for him."

R.E.T., which stands for Respect Equality Togetherness, plays R&B, soul, and slow jams from legends like Marvin Gaye, the Stylistics, the Commodores, and Rick James. But Ray tells me that pretty soon they're going into the studio to cut an original record. They don't have a distribution deal as of yet, but Ray hopes to sell discs at shows and "on the Internet." In the meantime, they throw in one or two original songs each night. It's hard playing what you want to play in the casinos. In Vegas, the stage managers still write up song lists for the bands, based on what they think their gamblers will want to hear. For a Black band, this invariably means Motown oldies.

"It's like," Ray says indignantly, "why do I have to play 'Sittin' on the Dock of the Bay'?"

A skinny white woman in a Utah Jazz t-shirt sits down with us. She seems to know Ray. She lights a cigarette. I ask Ray how he likes Wendover compared to his home of Reno. He says it's not bad. There's not much to do in the daytime but watch TV and catch a matinee, but the crowd at night is pretty good, definitely better than a few years ago.

"They're the best band around here," says the girl. "I seen them the first time they played. I used to work here."

"Back in '96, the crowd was all, like, Mormons," he tells me. "I mean, everyone had a beard. They didn't know what to make of us."

"When do you start again, Buckwheat?" says the white woman, lighting another cigarette.

Ray looks at me and raises a single eyebrow. After two decades in this business, he's heard it all. What else do you need to know, he seems to say. He finishes his drink.

Before he gets up, I ask him a final question. I want to know where the name Respect Equality Togetherness comes from.

"Well, originally it was Ray, Ewan, and Tony," he says. "But Ewan and Tony left the group, so I changed the name, and kept the letters."

When Col. Paul Tibbetts came to Wendover Air Base during World War II, his mission was so secret that he was the only one on base who knew what it was. The facility was brand new, with its identical barracks lined up on the salt flats like hay bales on the prairie. If you combined the airmen, their families, the railroad crews, and the miners, there were more than 20,000 people in the dusty outpost. Tibbetts knew that the plane he piloted from Wendover would change the course of history. He knew that the plane would be famous, and to be sure that it wouldn't have the same name as any other vessel, he christened it after his mother, Enola Gay.

Tibbetts's devastating mission over Hiroshima may have put Wendover on the map, but not for long. In 1977, the Air Force abandoned its Wendover base, and deeded the airstrip and barracks to the city. As the casino industry boomed on the other side of town, Wendover flung itself headlong into establishing a gambler's airport that would haul in the tax money. Ultimately the expected weekend junkets never arrived; Wendover declared bankruptcy and Tooele County took control of the airport.

The rest of the air base buildings have been rented at meager profit to various local concerns. What were once barracks now house a fifty-cent-per-load laundromat, a weight-lifting gym, and Ben's Used Things, which sells furniture, vacuum cleaners, and mismatched sets of china. The old chapel has been converted to apartments, with the steeple still intact; a mess hall has become the Wendover Christian Center. One airstrip is a commercial drag racing lane. Other buildings are boarded up or falling down.

One attempt to bring a share of Nevada's tourists over to the Utah side is the self-guided historical tour of the air base. Big signs mark the locations of the Enola Gay hangar, the chapel, and the airmen's barracks. The airport lobby includes a one-room museum with framed black-and-white photos and scale models of the base. Press a button and hear an audio reenactment of 1945 soldiers loading atomic bombs onto the Enola Gay, complete with war-era swing music in the background.

The largest intact building, according to the neatly lettered signs, is the "Officers Service Club, Gym, and Open Mess." Old-timers recall seeing Frank Sinatra perform here for soldiers, just after the war, back when the State Line Casino was hardly more than a roadhouse. Nowadays, locals know this building by its other sign: a hand-painted plywood number with a crude cowboy hat and saddle and the red-lettered words "Ramiro Ascencio's Salon Vaquero." This is Wendover's Thursday night club, and on a good night it draws a bigger crowd than any of the casino stages.

I'm here for the dance. None of us here knows that in two weeks the club will be closed down by the state police. For the time being all is festive. Children are playing. People are eating tacos from a truck in the lot. The security guard, a blonde woman who is the only other gringo besides me, informs me that tonight is a quinceañera, and admission is free. I pass through the lobby, where men drink bottles of beer, into the dance hall.

It is a big, square, high-roofed hall filled with music and laughter and spinning electric lights. It smells like old lumber and perfume. Couples are dancing on the plank wood floor, the woman in dresses and the men in cowboy boots and hats. Others sit at little round tables against the walls. There are hundreds of people. A balcony wraps around three of the walls, and at the far end, up on the balcony, plays the band. They're dressed in silky cowboy suits that remind me of some extravagant Fourth of July pageant.

They play the fast, tinny brand of Tejano music that blares from jukeboxes in Mexican restaurants. A green spotlight focuses on the singer, and down here on the floor they clap and holler when the song ends.

I am in the Silver Smith Casino lounge talking to Lisa Willcox about guns. It's across the street from the State Line and owned by the same company, and connected with a skywalk that bridges four lanes of pavement. The stage is nondescript; slot machines make slot machine noises. Pete Willcox told me that there was once a prettier showroom here at the Silver Smith, but it was torn out to make room for more slots; after all, he admitted, the bottom line of the gambling business is making money. The chairs are soft and round, the same ones they have over at the State Line. Lisa is telling me that the last time she was in Wendover she bought a 9 mm handgun at the pawn shop.

"My girlfriend was pissed when she heard I got it for 150 bucks," says Lisa Willcox. "In Vegas they go for 350, so I got a really good deal. The blue book is three, like, twenty on it, so I got it for half the blue book."

She has changed out of her stage costume but still wears the two-inch fingernails and one-inch eyelashes. She's wearing jeans and a white turtleneck sweater with purple and lavender stripes. It's the same two colors as her lipstick, which is applied over an area about twice the size of her actual lips. The topic of guns had come up earlier when I'd asked Pete and Lisa what they did to pass the daytime hours in Wendover, and Lisa had said, "Shoot guns, play golf, ride motorcycles." They like to drive their bikes to the ample open space around town and fire their weapons. Handguns, mostly. Pete told me he had some .30-30 rifles but he never shot them; he had just bought them because he liked their Western look. He also has a .22 that is so accurate, he says, that all you have to do is point it at a bottle, and the bottle explodes.

"You don't even have to pull the trigger," he said. "I swear."

Now Lisa and I are here at the Silver Smith to see the Coates Twins perform. More accurately, I am here to see the Coates Twins, and Lisa is here to sing with them. Pete has gone home to do some recording on his digital machine, which he told me was no bigger than the briefcase I have been lugging rather self-consciously through the casino. Both Pete and Lisa have assured me that I will enjoy the Coates Twins' music.

"They're been playing since they were thirteen, or younger," Lisa told me. "They met the president."

The Twins are on stage now, wearing matching black velvet pants and floor-length zebra-print overcoats. Along with a mustachioed lead guitarist and a young bald drummer behind a Plexiglas shield, they are playing a competent cover of a Jewel song. One Twin plays bass, the other plays guitar. Both sing. Both do the chicken walk. Yes, they really are twins.

There are three other people in the audience. A husband-and-wife truck-driving team are drinking Cokes. A drunk man has employed a second lounge chair for his legs and is lying down. Lisa tells me that when she and the Twins are in Wendover, they ride bikes together.

"They're real tomboyish," she says. "They grew up on dirt bikes, so they taught me to ride my street bike in the gravel. And I tried to peel out in the gravel, which I don't know how to do. I wrecked my bike."

A security guard is tapping the drunk man's shoulder. I notice now that he is passed out, sleeping. Without opening his eyes, the drunk man swings his fist at the guard. The Twins are playing "Keep on Rockin' Me, Baby." Soon there are four security guards. The man is smoking a cigarette, his eyes still closed. They grab hold of his limbs and he kicks and flails. The security guards are not sure what to do with the man; they confer near the front entrance. Lisa and I and the truck drivers clap as one song ends and another begins.

"Some people call me the space cowboy," sing the Coates Twins. "Some people call me the gangster of love."

Then Lisa gets up and lays her hand on the man's wrist.

"I want to talk to you but it's too loud in here," she says. "Will you come outside with me?"

The man bolts upright and staggers behind her to the foyer where the security guards are waiting.

"I didn't want to see you get carried out," she tells the drunk as he is escorted to the street. "It would have been ugly."

I would like to thank the Young or Old People, that ran off with 90% of our just harvested potatoes on or around the 14th of October 1999.

I would also, like you to know, that most of the Spuds you got away with, are the seed Potatoes, that I was saving to plant next spring.

I think that it's sad that you had to steal our food, that we took 6 months to grow. Well I hope that whoever took the Potatoes, enjoys them. That will be the first and last time you will ever get anymore of them from me, because I just won't allow it to happen again. If you don't believe me, just try it again next fall, and see what I mean. Here is some information that I think you should know. We live in Wendover Utah—on Pilot Avenue. Between 700—900 East. Also I would like you to know that its going to cost us over $75.00 to replace the Seed Potatoes you took from us. I hope that you don't choke too much when you bite into the spuds that you didn't put any effort in earning. I want to thank you so very much for you being who you are. I hope that you always enjoy living with yourself, and doing the bad things you are doing.

I may not find out who done this to us, but I do know that the good Lord will get you, if and when you get to Heaven. I hope that you will be able to rest in peace. I know I will. Thanks for nothing.

Bill J.
Wendover, Utah

—a letter to the *Wendover Times*

From the moment Ramiro Ascencio shows me his briefcase, I understand that he does not intend to lose this battle. It is the boxy leather type with a combination dial that Ramiro must spin with his thumb before clicking the latch. Inside is a thick stack of documents: licenses from the city, minutes from the zoning commission's meeting, clippings from the local newspaper. As he shows me each paper, he thrusts his forefinger at certain passages and reads them aloud.

"Permit for consumption of beer," he says. "It says so right here."

We are in the lobby of the Salon Vaquero, and Ramiro Ascencio has his papers spread out on the ticket counter. He has agreed to meet me here on his day off. He and his son were dropped off here by Ramiro's wife. She let them out of the minivan, then took the young daughter to the laundromat.

It is cold inside. Ramiro wears maroon sweat pants and a black leather jacket. Wind blows in beneath the front door and lifts the dust off the plank wood floor. He catches me looking at the ceiling, warped and water-stained, with the tape is peeling off, and tells me that he did the drywall himself. But then the roof leaked and ruined all his work, so he decided not to fix it until the county replaced the roof. The walls are covered with concert posters.

Promociones Ascencio Presenta
LOS CAMINANTES
Con Su Exito "Supe Perder"

"I'm taking my son to court with me," says Ascencio. "He heard the city manager tell me everything OK to open again. He's a witness."

His son, who is leaning against the ticket counter in a West Wendover High football jersey, nods with assent but not enthusiasm. He speaks Spanish to his father, and the few words he says to me are in unaccented English.

Ramiro Ascencio shows me his court papers. He is angry. He tells me he lost $8,000 on the night of the raid. He is not sure why the police seized his cash drawer. He has hired a lawyer and pleaded not guilty to five counts of serving alcohol to a minor. He does not understand these charges because, during the raid, the officers didn't find any minors drinking beer. Furthermore, the *Wendover Times* reported that Ascencio had been charged with five entirely different violations, all having to do with improper alcohol licensing. But the criminal charges from the State Alcoholic Beverage Commission are just part of the problem; Ascencio has also had his business license suspended by the city of Wendover, Utah.

Among the infractions are complaints of noise, not having restrooms, and no running water. Ascencio points outside at the portable plastic outhouses he's rented. "As long as they can pee and poo," he says, "everything is fine." As for water, the Salon Vaquero is not connected to the city system. For more than a year, Ascencio has been lobbying Tooele County, who owns the property, to extend water service to his building. It hasn't happened.

Ramiro finds his predicament suspicious. To begin with, the city never told him that they'd suspended his license; he read about it in the *Wendover Times*. When he took the newspaper to the city manager's office, he was told that they knew nothing about it. But he then acquired the minutes from the meeting of the Zoning Commission in which the suspension had been recommended. It turns out that the chairman of the commission, Randy Croasman, is also the publisher of the *Wendover Times*.

Just as I'm about to ask Ramiro if he thinks this publisher might have a conflict of interest, he tells me that Croasman is helping another local Mexican to open a new nightclub, just blocks from the Vaquero, that will hold Spanish-language concerts. When Ascencio called Croasman to ask him why he was publishing undocumented rumors in the paper, he tells me Croasman yelled at him angrily over the phone. He also informed Ascencio that Salon Vaquero was in violation of a code that mandated that no beer could be sold within 600 feet of a church. The nightclub is 580 feet from the Wendover Christian Center, which occupies an old barracks. Ascencio doesn't believe that his neighbors would have complained about such a thing; in fact, when their daughter married, they held the reception at the Salon Vaquero (Randy Croasman did not answer my requests to speak with him).

My next question for Ramiro is this: how did the State Liquor Commission, whose nearest office is in Salt Lake City, find out about the Vaquero in the first place? And how did the *Wendover Times*, which is a weekly that comes out on Friday, have such a detailed report of the raid that happened late Thursday night.

"I don't know," Ramiro tells me. I look at his son, who looks away.

Does he think it was the newspaper man?

Ramiro shrugs and smiles, as if to say, you didn't hear anything from me.

I ask why, with all the trouble from the city, he didn't just open his club across the border in Nevada. He tried that, he says, and held a couple concerts in an auditorium in West Wendover.

"But the landlord don't like Mexicans hanging around in the parking lot," Ascencio tells me. "So he kick me out."

Truck of The Week from the Rainbow Hotel Casino
Suites

It's the 77 Express Stargazer from Lowell, Michigan. Drivers Ken Stone and Ken Orcar operate this 1999 Kenworth, powered by a 500 Detroit diesel. This week the truck was hauling paper and cheese from California back to Michigan. The truck is highlighted with chrome and has over 130 lights on the outside.

The truck will soon have a Rainbow Hotel Casino decal on it as the sponsor of the carpet for the cab and under the tractor during truck shows in several states.

—advertisement in the *Wendover Times*

There are seven of us around the table in the Silver Smith lounge. The Coates Twins are on set break, and I'm there with the entire band, as well as Lisa Willcox and a man in a shirt and tie who is in charge of hiring bands to play here. In my corner, Lisa Willcox has introduced me to the Coates Twin who plays bass guitar. Lisa says I'm a writer doing a story about Wendover music, and Bass Twin's interest is piqued. I offer up two copies of *Great God Pan*, the magazine I publish, to prove my credentials. Lisa has sent for two drinks—a Coors for me and a virgin piña colada for herself—and paid for them with vouchers. Bass Twin is drinking a can of chocolate SlimFast.

While we talk about various subjects—the quality of different recording devices and how much the different casinos pay—Lisa Willcox and Bass Twin thumb through the magazine. They seem a bit tripped up by the story on Bobby Beausoleil, a cohort of Charles Manson, and by the advertisements for Feral House books, which include such titles as *Satan Speaks*, *The X-Rated Bible*, and *Lords of Chaos: The Bloody Rise of the Satanic Metal Underground*.

"Look here," says Lisa, reading the ad, "Jehovah commands Hosea to marry a whore."

Meanwhile I'm trying to make conversation with the rest of the table. My repeating of Ramiro Ascencio's claim that Mexican ranchera bands earn $10,000 per night is refuted by a chorus of disbelieving scoffs from the professional musicians. But the man in the tie concedes that it could be true. "A lot of those stars, we've never even heard of."

"Like Selena," says someone. "She was huge in Mexico before anyone up here knew who she was."

Lisa looks up from the magazine and says it would be fun to do Selena in her show, but doubts that her audience would recognize her. Her crowd tends to be older, she says. I ask if anyone has ever been to the Salon Vaquero, and they shake their heads. They've heard of it, though.

"I was thinking of going to that," says Lisa Willcox, "but my friends said I better not because it's dangerous. I wanted them to teach me to dance better, for Gloria."

Now it's time for the Twins to go back on. I ask Bass Twin if there's a time we could talk in the next two weeks.

"We're only here for one week," she says. "So why don't we do it the week after that?"

Then she turns and walks up to the stage and I'm left with Lisa Willcox and my briefcase of magazines. I'm not sure what just happened. Lisa stands up to follow the man in the tie to the buffet; he's going to comp her a free dinner. I get up, too, and ask her if she thinks the magazine has offended the Bass Twin. Lisa nods.

"You see, the problem is, she's like me. We're both Christians. And it's hard to see the references to Satan, and all this about Hosea marrying a whore. When you love the Lord, it's hard to see that."

The man in the tie motions her away, and she slings her purse on her shoulder.

"And even in your article about camping there's a . . ." she continues, smiling, searching for the right word. I understand that she is trying to be helpful. "There's an unfavorable reference to the male anatomy. And when you tell someone you're born again, you don't want to see that stuff on one page and yourself on the next."

Then she's gone. I sit back down. The music starts.

I spend the evening drinking Coors and watching the rest of the Coates Twins' show. It will be a long and unusual night. It will surprise me, the things you see and hear if you sit that long in a casino lounge in Wendover, USA. Later on, a man who is half my height and twice my age will say to me, "I used to be a beautiful woman, so why don't you fuck me?" A drunk Hawaiian, barely able to stand, will ask me to join his rock band called Tropical Flame. A slightly built man of fifty with sideburns, a black silk shirt, and prison tattoos on his forearms, will dance with a young woman from Salt Lake City, and with flamenco-like grace, wrap his knees around her in plain view of her father and fiancé. Meanwhile, the father, wearing a surprisingly orange t-shirt with Tommy Hilfiger's signature across the chest, will spring onto the dance floor and cross his arms and kick his feet in what looks like a Russian folk dance.

But in the meantime, none other than D Money has arrived, and been invited on stage to sing a number. They play "Brick House," and D Money is right in between the Twins, they in their floor-length zebra-skin coats and he in his black silk pajamas. He's giving them sidelong, lascivious smiles, smacking his tongue up against a formidable gap in his front teeth. Bass Twin leans back on her heels with a skeptical look on her face. D Money is electric. He's spinning and grinding and tapping and slapping the soles of his patent leather shoes. He has on white socks. Then one at a time, he slinks toward a Twin and gets behind her with a hip-thrusting humping motion, all the while waving and grinning to the crowd. The audience loves it. They cheer. The Twins turn red and look away.

Ramiro Ascencio and I are inspecting the men's room in the Salon Vaquero. There are pipes along the wall where toilets and sinks should be attached. But there are no such fixtures. There is no running water in the building, but

Ramiro assures me that, in the case that water service is suddenly established, he is ready to install toilets at short notice.

"Now I show you the ladies' room."

The ladies' room looks pretty much the same as the men's room.

We cross the lobby and Ramiro pulls aside a hanging plastic sheet and leads me to a back room used for storage. It's a big cold chamber. On the floor, pink and yellow toilets and sinks and urinals lie on their sides, covered in dust. He goes over and nudges the porcelain with his foot.

"You see?" he says. "I have the toilets."

The only other things in this big, drafty storage room are a fleet of plastic sit-on-top toys.

"In this room, I want, how you say, for the children."

"Day care?"

"Yeah, so when they bring the family, they can dance while the kids play in here."

Ramiro tells me that the problem with raising kids in Wendover is that there is nothing for them to do. Since they're not allowed in casinos, they spend their Friday nights driving out to the desert and drinking beer. They start as young as age twelve, he tells me, and they get addicted.

"That's how come I want to open the club three nights a week," says Ramiro. "Fridays for kids, Saturdays for adults, Sundays for families. The kids need somewhere to go."

We make our way to the main hall. I can see daylight between the planks of the enormous pitched ceiling. The paint has peeled off. The rafters are covered in bird scat. Ramiro tells me that when he first moved in here, he had to shovel bird shit out of the long-abandoned hall.

"This deep," he says, pointing at his shins. "We also paint the downstairs. See?"

Ramiro Ascencio takes me upstairs and turns on the music. The ranchera blasts from a wall of speakers. The windows rattle. The louder the music gets, the emptier the room feels. Downstairs, Ramiro's wife has arrived and is straightening tablecloths and arranging chairs. Their daughter rides a plastic tricycle across the dance floor.

I ask Ramiro if he ever played in a band, and he says no, but now and then he'll get up on stage and sing a few numbers.

Then, for reasons I don't understand, Ramiro begins to tinker with the spotlights. I'm not sure if they're broken and need adjustment, or if he's trying to re-create for me the effect of being here during a dance, or if he just likes to play with them. He points a light at the spinning disco ball; melons of lights roll in circles around the dance floor. Trumpets ring out from the speakers. Ramiro flips on a big spotlight and a green circle appears on the empty stage. It's just me and him and his family and the loud music, mid-morning on a Saturday. Two months later he will win his court case and be acquitted of all charges. The judge will remark that the confusing and misleading nature of the Wendover permits made Ascencio's mistake understandable. Then he will try his best to bring the dance hall into compliance with zoning codes, and bring the Vaquero back to life.

Ramiro Ascencio spins a dial and the circle of light expands, then contracts, and he aims it onto the mike stand at head level, and on the back wall appears a small green circle with the shadow of the microphone. He leaves it there, satisfied, and we stand there together listening to the music and watching the lights.

I'm watching the second set of Pete and Lisa's show at the State Line. Lisa has just finished Cher, and the crowd was crazy for it. She has it down, complete with Cher's snotty banter: "You guys have been a real peppy crowd," she says through her nose, "but I gotta go now."

The room has filled up considerably. There are close to a hundred people. In front is the road crew that has been in town, working on Interstate 80. There are three women and a dozen men, and all have white hotel towels wrapped around their necks. They purport to be having a toga party, and they call for cocktails by the trayful. It's a good audience; loud and drunk and boisterous, but not rude. One man knelt stage-side while Lisa blew him a kiss. As the next song begins, they play bumper cars on the dance floors in their lounge chairs which, I learn, have wheels on the bottom.

Pete comes out as Tony Bennett, doing "Stepping Out," but midway through the song, Tony calls out George Burns, and Pete suddenly has thick-rimmed glasses, a cane, and a hobble. He begins a series of impressions of movie stars: Jack Nicholson, Walter Matthau, Clint Eastwood. I know from our earlier conversation that this is Pete's favorite part of the show, the part he considers the most intimidating and risky.

"Sometimes they like it, sometimes they don't," he had told me. "I'm kind of at their mercy. When you get vulnerable—when you give the audience the chance to really like it or not like it—that's when it's the most exciting."

Now Rocky Balboa is trying to sing "Stepping Out," and the crowd howls. They love it. A group of gamblers is hesitating at the cabaret door, wondering if they should commit.

"It's a free show, pilgrims," says John Wayne on the stage. "Come on in. We won't bite ya."

They come in and take a table and the crowd cheers. One of the road workers lets out a hoot. I am thinking about what Pete Willcox had said about taking risks onstage. He had compared it to a boxing match he'd seen the week before.

"He was really a big guy," Pete said. "Two hundred forty to two hundred fifty pounds. I wish I could remember his name. And he was fighting someone who was about two hundred fifteen, who had just had a hundred rounds sparring with Lewis—Lennox Lewis—and he knocked the kid down twice. Then he got up and knocked him down. And four rounds later: bang, knocked him out again. Oh man, it was jarring. It really was. That was the most explosive fight I've seen in the last five, six years.

"Now, you can stand there and outpoint a fighter, just with jabs, but if you'll take a chance, and start throwing roundhouses or extra rights, you stand a chance of getting knocked out. But you also stand the chance to knock the other guy out. That's what happens in entertainment. You do just safe bits, and they go over. But to try these impressions and humor—if that goes over, it's really rewarding."

For the show's finale, Pete Willcox comes out as Ray Charles. No blackface, but with the sunglasses and shuffling feet, he's got it down pretty well. Then Lisa joins him in a spangled minidress and a red bob. She's the "Uh-huh" girl from the Diet Pepsi advertisements, and they sing, "Hit the Road, Jack." The crowd has settled down a bit, but is still attentive, and applauds. They finish with "A Woman is a Woman but a Man is Just a Man," a choreographed number featuring Pete bumbling around stage and Lisa wagging a playful finger at him. He improvises some loose-legged dance moves and she rolls her eyes to the crowd. They seem to be enjoying each other, and the crowd can see it. Pete grins shamelessly. Lisa laughs and smiles. The road crew yells and the rest of the crowd claps their hands.

"Sometimes when we're on stage, usually at the start of the show when the light comes on us like that," Pete had told me, spreading his fingers to demonstrate what it's like to be in the spotlight's halo, "I almost feel like Adam and Eve in the Garden of Eden. Kind of like she and I against the world, and no matter what our troubles are, at least we're trying here."

The show is over, and within five minutes the showroom is empty and the blue velvet curtain hangs lifelessly where Pete and Lisa Willcox had just stood in an embrace.

"There's a good moment there," said Pete, "that always touches my heart somehow."

Cave Men

As a young man drifting in the desert, I acquired a valuable bit of wisdom: when you come across a cave, you should go inside, and, if possible, spend the night. This chestnut has served me well through the years, and came in handy in the spring of 2008, when my friends and I were on another of the haphazard, marginally safe expeditions that we undertake each year when the West's sudden snowmelt floods its valleys with cold current.

This time we'd chosen the Owyhee River in the desolate southeastern corner of Oregon, a river so rarely floated that it doesn't require a permit. This, of course, is another way of saying that our applications for more popular rivers had been denied or, in my case, sat blank on my desk until several days after the due date.

And so two days in, having just run a rapid called Bombshelter, we found ourselves snaking between sheer rock walls while a headwind blasted us with grit. One paddler had got his inflatable kayak pinned in a tiny alcove, and had to be kicked free by another.

By then he was rattled, and the next wave dumped him into the whitewater, from which we eventually fished him out, the second such rescue of the day.

Then it started to hail.

I should mention that a day earlier, at the Three Forks launch ramp, after a couple of hours of drinking beer and bouncing across dirt roads, we concluded that the raft was overloaded and jettisoned some supplies. Our choices, influenced by the ninety-degree heat and the beer, now seemed like poor ones.

Items that remained on the raft included an iron-wrought set of regulation horseshoes, two bottles of top-shelf bourbon, a small cedar chest of Brazilian cigars, and a ninety-four-quart ice chest packed with five cases of beer. Items left behind in the truck were fleece jackets, paddling gloves, and my tent.

It may sound now as though we were simply in over our heads. Actually, five of the seven of us had been river guides, and one a river ranger. But then, that level of experience allows a certain slackness, which can sometimes result in bold and rare incompetence.

Now wet and shivering, with the gales blowing the raft upstream, we fought our way downriver, and there we saw the cave. It was three o'clock and we were still six miles from our intended camp, but without discussion, we paddled to shore and hauled all the coolers and boxes and dry bags into the gigantic cavern.

And what a fine cave it was! Its white-sand floor was dry and soft, sleeping seven comfortably with ample room for fold-out kitchen tables, campfire, lawn chairs, and a regulation-length horseshoe pit. We quickly got into dry clothes, watching the rain blow sideways just mere feet from our warm shelter, where we would hunker down for the next twenty hours or so.

For some reason, we had been unable to convince any wives or girlfriends to come with us.

Initially, a few had signed on to float the lower stretch of the Owyhee (pronounced oh-WHY-hee), which has been called Oregon's Grand Canyon, with mild rapids, stunning vistas, and riverside hot springs. But in the days before the launch, they had backed out one by one, and simultaneously our itinerary morphed, governed by the same unspoken power that steers a Ouija board.

By the time we'd driven fifteen hours from Montana, across Idaho, and into the Oregon desert, we had scrapped the bucolic float and agreed to instead paddle the middle stretch, with Class V rapids—the second most difficult in the international rating system—notorious headwinds, and a twenty-foot waterfall.

We launched in May, during the first heat wave of the year, in a wide canyon where the three forks of the Owyhee joined. This desert, where the corners of Oregon and Idaho butt against northern Nevada, is some of the most rugged in the country, with just a few outposts; many of these, like Jordan Valley, were founded by hardscrabble Basque homesteaders.

The dirt road wound down from the dry plains into the green canyon, where the river meandered through lazy turns, soaking the willows and horsetails that sprouted from the banks.

We shoved off, paddling five hard kayaks, two inflatable kayaks, and one raft with oars. As we floated, the canyon flanks were silvery green with sagebrush, dotted with black chunks of volcanic rock and bursts of yellow where the arrowleaf balsamroot bloomed like big daisies.

Within a mile, the walls steepened and we tied the boats onshore to scout the first rapids, a series of ledges above a rock garden that continued around the bend, out of our sight. We successfully paddled the first drop, but then in the rock garden, Tiff flipped and came out of his boat.

I was trying to help him to shore in the pool below, when I noticed flotsam—a jug of orange juice, a fly rod, an oar—and looked back upstream to see the raft surfing in a hydraulic, a recirculating hole, with its captain, Nate, scrambling to the high side to keep it upright. After five minutes or so, the river released him, and we regrouped in the calm water.

The next morning, camped on a beach where wild hawthorn flowers blossomed, we vowed to take the whitewater more seriously. The reason we'd lost gear the day before was the lazy rigging job at the launch. Today's first step would be to tie things in more securely.

"Where are the rest of the straps?" I said.

"We left them in the truck," someone replied.

So we rigged the raft with a spool of laundry line and hoped for the best. It was then that I realized that we were about to paddle a Class V rapid, something I had never done in a kayak. I had misread the brief description of the Owyhee on the Internet, and thought we'd be portaging all the big rapids. So when we arrived at the Half Mile rapid and hopped over the boulders and sprigs of poison ivy to scout it, the water scared the hell out of me—all narrow slots and chaotic holes and sharp pour-overs.

I decided not to tell anyone it was my first Class V. It might jinx me.

Had I thought carefully about the rapid's name, I might have noticed that the part we were looking at was no longer than a quarter of a mile—which left a big unknown around the corner. But we could worry about that later.

So we returned to the boats and, keeping a careful formation, paddled the upper drops. Everyone nailed their lines.

Confident now, we floated willy-nilly into the lower stretch and quickly realized that the meat of this rapid was yet to come. We dodged rocks and flipped in holes—pure combat boating. I braced on the paddle with all my weight just to stay upright.

Then I noticed Mick standing on a rock in the middle of the river and figured he had stopped to take photos, or something, only to realize that he had no boat. His yellow kayak was cartwheeling downriver.

Stranded, Mick had no choice but to swim. He eased himself off his rock, and was swept into the froth, arms and legs flailing as he pinballed through the rocks and emerged sputtering in a pool below. On a sandy beach, we celebrated still being alive by eating pastrami sandwiches and potato chips, and drinking all the cans of beer stored in a mesh bag hanging off the raft to keep cool. As we lunched, the sky clouded and the wind picked up. I put on a wool hat.

Downstream, the canyon deepened. Sheer walls rose up both sides and buried the river in shadow. Looking down into the foreboding narrows, I remembered the thing I love and fear about running rivers: you have no choice. With more options, I would probably try to find an escape. But in a walled canyon, the only way is downriver.

·+·

It was in this giddy state amid pouring rain that we reached our savior cave. In our exhaustion, no one had the energy for full-court horseshoes, but—thank God for innovation—we improvised a game that allowed us to chuck the shoes from a seated position in lawn chairs. I cooked a pot of chili con carne and we mashed a bowl of guacamole.

When the rain finally stopped, we emerged from the cave into moist yellow twilight, scrambled over the basalt boulders spongy with wet lichen, cast a few flies into the current, and listened to the river gurgle and boil.

By morning we were thoroughly refreshed, and despite being able to see the fog of our own breath in the cold air, were more or less ready to paddle again.

"This cold front will blow right through," someone said. "This is the desert."

When we reached Widowmaker, the Class V+ falls, we shouldered our kayaks over house-size rocks, and lowered them on the other side with a rope. Then with ropes affixed to the raft's stern and bow, we inched it down the rocky banks, pivoting off rocks, then finally eased it over the drop into the safe pool below.

Then it started to hail again.

The cold weather didn't blow through, and after another afternoon of shivering and fighting gales, we finally paid the price for our lax planning. The beach camp we found wasn't horrible, but it was a poor substitute for our cave.

We stayed up late that night, huddled low around a fire to keep the blowing sand out of our teeth, wishing the rain would stop, killing the bourbon and tobacco.

But who really cared if we got wet and miserable? We were only a day's paddle from the car, and though we were sure it would be a long, cold, windy day, it couldn't be too bad.

We'd been out three nights and hadn't seen another soul. I had watched an osprey circle in the canyon updrafts. It was actually kind of fun, if you thought about it.

We gathered more driftwood and the flames rose higher. Nate leaned closer to the fire and pulled his collar over his ears.

"I'm wearing six cotton shirts," he announced. "I left my jacket in the truck."

The Fortress of Nice

The first words spoken when I stepped onto a shooting range where cops were learning to fly drones over American towns: "You need some sunscreen and bug dope?"

The holder of DEET was a North Dakota deputy I had followed seven miles from Grand Forks on straight roads through flat squares of soy and wheat. At nine in the morning the sun was high and hot, moisture and insects humming above the turf. Affable fellows loaded Cokes into ice chests.

Unmanned aircraft are booming here—*MarketWatch* declared North Dakota the Silicon Valley of drones—which is why cops were training, startups were startupping, and a magazine's editors had dispatched me, perhaps a dubious choice, considering I still carry a phone of the flip variety and my ignorance of drones was complete save for my hope that one not peep through my window.

I was led to a gray-topped officer bedecked with gun and handcuffs and a tan polo embroidered NORTHEAST REGION UAS UNIT. Alan Frazier was a professor of aviation at University of North Dakota and chief pilot of this interagency team. He gripped my hand viselike and said, "Some of the guys might use pretty strong language, and since that's not pertinent to your story, there's no need to include it." I tend not to debate men carrying handcuffs.

Beside a portable shade canopy, officers were learning to chuck a fixed-wing airframe that looked like a toy. "Nice and straight," coached an instructor. "Think: javelin throw." A policeman hurled the plane while the pilot, face buried in what looked like a lampshade, hit the throttle on a handset. The prop whirred and the plane soared.

The cops didn't look very coppish. They wore shorts and sneakers with teeny socks, tees emblazoned with hockey teams and 10K runs, wraparound sunglasses, and bills of ball caps crimped just so. White-male-wise, we were at 100 percent.

"Here comes the crash," someone told me. "We love this part." The plane belly-flopped on the grass and burst apart, wing and tail tumbling catawampus as the plastic ball that houses the camera bounced like an unripe cantaloupe. We hoorayed! Ingenious design allowed the pilot to reassemble it quickly.

A red-headed fellow stepped up. Pale as milk, packing a cannon, he flung the drone directly onto the turf, upon which it broke apart, inciting hoots. Perhaps the weight of the pistol had run his equilibrium asunder.

Beneath a second canopy, officers ran a quadcopter. As they sprawled in camp chairs I remarked that it looked like vacation.

"Nah, we'd be fishin'."

"Or drinkin'."

"Shame to have beer holders on these chairs but no beers."

Nicest guys! At any moment a game of horseshoes could break out! And it turns out that horseshoes would have been as exciting as learning to surveil. Don't get me wrong: the Qube was incredibly cool, the way it purred like a dragonfly when the rotors spun, lifted gingerly off the grass, and flew cloudward. But then all it did was run a grid over a soy field and relay video of—you guessed it—soybeans. Drag your finger across the tablet, the drone follows. Press a button and it finds its way home and shuts itself down. (I could use an app like that some nights when I leave the bar.)

I asked, "So could you chase O. J.'s Bronco down the freeway with this thing?"

"The FAA won't let us pursue," a deputy said glumly, "and besides, it tops out at thirty miles per hour."

They use drones for unsexy tasks like photographing car accident scenes. One potential use would be to locate a child lost in a cornfield, the mention of which always drew an approving murmur. My paranoia felt newly selfish: what kind of monster prefers a droneless world in which toddlers feed the coyotes?

When I asked if citizens of their towns resisted the prospect of camera planes overhead, the officers set me straight. Anything a drone does is already legal in helicopters and airplanes. The real innovation is price: about $20 per hour versus $575 for a helicopter. As for surveillance, they told me, we are already photographed at stoplights every day. Drones are no big deal.

Thus the down-homey mood of Cops with Props. I had expected tight security but instead the most controversial upshot the Chief Pilot could imagine from the presence of a reporter was F-bombs plopping into print.

And that would not be nice.

Frazier wiped his brow. "Could I get a few guys to fire up the grill?"

·+·

The first things you'll see, speeding from Grand Forks airport, plunked down in corduroy crops, is a red, white, and blue quonset hut that screams GENEROUS GERRY'S FIREWORKS SUPERSTORE, and you'll think: ah yes, come here to do dangerous stuff that is elsewhere banned. North Dakota is fashioning itself the Kitty Hawk of unmanned aircraft, a quixotic bid when you consider that most aerospace and software behemoths—the ones that design drones—dwell in the mega-economies of California and Seattle. And yet, it's happening.

Quick let me clarify: nobody official calls them drones. They say unmanned aerial vehicles, unmanned aerial systems, remotely piloted aircraft. UAV, UAS, RPA. Drones, as one pilot told me, is a four-letter word around here. Another conceded that the word had a "delicate public perception"—but I'm getting ahead of myself.

The obvious reason this flat state welcomes drones is that it has fewer people and things to collide with should your aircraft, as one airman euphemistically put it, "come into contact with the ground." But there's much more to it. In past decades, Grand Forks Air Force Base, once home of B-52s and Minuteman missiles, was repeatedly BRAC'd (Base Realignment and Closure), but instead of crying over lost nukes it lobbied for drones. Now with zero manned craft it flies the Global Hawk and Predator.

It's not limited to military. Customs and Border Protection chose Grand Forks for its northern fleet. In 2009, the University of North Dakota launched the nation's first undergraduate program in UAS piloting, and with 180 students, it remains the largest. In 2014, North Dakota was chosen by the feds as one of six official test sites, and the entire state permits flights at altitudes of 1200 (as opposed to 200 in most of the nation). Northrop Grumman plans an R&D center at Grand Sky, a proposed UAS business park adjacent to the base. In 2015, ComDel Innovation manufactured the first drone in the state. Startups launched with cool names like Botlink, SkySkopes, and Field of View.

I arrived slightly scared. Senator Lindsey Graham promised, "If I'm president of the United States and you're thinking about joining al-Qaeda or ISIL, I'm not gonna call a judge, I'm gonna call a drone and we will kill you." I watched grainy footage of targets exploding in Pakistan and Yemen. As for the personal copters you can buy for a few hundred bucks and fly without a license, like the one that came into contact with the White House lawn: what a neat way to deliver anthrax or stalk your ex! Of course the public is alarmed by these flying robots.

What I did not anticipate was the onslaught of chumminess. My first stop was the Northern Plains Unmanned Aerial Systems Test Site, where the director, Bob Becklund, a lean pilot, all fighter-jet competence in a crisp black polo and fair clipped hair, seized my hand and said, "My suspicion is that by the end of the week you'll be pretty enamored with the place."

By golly he was right.

I junketed from one official to the next, and to a man they were polite and disarming. A brigadier general decreed that folks here were not just nice, but *North Dakota nice*. A professor of aviation gifted me a medallion stamped with the school logo and VENTURUM TEMPUS PROSPECTUS: Looking to the Future! At each stop plotted by a cheerful PR crew I was regaled with the vocabulary of promise—disruptive tech, green fields and blue oceans, turnkey and build-to-suit, incubators and accelerators—and the cool jargon of military pros: "Our ops tempo is off the chart."

At the university I simulated flying a drone over the Pentagon, easily scoping a target by clicking it in the crosshairs.

A toothsome trio of camo-clad handlers chauffeured me around the Air Force Base. The eyeless Global Hawk hulked in its hangar, as sleek and muscled as a bottlenose whale, yet its jumpsuited pilot was all smiles. "I've taken an aircraft off, gone home, had dinner with my wife," he said, "then gone to sleep, come back the next morning, and landed the same aircraft." I was permitted to run my fingers along the chilly-smooth composite hull of the Predator, and the border patrol pilot let me sit at the console and pretend to launch it. When I asked if he preferred the drone, er, I mean the UAV, over his old Navy jet, he said, "It's always seventy-two degrees in the ground control station. And you sit in a more comfortable chair."

Down to earth! I didn't suspect a single one of them of wanting to spy on me!

Grand Forks itself exuded warmth and trust, a tidy little town: not too big, not too small, not too rich, not too poor. Thanks to an oil boom out west, North Dakota's economy and population lead the nation in growth. The state leapfrogged Alaska to become our forty-seventh largest state, closing in on South Dakota. Just as crude is fracked to the surface, so is money frucked to the east, where roughnecks deposit wives and children in the solid schools and leafy lanes of Fargo and Grand Forks, far from the oily man camps.

As I cruised its wide streets cranking Polka Hour in the rental, I saw evidence everywhere of neat prosperity. I stayed in a spanking new motel located out by the—well, it didn't appear to be near anything, except the interstate and a cluster of similar motels that aspired to "inn" and "suites" but resembled pieces on a Monopoly board, plunked down on freshly poured concrete with sprigs of trees wired between steel posts. Outside my window hulked a titanic apartment block, the work of an earnest but uncreative Lego prodigy, a NOW RENTING banner hanging limp. In a bulldozed field a front loader erected the plywood shell of a model home, identical foundations down the line, pre-assembled wooden trusses waiting in stacks. As just one informal yardstick of its growth, the city of 56,000, a three-day drive from either coast, boasts three sushi joints. At a palatial garden on a slick suburban strip, the waitress told me that she and her husband, who were Chinese, had left New York for better jobs here.

But the influx of people and money does not appear to have altered the place's agreeability. I had come to view our most advanced machines of war and espionage, just two hours from an international border, but instead of body searches and iris scans, upon registration at the motel I was required to sign a paper promising never to bring into my room—a hockey stick! A sign in the elevator read:

We suggest that if your plans are to "PARTY" after
midnight, that you please take it to somewhere else. Be
respectful of others and everyone will have a great stay.

Forget jihadists and cartels, the greatest threat to homeland security around
here is post-rink horseplay by the Minnesota-Duluth Bulldogs.

Pressing my nose against the truck window as I exited the Air Force Base
with my camouflaged handlers, I said:

"Is that really a golf course?"

"Yes."

"Eighteen holes?"

"I want to say it's nine."

·+·

Even as I verged on trusting the whole world, I could not quell those niggling
fears. At an oaken conference table where a border pilot said, "We have assisted
with some meth, some gun cases, some pot. We haven't got any cocaine up here,"
I found myself studying his sidearm and wondering why he was packing inside
a conference room, on a heavily restricted military base, and as I inventoried
our party of officers and defense contractors and one lone anarchist (me), I
easily predicted who among us, when push came to shove, would be forcibly
subdued. I had intended to find out what drones were actually photographing
in border towns like Eureka, Montana, and Pinecreek, Minnesota, but when
the time came to ask, I don't know, I guess I spooked.

My phobia was met with only upbeat assurances. "Issues like privacy will
be handled by the courts," Becklund told me. "Will they get in the hands of
the wrong people? I'm sure they will. But from a government point of view,
privacy is not a big issue."

"If you're not doing anything wrong, what's the big deal?" agreed his
colleague Mark Hasting. "Honestly I think it's an egotistical view that someone
wants to watch us."

"If you don't have anything to hide," reasoned one young pilot, "then
why are you hiding?"

The Gordian Knot of agencies does little to ease the sense of impenetrability. The Test Site is not actually a bricks-and-mortar proving ground with hangars and runways, but an amorphous entity mandated by the Federal Aviation Administration, in partnership with UND Aerospace, ND State University, ND Aeronautics Commission, ND Aviation Council, and the Adjutant General of the ND National Guard, but largely funded by the ND Department of Commerce, which also funds Grand Sky business park, a partnership with the US Air Force and Grand Forks County. The Test Site is housed adjacent to, but not inside, UND's Center for UAS Research, Education, and Training, and both are literally connected by a tunnel-bridge known as a gerbil tube to the Center for Innovation, a project of Innovate ND, also partially funded by the Department of Commerce. Both the Air National Guard and Customs and Border Protection operate Predators at the Grand Forks Air Force Base, where UND researchers are developing a Predator training simulator. Meanwhile Alan Frazier's Northeast Region UAS Unit links the Grand Forks Sheriff's Department and the Aviation Department of the Aerospace School.

Got it?

While boosters touted the friendliness and transparency of the UAV industry, government agents were predictably opaque. I later learned that the unarmed border patrol drone introduced as a Predator-B was officially called the Reaper. Even though nobody would explain the name change on the record, I understood the bad PR that would result from patrolling our closest allies with the Personification of Death.

Beneath the friendliness, secrets were still secret. When I asked the Global Hawk pilot the purpose of flights over North America, he cautiously demurred, while my handler jotted down notes. Because of nondisclosure agreements, Becklund could not tell me which companies were flying at the Test Site. I met pilots who remotely flew Predators from Fargo, but when I asked the nature of their missions, they clammed up. An Air National Guard spokesman conceded that "as a matter of public record" such missions existed, but told me nothing more.

If you have nothing to hide, I wondered, then what are you hiding? After two days in-fortress, I was developing a complex of military-industrial proportions.

·+·

I needed a drink. The Speedway is a brick cube on a shadeless Grand Forks avenue. The parking lot smelled like bacon. Inside, Matt Dunlevy and Jack Wilcox, midtwenties, gulped dark beer from glass steins as big as their heads. They were owners of SkySkopes, one of three licensed UAV operators in the state. Matt wore basketball shorts and a t-shirt, and rubber sandals. A former history major who quotes Oppenheimer, he was prone to pronouncements like: "Being an entrepreneur is a romantic ideal."

Also at the booth, beneath a gigantic TV showing basketball, a phone smushed to one ear and a finger in the other, obscured from view by a plastic tumbler of Coke and ice, was SkySkopes' pilot, Connor Grafius, oxford buttoned to the neck, black Wayfarers propped on cropped blond curls.

"We are looking for a range extension," Connor said into the phone. "A blanket COA to 200 feet. You have to exclude the military installations."

"We're on the phone with the FAA now," Matt told me. Two days from now, SkySkopes would fly its first commercial mission: to inspect a cell tower 300 miles west of here in the Oil Patch.

"What's COA?" I said.

"Certificate of Authorization."

"Your phone sucks," Connor said, hanging up and passing it back to Matt. He sipped from his straw. The reason he drank pop was that he was only twenty years old.

I liked these guys. While most of the industry struck me as top-down pork, these innovative kids had a vision, and were starting from nowhere, or close to it. Their openness was the opposite of the fortress. When I'd met them earlier that day, they had pulled an octocopter out of their car and launched it in about five minutes. Then they'd let me fly a cheap drone. In their hands, drones didn't seem like sinister weapons, but brilliant gadgets to make life fun and easy. That very day I read about California lifeguards who cleared swimmers from the beach after spotting a shark with a drone. In Uganda, researchers transported human blood by drone. I could get behind this. SkySkopes could prevent linemen or pilots from risking their lives to study skybound cables—and make a bucket of money in the process. Their smarts and ambition and enthusiasm made me think they were going to succeed. Forget journalistic objectivity: I *wanted* them to succeed.

Drones are evolving faster than the regulations, which is why Connor essentially had to explain to the FAA what he was trying to do, in order to get permission to do it. For many years the only drone users were the military, who operated outside agency purview, and hobbyists, who were largely unregulated. Now that is all changing. In 2014, the FAA began to issue commercial permits, launching a new industry. Among the licensees were Dow Chemical and Amazon, but most were small operators such as SkySkopes, who just three weeks after permitting had a $5,000 contract. They did not know of anyone in the country who had done this yet—at least not legally.

"There's really no one to ask for advice," Matt told me.

While Matt was the businessman, Connor was the ace. A junior in the UAS program at UND, he began flying and building remote-controlled planes when he was fifteen on the shores of Lake Minnetonka. A kid who loved video games, he mounted cameras on his planes, piloting them by feel as he strapped on a pair of video goggles. Passersby might have been perplexed to wander upon this wispy teen, basically blindfolded, operating a stick and throttle, enraptured by what he saw in his headset.

"It's the greatest thing I'd ever seen," he told me as he picked at his french fries. "The sensation, the peripherals, it's like you're flying. When people asked what I was doing I'd say: Just look into these goggles and you'll freak out."

I asked why other companies weren't doing the same as them.

"We're hungry," Matt Dunlevy said. "They're not."

·+·

Flare stacks in the Oil Patch threw yellow fire toward the sky. When I'd told the Grand Forks cops I was coming here, one had said, "Do you have a gun?" I expected to see human heads mounted on stakes. "It's one thing to see pictures of it," said Jack, "it's another to actually experience it." He had been driving since three in the morning.

I had wondered why the state Department of Commerce was so involved with drones. So here's why: tethered for decades to ag and energy, North Dakota hopes to parlay the oil boom into a bust-proof tech sector. Oil enriches state government, which in turn funds the Test Site, Grand Sky, and ND Innovate, which funds startups like SkySkopes.

At the gas station in a brown outpost called Ray, they donned yellow safety vests. Connor in particular did not look much like a roughneck. He wore a checked oxford, tan levis, and unlaced boat shoes. At the pump he almost collided with a man packing two firearms. "He looked me right in the eye," Connor reported, "and was, like, what are *you* doing out here?"

"He'd probably shoot down our drone," said Jack.

As we pulled onto the highway, Jack's seat belt warning beeped.

"That's an OSHA violation," Connor said.

"I'm pretty excited," Matt told me. "I didn't sleep successfully."

We pulled down a gravel road to where a cell tower rose from the fields like a pencil on a pancake. A tattooed workman with pony tail beneath his hard hat held up a waiver that I signed without reading. He regarded Connor's Topsiders and said, "If the safety guys show up they're gonna say something about your shoes."

Two older men arrived in a pickup—neat gray hair, and jeans and boots and hard hats—and offered their names but didn't say who they were. Guys From Corporate, I deduced. The problem, explained GFC, was water. Strands of black cable snaked to the top. Rainwater somehow entered the plastic sheath and poured into the circuits below. Was it faulty weather-stripping where the cable passed through a steel housing? Or had the cable been nicked through careless installation? Thousands of towers—millions of dollars—hinged on the answer. But it cost $1,500 to send a climber, who might not figure it out.

Connor hefted a black case from the back of the car, wheeled it across the gravel, and opened the lid, revealing the menacing black widow. He straightened its spindly legs, each tipped with bright red. SkySkopes did not actually build the drone. They bought it online. Connor's talent was mounting and interfacing camera, gimbal, and software. He connected wires and batteries.

"You have done towers before, right?" said GFC.

"Yeah," said Connor.

"Is it easy to fly one of these things?"

"Not by a tower."

"How close can you get?"

"Very close." Connor turned to the Tech. "Does this tower produce any frequency in the spectrum of 2.11 gigahertz?"

"You guys have insurance in case something goes wrong?" said GFC.

"Up to two million," Matt interjected.

"Does anyone have a spare zip tie?" said Connor.

As the GFCs beheld the eight-legged creature, their skepticism softened. Because that's the thing about drones. They're really cool. Everyone stooped down to examine it.

"That's a pretty mean fucking gadget," said the Tech. "I'm not sure if I want to take pictures or start shooting."

"Do we want one?" said GFC with a chuckle. "I'm going to talk to my wife."

"I want this job!"

"A geek's delight!"

Connor powered the drone and a melody beeped.

"It comes with music!" cried GFC.

"That's its horn," said Connor.

"Can I take a picture?" said GFC. "I realize it might be your secret sauce."

"Clear," Connor called. "Powering up."

The thing whirred like a hummingbird as its eight rotors spun. It lifted off the ground. As Connor slipped on his sunglasses and piloted it upward, the rest of us did the only thing male humans can do upon encountering an unmanned helicopter: took pictures of it.

Connor's gaze alternated between the drone itself and real-time video on the monitor. Jack operated the camera, Connor gave commands. "I want you to look down at those guy wires. Look straight. Now look up."

"I always get scared," said Matt, pacing.

Connor's shoelaces flopped on the ground. But he was as cool and crisp as a mint hundred-dollar bill. GFC peered at the screen and said: "There: right there. That's what I need." Connor held the drone steady and Jack zoomed in on the junction where the cable entered the steel housing. "Yes, that's it." There was a sense of wonder: the marvel of technology—the magic really—that we could be scoping in such detail twenty stories off the ground. Those magnificent lads and their flying machines!

The drone wove between steel wires as it climbed. Depth perception was impossible. Connor propped his Ray-Bans on his forehead and studied the monitor, saying to Jack, "Look up. OK, look level," then dropped the glasses onto his nose and held up a hand to block the sun.

I was enjoying myself! Not only did I love watching the thing pirouette between the wires, I felt like the crotchety GFCs were getting a smackdown.

I heard a thwack way up high. My head snapped up just in time to see the octocopter jerking sideways, spinning out of control.

"Uh-oh," said Connor. He throttled up and pulled it away from the tower. The drone lurched and swiveled, rotors whined, landing gear deployed, and before I could count five the thing slammed down in the wheat, bounced, and toppled in a heap.

·+·

I ate an omelet draped in Kraft singles in Carrington, a husk of a farm town, in a motel called the Chieftain whose twenty-foot red-skinned statue qualified as the region's primary monument. I was here to watch flights, operated by the Test Site, at the North Dakota State University research center. Nearly every civilian I had met agreed that the way to make money with drones was in what they called "precision ag," which soothed my inner dove in a swords-to-ploughshares way. The previous evening I had walked the shuttered downtown, flyers for farm auctions tacked to empty storefronts. Sipping coffee, I eavesdropped on the booth of old-timers next to me.

"I'll tell you how to win the next war," said in a man in a western shirt: "Find a way to turn off everyone's phone."

"Anymore, you can't pay your water bill without a computer."

"I live an old-fashioned life and I just refuse to move along," said a woman. "I've never used an ATM machine."

I had finally encountered someone skeptical of the marvels of the future! Just as the cop posse saw drones as a mere improvement of efficiency, so did most civilians think that analyzing crops with unmanned aircraft marked indisputable progress.

"I haven't met anyone opposed to drones," said John Nowatski, a researcher at NDSU, "except crop dusters, and urban people."

Setting aside the fact that four of five Americans are urban people, these machines certainly alter the way we grow food, and this farm state leads the revolution. Fields heretofore crisscrossed by squads of sweating earthbound humans will be inventoried in minutes by air. Nowatski speculated on a partnership between an airframe manufacturer, say Boeing, and an ag corporation, say Monsanto, which would photograph the entire state daily and store data on the cloud, from which a farmer could download infrared images. Botlink CEO Shawn Muehler proposed a model in which a farmer's own inexpensive drone, piloted by smartphone, flew overhead and transmitted real-time data that instructed the tractor to apply fertilizer and pesticide and irrigation. It would save water, chemicals, and money.

Nowatski told me that when he grew up on a farm, the average size was 400 acres. "Now it's four times that, and Big Data will make that kind of consolidation more likely. It's good for the price of food in grocery stores. It's good for people starving all around the globe."

We watched the fixed-wing craft buzzing overhead. I thought about the old-timers filling their cups with watery coffee at the Chieftain, probably paying their tab with buffalo nickels.

"What about for people in North Dakota?" I said.

"It will be harmful for Carrington," said Nowatski. "Not as many people in schools, in restaurants, drinking beer. We're going to see fewer and fewer people on the land."

But I didn't want fewer North Dakotans—I wanted more! I *was* enamored with the place, and the people. When the sushi waitress back in Grand Forks suggested that I try the Sex on the Beach Roll, I had been in North Dakota long enough that I blushed! At a rival establishment, the delicacy had been PG-13'd to "Beauty on the Beach Roll," better reflecting the local decency.

Three nights before, after my visit to the base, I had driven to the banks of the Red River of the North in Grand Forks, where I unfastened my necktie and shimmied into shorts and ran along the trails. I have been to a lot of parts of America and let me tell you, none is finer than the green slopes of the Red River on a summer solstice evening: thick stands of cottonwoods bursting from the loam, June fluff aglow in the dappled rays of northern sun as it eases horizonward inch by inch. I tasted the sugar of silver leaves on my lip. I floated over acres of sod. A pair of lovers cuddled on a bench. The golden light was lush in my lungs, and I wanted to throw a football, roll in the turf, procreate, pledge allegiance to the republic. This was a homeland worth protecting.

The elysian splendor is no accident. The Red River, after bisecting Grand Forks, flows toward Canada where in spring, ice dams block its waters. In ancient times the floods blessed the flat valley with fertile soil, but nowadays they pose difficulties. In 1997, the river rose a biblical fifty-four feet and deluged the city. A less plucky people might have pulled stakes for higher ground. But Grand Forks demonstrated the can-do ingenuity that settled the frontier and put a man on the moon. Atop earthen levees they lined the city with a fifteen-foot stone wall.

The result is like a medieval kingdom, protected from invaders. During floods, the gaps where the bridges enter the keep are blocked with sheets of metal, sealing the city from the waters. Along a strip of pleasant eateries the wall is only waist high so townspeople can gaze happily at the gentle Red, and when the waters rise, they install steel barriers and lick their ice creams in peace as wild nature laps at the door.

The kingdom is equally insulated from the bitter debate about whether or not citizenry should grant the use of drones to its government. In California, activists have protested Northrop Grumman and General Atomics; in Nevada they picket Creech Air Force Base. But not here. The chair of a committee that regulates drones told me that there had been little disagreement. She pointed out that, anyway, we are constantly photographed in banks and malls, and the GPS in our smartphones tracks us better than any aircraft could. When I replied that smartphones were an elective technology—that you *chose* to purchase one, same as you chose to use the Internet or drive a car—and that no citizen ever voted to allow police to film us from the commons of the skies, she and everyone else in the room looked at me as if I were some Amish person who had just explained why suspenders were godly but belts of the devil.

When I quoted Senator Graham on killing with drones, people looked at the floor in embarrassment, and one professor offered that North Dakota avoids the extremes, as evidenced by its selection of one senator from each political party. I asked the skippers of aeronautics if North Dakotans tended to trust the government, and someone said, "They trust *everyone*." Alan Palmer, a retired brigadier general, laughed and told me, "If you were a terrorist who wanted to enter the country, you should fly to Winnipeg, and drive to North Dakota, and if you broke down on 29, someone would help fix your car!"

I mention this not because the Manitoba border needs beefed up, but because it made me wonder: why are we droning Canada anyway? The border patrol deployed a Predator—or was it a Reaper?—to resolve an armed standoff with a rancher. The Department of Homeland Security reported that border drones cost twelve grand per hour to fly, five times the original estimate, and that CBP "cannot demonstrate how much the program has improved border security."

The double-edged truth about drones is that they will quickly change our lives for the better, their pioneers displaying ingenuity and imagination that from Edison to the Wright brothers to Steve Jobs makes the world love America; and, also, our government will continue to deploy them for spying and killing, without the knowledge or consent of citizens.

There is a sense in the north country, as the elevator sign said, that if we merely respect one another, everyone will have a great stay. The quaint attitude lingers from our grandparents' America—one I no longer live in, one I sometimes wish we could return to—and what breaks my heart is when I watch that black-and-white footage of targets exploding, I do not imagine myself the patriot pulling the trigger, rather the mope in the crosshairs, who either by choice or clerical error got myself listed as enemy of my own country—the one that I love, its Red River and rich soil—and as a result got clicked on by some perfectly nice fellow at a console in the heartland, seventy-two degrees summer and winter, in a very comfortable chair.

·+·

I assumed SkySkopes would be discouraged. But after we split into two cars and drove to Minot for lunch, Matt recapped the ride: "Connor took a nap and I was bumping some beats." We found our way to a cantina where Connor got carded.

The mishap actually proved the rightness of their vision. No one was hurt, the tower and wheat field were not harmed, and the damage to the drone amounted to only thirty-five dollars. The landing gear properly deployed to protect the camera and gimbal. Had they packed more spare parts, Connor could have repaired the thing on the spot. A month later they scheduled to finish the job, and Matt told me that other missions were underway.

In the future, they determined, they would bring a second drone, just in case. SkySkopes was unfazed, and my faith in them was undeterred. Even the Wright brothers crashed a few planes.

"Another thing," said Connor, sipping his Coke. "We need parachutes."

As for me, I had come north afraid that drones would enable my country to invade my privacy, only to learn that it was already invaded—usually with my own consent. In the airport shuttle a mounted camera winked at me. Octocopter ads flooded my Facebook feed. I had Googled words like drone and Predator hundreds of times. Someone is watching, recording, collecting data, but the person isn't Them, it's Us.

Outside the walls, the rivers rise, our enemies multiply, and the world is going to H-E-double hockey sticks. But inside the fortress the sun is shining, the soil is fertile, and the Beauty on the Beach Rolls are as wholesome as anything I've had on the coast.

Potter and Keats

When I heard the news of Dean Potter's death—the rock climber crashed while literally flying across Yosemite Valley in a wingsuit—I was transported back thirty years, my sixteen-year-old self dangling from two bolts drilled to the side of a Yosemite cliff. It was my first multi-pitch climb, meaning that the route was longer than the 150-foot rope, so at the halfway point I hung in my harness for a half an hour to belay my partner. My fear was evident in the pounds of gear dangling from my waist—not just hardware but also rookie accoutrements like a guide book, water bottle, rain jacket, and sneakers for the descent.

Just then a blond apparition appeared below us. As we fiddled with ropes and carabiners this man, naked but for gym shorts and rock shoes, floated up the cliff as easily as a birthday party balloon. He passed just a few feet to my right, breathing calmly, giving a polite nod. His shirtless torso was sculpted and suntanned, golden curls flowing toward his shoulders. Lashed to his waist was a bag of gymnast's chalk with which he dusted his fingers. He moved like an angel, smearing his boot over granite flakes, testing for a fraction of a second, before smoothly stepping higher. Between his teeth, like a blade of grass, glinted a piece of metal; I was close enough to discern that it was, incongruously, a fingernail clipper.

The shimmering domes of Tuolumne Meadows fell silent beneath us— and indeed the entire world disappeared as this otherworldly being climbed toward the heavens, apparently unbound by gravity or material possessions or any of the chains that binds mortals to Earth. The vision remained etched in the plasma of my memory all these years, but it wasn't until recently that I understood why:

I had seen a God, flown down from Mount Olympus, walking among men.

I knew immediately who this man was. Indeed, posters of him plastered my bedroom wall. John Bachar was one of the great climbers of his day—of all time—and was in some ways the model upon which Dean Potter would one day mold himself. In the 1970s Bachar pioneered free soloing—climbing without ropes—which is what he was doing when he soared past me that day. When I saw him in 1986, climbing was still a peculiar subculture, tinged with hints of anti-consumerism and Eastern mysticism. There were no indoor rock gyms or sponsored competitions or apparel companies offering climbing "lifestyle." That stuff wasn't far off. The climbing world was in schism, pitting traditionalists like him—who valued form and purity of style above all—against "sport climbers," who were determined to push the level of difficulty by any means necessary, adopting European techniques such as rehearsing moves while hanging on the rope, or placing protection bolts on a proposed route beforehand, rather than "on lead."

The battle ended in a rout, with sport climbing all but erasing traditionalists. Bachar, once the golden boy of American climbing, was dismissed as an anachronism, a crank. Rockclimbing quickly shifted from a fringe sect, like Tai Chi practitioners, to a mainstream sport, like skiing or surfing. Something called "speed climbing" has been introduced to the X Games, and the International Federation of Sport Climbing is lobbying hard for inclusion in the Olympic Games. But for a bookish scrawny kid like me unable to make varsity teams or for that matter paddle a surfboard past the waves, the esoteric art Bachar practiced was a revelation: being a lightweight and a daydreamer were assets rather than flaws, and it was the first time I had found my body capable of anything beautiful.

There was something noble about Bachar's refusal to compromise when the sport he pioneered suddenly became commercially viable, indeed to insist that it was not sport at all but rather a mystical means of creative expression, more akin to ballet or bullfighting. Over the years I quit climbing and drifted away from that world but always admired Dean Potter from afar, reading of his latest feats, whether free soloing routes that Bachar never would have considered, slacklining between towers, or flying off the Eiger in a wingsuit. In the era of YouTube and GoPro, Potter achieved far more fame than Bachar, and yet both men were chronically misinterpreted as daredevils with a death wish.

Potter's death was cause for widespread harrumphing among armchair moralists. "Dean Potter thought he was flying. He was just falling," scolded Timothy Egan in the *New York Times*, wringing his hands over "the cultural celebration of sport-assisted suicide." Among the legion complaints were that Potter was selfish, a narcissist, and an irresponsible lawbreaker whose remains would have to be scrubbed off the rocks at taxpayer expense. As for his supposed spirituality, the critics said, the fact that he filmed and posted his exploits on the Internet proved that he was just a publicity hound. If he were really soulful, goes the reasoning, he would have only BASE jumped in private. Furthermore, sniffed Egan, Potter's pretensions of being not just an athlete but an artist were just that: "There was certainly a bit of stoner stunt ethos to what he did, the dare that follows a question, 'Dude, wouldn't it be awesome if we could fly from Half Dome?'"

Setting aside for a moment the sneer, let's face the proposition straight on. Maybe Dean Potter was an artist. And if so, what was his art?

·+·

In June of 1818, the twenty-two-year-old aspiring poet, John Keats, left Lancaster for a two-month walk across the Scottish highlands. "I shall learn poetry here," he wrote, "and shall henceforth write, more than ever, for the abstract endeavor of being able to add a mite to that mass of beauty which is harvested from these grand materials, by the finest spirits, and put into ethereal existence for the relish of one's fellows."

The cross-county hike was the latest in a series of impractical—some might say self-destructive—choices made by young Keats. Two years earlier he had quit the profession for which he had trained—physician—and announced his intention to write poems for the ages. His work was not just run-of-the-mill rhymes about love and flowers; his were epics of the gods, rife with satyrs and fauns and all manner of unearthly beings. His early poems was widely ridiculed for their aspirations of the eternal.

On his walk, the "grand material" from which he hoped to wrest poems was nature itself. Yet he quickly understood that language was unable to capture the grandeur. "The space, the magnitude of mountains and waterfalls are well imagined before one sees them," he wrote, but once witnessed in person, they "surpass every imagination and defy any remembrance."

Along the way he climbed Great Britain's highest peak, Ben Nevis, reporting that, "After much fag and tug and a rest and a glass of whiskey apiece we gained the top of the first rise." He was staggered by the wilderness. "I never forgot my stature so completely," he wrote. "I live in the eye, and my imagination, surpassed, is at rest." After six weeks exposed to the soggy elements, he lamented that, "My Sore throat is not quite well and I intend stopping here a few days."

Whether Keats's epiphanies of impermanence in the highlands caused his artistic maturation is up for debate. What is fact is that the cold he caught was permanent. His lungs never recovered, and within three years he would be dead of consumption at age twenty-five. In those intervening thousand days he wrote a batch of humankind's greatest poems. What changed was not his obsession with gods and immortality; rather, the later poems counter his dreaminess with an awareness of his own inevitable death. In "Ode on a Grecian Urn," even as he swoons over the timelessness of the figures etched forever in clay—"More happy love: more happy, happy love!"—he senses his own tubercular body watching from far above, "a heart high-sorrowful and cloyed / A burning forehead, and a parching tongue." In "To Autumn" he sings not to the much-celebrated buds of spring that promise new life, but to the ripe fruit on the verge of decay, the "full-grown lamb" a season closer to slaughter, and the inevitable approach of winter and death: "Thou watchest the last oozings hours by hours."

Reading Keats we are simultaneously aware of the soaring beauty of our existence, its nearness to the immortality of the gods—and also its looming end. What if Keats had never walked the Scottish moor, never caught consumption, never spent three years staring death helplessly in the face? Would he have relished the rapturous beauty of his numbered days on Earth? Would he have articulated the fundamental tragedy of humankind, that in order to live we must certainly die?

In the years after seeing John Bachar ascend past me, I did some free soloing myself. I was too young to understand how my death would have devastated my family, but I was old enough to know that exceeding my abilities would kill me. I was careful enough—and lucky enough—not to fall. I soared as best as I could, but I lacked the courage and skill to reach the sun. I took up other, less dangerous, pursuits. As for my hero John Bachar: like Potter, like Icarus, he eventually fell to his death.

When Dean Potter died I felt an unbearable loss. Even though I had never known him, I grieved. I spent a few days watching his videos. In one, while climbing without ropes hundreds of feet off the ground, he misses a hold and falls—apparently to his death—but then from within a cloud of ether pulls a parachute cord and floats safely to Earth. In another he walks a slackline between two stone towers, framed by a milky full moon, and appears to literally walk across the moon. Unlike Neil Armstrong he requires no spacesuit or rocket ship; he goes barefoot. In perhaps the most gorgeous expression of what he called his "dark arts," Potter leaps from the Eiger and flies in his wingsuit for three minutes, twenty seconds, descending nine thousand feet and soaring almost five miles.

Potter demonstrated two things that I learned from Keats. First, as language was not adequate for the task of depicting nature, Potter pursued perhaps the most romantic quest of all: to merge with nature, to become a silent feature of its cliffs and skies. Second, watching Potter I felt at once the unabashed glory of being alive—and the pitiless fragility of it. It's so beautiful, and yet he could die at any second!

Here lies the evidence, according to some, of his irresponsibility and death wish. How dare he get so close to dying! But here's the thing: sitting at my desk, stepping into the bathtub, driving in a car to the supermarket, I too could die at any second. And so could we all. I don't mean that these activities are as dangerous as BASE jumping, but rather that while the time and circumstance of our death may not be pre-determined, its certainty is. Art's oldest aspiration is to transcend our short mortality—to last forever, like thunder and the sun and the gods—but Keats only got twenty-five years, Dean Potter only forty-three, and if anything will outlive gilded monuments it is their embodiment of the simple truth: to live we must die.

Critics will snort that Potter couldn't be a real artist because he wasn't clever enough to explain himself like a museum curator: "Dude, wouldn't it be awesome if we could fly from Half Dome?" But language is only one medium of accessing the eternal, and artists of all persuasions, from musicians to painters, ballerinas to bullfighters—even climbers and surfers—reveal beauty and truths for which words do not suffice. I for one am grateful that Potter poured his soul into jumping off cliffs instead of, say, writing short stories, or op-eds, or getting an MFA, or strumming indie rock. For all the clichés that artists spin about risking their lives for their art, here's someone who actually risked it, and the job of explaining himself to the rest of us is not his, any more than the task of explaining her song lies with the nightingale. Potter's videos—and life—are works of art of the highest order. When I'm old and frail and unable to scale mountains on my own, I imagine that watching him fly will bring me as much pleasure as *Anna Karenina* or "What's Going On?" or *The Godfather*.

Yes, Dude, it would be awesome to fly from Half Dome, and it will forever be awesome that you did it! Thou wast not born for death, immortal Bird! Like those figures on the urn, like the song of the nightingale, like the gods in the sky, Dean Potter and his flight will, I suspect, outlive us all.

Tinier Than Thou

Remember not too long ago, maybe 2012, the slew of blogs and Tumblrs and films that heralded not just a new type of house but a movement, a post-collapse quest for simplicity and freedom, a rejection of waste and "stuff" and, just like Thoreau in his cabin of yore, a crusade to chomp life's essence and suck its marrow? Museum-quality photo books showed how to stick it to the man in 400 square feet or less—with the clean lines and blond oak that made us drool onto the pages of *Dwell* magazine. Of all the earthy trends to emerge since the 2008 crash—local food, urban farms, permaculture—none have captured adoration like tiny houses, spawning no fewer than seven reality shows. You won't find a series about cloth diapers.

It appealed to me, someone who has lived in some of the tiniest homes out there—a Subaru wagon, a Toyota pickup, an SUV with the back seats removed. When it comes to car camping, I wrote the book. Seriously. It's called *Car Camping*. What's more, I own a 1965 singlewide that measures just 570 square feet, with pine cabinets like you'd find in a sailboat, on an acre outside Moab, Utah. I've always thought that if I owned less, worked less, and spent less, I would be more free.

But my vagabond days are behind me, and as I sped toward the second annual National Tiny House Jamboree in Colorado Springs last August, I was undergoing my own tiny crisis. My wife and I had bought a tiny car that got nearly forty miles per gallon. We'd even upcycled a Mexican roof mutt into our own tiny dog, who consumed at mealtime less than one cup of kibble and canned pumpkin and whose tiny poops hardly registered at the landfill. Meanwhile we'd upsized to a two-bedroom bungalow—our biggest yet. Even as I understood that appetites like mine were plundering the planet, I could not stop wanting a third bedroom. As for the car: it was the first I'd ever owned that was too small to sleep in, so if the weather turned bad I might have to get a hotel room, and wouldn't that indulgence offset the efficiency?

Was small actually beautiful? I was tiny-curious.

·+·

In my imagination, the Jamboree promised a quaint circle of funky sheds inhabited by anarchists who'd pass the porch-bound evenings picking banjos, sipping moonshine, and comparing insulation R-values. But because last year's hordes had packed the grounds of the Western Museum of Mining and Industry, backing up traffic, this year the Jamboree supersized to a field at the Air Force Academy. My subversive fantasies were deflated by the armed guard at the academy gates, who demanded my license, weapons, explosives, and drugs.

I followed a stream of Tiny Jammers driving through the piney hills to the stadium, one minivan painted with TINY HOUSE OR BUST! FIND US ON FACEBOOK. We throngs—nearly 60,000 before the weekend was over—filed our vehicles into long rows, then stampeded toward the entrance on foot. Saturated with the carnival cloud of a pork smoker on wheels, ringed by porta-potties innumerable, a field of yellow grass and gravel was packed with dozens of trailers on blocks, lines of looky-loos at the steps. A string of booths showcased off-grid accoutrements from solar panels to composting toilets to twig-burning cookstoves.

I had a date at the Tiny Stage to get to the heart of this phenomenon. A roster of the movement's Luminaries would clarify the Tiny House Philosophy, which, it turned out, had little to do with bookshelves-as-stairs or sinks-in-closets. One philosopher, Kent Griswold, founder of Tiny House Blog, a gray-headed avuncular type in cargo shorts and sneakers, confessed that he didn't even live in one. No matter. All could benefit from its principles:

> Reduce your belongings.
> Get out of debt.
> Do work that you love.

Sager advice has never been given; indeed, these very principles had guided my own adulthood. But if living tiny doesn't require a dollhouse, then what were we all doing here?

The first Luminary I met was Nina Zamudio, whose tale was pure bravura. A native Californian, Zamudio had worked her way through college, was earning a good income, and had even bought her mother a home. She had achieved the American dream. Then she divorced and moved out of her 2,800-square-foot house in Orland to take care of Mom in Chico. Now forty-nine, with lustrous black hair and an irrepressible smile, Zamudio told me that after her mother's death, she'd spent months getting rid of everything. Her mother's place was only 1,200 square feet, but the empty house felt hollow and lonely, her solitary voice echoing off the walls. She attended a workshop with Jay Shafer, a fifty-two-year-old designer and builder hailed by Oprah Winfrey as the Tiny House Man, author and publisher of the 2009 movement bible *The Small House Book*. Transformed, Zamudio sold the house and rented her first tiny home. She moved to Texas, where—helped by a crew of friends and strangers—she built an eight-by-twenty-foot house on wheels. A church allowed her to park on its grounds. She found a new set of friends at the Dallas Tiny House Meetup group, not to mention a boyfriend.

Zamudio inspired me. Who doesn't want to rebound from adversity with panache, to be reawakened at middle age, to forge meaning amid drudgery and isolation? Tiny Housers' zeal approaches the religious. "It's not really about the tiny house," one told me. "It's about values, a way of life." Another said, "Your whole life changes when you live in a tiny house." As with any sect—or recovery group—its core is the narrative of personal transformation, whether being saved or getting sober. Here the stories pivoted around Turning Tiny. Before Tiny, there was an unhappy marriage, unpaid bills, stifling office work, a home of 2,500 square feet or more; after Tiny came freedom, new love, debt relief, self-employment, and, of course, a handmade nest. When Tiny Jammers asked one another "Are you building?" it was no minor inquiry but rather the existential question, and when someone responded "Three months now," a giddy thrill bubbled into the air, because we knew they had been reborn.

·+·

Duly evangelized, I set out to view the homes. But instead of the art brut of mad visionaries, I found professionally built sales models. An attractive rig from Northern California's Tumbleweed Tiny House Company, the nation's first and biggest manufacturer, cofounded by Jay Shafer himself, was outfitted with a flat-screen TV, faux-log stove, air conditioner, and washing machine, charged by a rumbling generator and encircled by a bevy of attractive salespersons in shirts that read DREAM BIG GO TINY. Cost of this model: $91,000. Inside I heard one Jammer say, "Did we bring the snacks or leave them in the car?" One of the "workshops" was a pitch by Ikea reps.

Better to call this the Tiny House Trade Show? As for the gadgets, as much as I admire a diminutive toilet, serious homesteaders make humanure by pooping into a bucket of sawdust. And a twig-burning stove can be fashioned from a No. 10 peach can. If we are trapped in a cycle of earning and spending, I wasn't sure that any purchase would free us.

A schism in the House of Tiny! While the Luminaries espoused buying less stuff, what was happening across the field was the peddling of merch, all of it cool, none of it cheap. While a panel of real estate developers discussed the potential profitability of tiny-home villages, a petite woman from Portland, Oregon, who lives in a hundred-square-foot wagon leaped to her feet and hollered, "What's the square footage of the homes you live in?"

My unscientific polling suggested that most Tiny-come-latelies were drawn in by television shows—and indeed, casting agents infiltrated the Jam, passing out cards for Tiny House Arrest, He Shed She Shed, Tiny WhoreHouse, Tiny House Mogadishu, Tiny House Swept Out to Sea (maybe I made some of those up), and even Tiny House Hunters, which documents not building a wee home but shopping for one. I surmised, perhaps unfairly, that people on these shows are less interested in dismantling the consumerist paradigm than in getting on teevee.

I rushed to the stage for the first real celebrity, a thirty-six-year-old freeskier and carpenter named Zack Giffin who chanced into hosting Tiny House Nation, FYI network's surprise hit that documents designing and building by reg'lar folks. Tan and blond and unshaven, Giffin took the stage in skate shoes. If Jamboree-goers were expecting bromides about rugged individualism, Giffin's sermon felt more like Big Government liberalism, complete with "economic segregation" and "the stigma of low-income housing." He declared, "Zoning is a good thing," an apparent blasphemy to a flock that detests regulation—a topic so tangled that I'll have to return to it later. Which is not to say that he dismissed craftsmanship. He praised Shafer's elegant designs: "Without him, we wouldn't be here."

Two hundred people lined up to get an autograph, take a selfie, or ask some tech question like "How do I install a P-trap under a tub so that it won't break off if I hit a speed bump?" Giffin spent five minutes with each, giving hints on hot roofs and DC inverters. His fans crossed the spectrum: bearded hipsters, married lesbians, a woman who literally rose from a wheelchair to embrace him, an active-duty soldier in a cowboy hat with bald eagles painted under the brim who, after waiting more than an hour, pressed a card into Giffin's palm and said, "I hit you up on Facebook but you didn't respond."

"Oh, I'm sorry."

"Check out my YouTube site on bug-out survival."

Also in line was Zamudio, with a skinny fellow in cutoff tan jeans and a navy t-shirt and wide-brimmed felt hat. I speculated out loud that Giffin was the Jam's biggest draw. Zamudio motioned to her companion. "This is Jay Shafer."

The godfather himself! Shafer blushed at the praise and then shook my hand, his blue eyes twinkling, an impish grin above a chin of gray stubble. His gangly arms flapped at his sides, like a marionette in the wind.

Shafer had been living tiny since long before the 2008 recession. In 1999, he built the first Tumbleweed, perfectly symmetrical with wood-plank siding, a nub of a porch, and a lancet window under a gable, a motif he described as "American Gothic meets the Winnebago Vectra." A movement was born.

But before I had a chance to speak with him, he disappeared into the woods.

Recently I found myself looking at an ad for the most modern innovation in housing. "Beautiful design—top quality materials—decorator-styled interiors—nationally famous appliances." The sell spoke of low cost, minimal upkeep, and high resale value. The woman on the retro sofa between a pair of art deco lamps was super hip.

Would you be surprised that the ad comes from a 1960 issue of *Trailer Topics* magazine? I recognized the boxy windows and wood veneer of the Detroiter Mobile Home because I once rented one of the same vintage. No more than 400 square feet, it was perfect for this dirtbag bachelor and his fleabag heeler. Yet I dispute its promise of high resale. When the land beneath the trailer I rented was sold, my castle was literally scraped from the lot at great expense to its owner, who thought he had made a wise investment. According to federal housing regulations, mobile homes built before 1976 cannot be legally occupied unless grandfathered in.

Tiny houses have struggled against zoning codes, which set minimums of 1,000 square feet or more. Proponents bypass this by placing their homes on wheels, thus qualifying as RVs—which can't be full-time permanent dwellings. A community of four tiny houses in Portland has developed in the backyard of a conventional house, which dwellers pay rent for and use its shower and kitchen. Therefore, they contend, they are not living "full time" in their tiny homes. Current options for a spiffy home on wheels are to fly below the radar and hope to avoid getting booted, move to some unregulated hinterland and contend with long commutes and isolation, or grapple with the law.

Some days, my wife and I fantasize about going to live on our paid-for acre by the creek in Moab: no rent, no mortgage. But the trailer just seems too small. As for upgrades: in bankerspeak, the trailer is not an asset but a liability. I can't get a loan to enlarge it, and if I try to sell it, no bank will issue a mortgage. Unlike with a real house, the only incentives to repair my trailer are sentimental love and desperation. Due to a perfect storm of zoning, flood maps, and building codes, the only legal thing I can do to my trailer is scrap it and build a full-fledged house, which I can't afford. Hence my attraction to the quasi-legal tiny.

·+·

That night I pitched my tent at the designated campground, a mowed field thirty minutes from the Jam on the flanks of Cheyenne Mountain, whose granite bowels house some of North America's top-secret nuclear missile defenses. None of the Luminaries stayed here. I saw a grand total of two tiny houses: a professionally built Mobile Relief Office, marketed to insurers to process claims after disasters, and a minuscule trailer molded of lacquered fiberglass that belonged to a family from Denver. Its maiden voyage had warped its door. In the morning, a child gave me a tour, pointing at the drain on the floor that allowed showering.

"Can you sleep in here?" I said.

"You have to fold down some hatches and put in a mattress."

"Where did you sleep last night?"

"In the tent."

I met a young couple from the Midwest who were living in a van and who aspired to drive it to Portland, where they'd heard you could park on the streets without getting hassled by cops. They asked me to like them on Facebook.

There seemed to be a fundamental flaw in the Tiny Dream: it promised financial freedom and affordable housing, yet in most cases it involved buying what amounted to an RV and still not owning land. Some adopters retreated to conventional homes, renting their backyard pirate dens on Airbnb: "We are letting people into our home, in hopes to inspire others wanting to make the change to tiny a little easier," advertised one couple from Everett, Washington. Did they mention the eighty-three dollars per night?

By 2015, tiny houses had devolved into grist for a *Portlandia* spoof in which a hipster writes a novel while sitting on the john and his wife cuts toast on his back, plus unintentional parody like the actual Portland couple trying to crowdfund $30,000 to build a home, rewarding donors with homemade Christmas ornaments. "With the struggle of finding affordable housing," they reasoned, "we feel that we need more time in this amazing city. The answer for us . . . tiny living."

Maybe tiny houses don't make good homes so much as they make good stories. Christopher Smith and Merete Mueller, the thirtysomething auteurs behind the 2013 documentary *Tiny*, filmed their build in the high Rockies, made the festival circuit, and landed a string of speaking engagements. But without running water in the subzero winter, they hauled the thing to a backyard in Boulder before Smith lit out to Los Angeles and Mueller to New York. "I would have been impressed to learn about a significant lifestyle change that lasted," wrote one disgruntled viewer on the film's website. "I am forced to believe that the film was simply about Chris making a film." To be fair, Thoreau hardly lived in his Walden cabin, either.

Building a tiny house is to living simply as getting pregnant is to raising a child. The hard part is not the designing, building, blogging, and networking: it's committing to a place and living within your means.

·+·

Back at the Jam, I asked around for Jay Shafer. I heard only the stuff of legend. Boarding a plane in California to come to the event, he had posted on Facebook for an airport pickup, and by the time he touched down, five strangers had volunteered. He offered one of them the extra bed in his hotel room, which was four times the size of his house. He tried to walk the three miles from the Drury Inn and Suites to the Jamboree, crossing six lanes of I-25 before turning back at the high fences of the Air Force Academy. I bumped into Zamudio and asked if Shafer was manning a booth.

"Jay Shafer doesn't need a booth," she said. "Jay Shafer is a booth."

My initial assessment of zero DIY homes turned out to be false. There was one. It was an eighty-four-square-footer built by Dee Williams, a fifty-three-year-old from Olympia, Washington, who in flip-flops and rolled jeans, with gray bangs and a quick smile, is perhaps the godmother of tiny houses. After being diagnosed with a life-threatening disease at age forty, she sold her regular house and built her dream, even penned a memoir. Hers was a singular attraction: the only house actually constructed and inhabited by its owner.

The line to view it was long.

"I hear you started all of this," I said.

"Nah," she said with a throaty laugh. "I heard about it from Jay Shafer."

I'm generally skeptical about the wonders of design. Thumbing through *Dwell* around that time, its pages fragrant like money, I came across some fund manager's off-grid compound intended to "celebrate nature," and I thought: If you really want to celebrate nature, you could start by not building your goddamn house in it.

But being inside Williams's house gave me a feeling of peace. Nothing fancy, nothing extra. The cedar walls hinted at contemplation. I stood with her for half an hour, talking about the freedom of owning few things, of her years in her van as an itinerant rock climber. A thundershower broke open and we stood together under an umbrella. Williams posed for pictures and answered questions. She rolled her eyes toward the sales models and said, "Can they squeeze a clothes dryer above the dishwasher?" She watched the muddy unwiped shoes enter and exit. "Look at those people taking umbrellas into my house," she said. "I'm going to close it up." And she did.

Shafer arrived, all sparkly eyes and elfin grin, clad in the same cutoffs, t-shirt, and flat-brimmed hat as the day before. He greeted Williams, then darted behind her house. I wandered back there. He was gone. I suspected that I was not dealing with a mere mortal but a magical being. I chased him into the woods.

Rounding the first stand of trees, where I guessed I'd discover him frolicking with a pot of gold at the base of a rainbow, I nearly bumped into him, and he recoiled in surprise. His fingers curled around a small green carton. I felt like a jerk for following him. I looked at the object in his hand.

I said, "Are those menthols?"

"No. They're organic."

"Can I have one?"

Yoda was hiding from his Jedi knights to get a fix. As I smoked his tobacco, he told me that his new company and plans for a tiny village had stalled.

"Life got in the way," he said. Although from a distance he could pass for thirty, Shafer is past fifty. I saw the lines around his gleaming eyes, the gray in his stubble. "I've had a lot of AFGOs."

"What's that?"

"Another fucking growth opportunity."

Shafer was raised in a large suburban house in Orange County, California. "I never had a true sense of home," he said. After attending the University of Iowa, he got a master's in fine art in New York City. But urban life didn't suit him. He returned to Iowa City, where he taught art, living in a pickup and later, an Airstream. Although he considers himself secular, as an artist he was drawn to sacred symbols and icons. "I got tired of building shrines I couldn't live in," he said.

I asked him if he'd been on any of the tiny-house shows.

"I was on Oprah."

"What was that like?"

"Like watching Oprah on television, but in 3-D."

During a commercial, she told him that he had inspired her to get rid of one of her mansions. "I wish she would have said it on camera."

Shafer went on to describe design in a language I had not heard at the Jamboree—or anywhere. "Integrity is my word for God," he said. It was wrong to conceal structural elements or disguise materials, and purely ornamental features were like a comb-over. Both attempted to convince us that the homeowner (or the hair owner) felt secure but of course revealed insecurity. "My best designs come only when my ego gets out of the way, when the higher power flows through me." He had a sense of humor about it all, too. "I spent weeks trying to design a dining table that would convert into a coffee table. Finally, I figured out that all I had to do was turn the thing on its side."

He described himself as a "meaning addict," always looking for higher significance in material objects. "A gate in a picket fence that opens onto a narrow path that leads through a yard to an open porch that covers a door," he said, "is a set of symbols we recognize as signposts guiding us through increasingly private territory toward the threshold of someone's clandestine world."

I finally got it. I had not understood why Williams's house had felt so authentic while so many of the blocks on wheels felt awkward or false. This subculture, although it seemed to be about nifty gadgets and Murphy beds, was at its heart the expression of our longing to find our place in the universe, to become as beautiful and functional as nature itself.

·+·

I heard a lot of talk at the Jamboree about "home." A young waitress from Jackson, Wyoming, faced with leaping rent, had bought—financed, actually— a Tumbleweed house for around $90,000 and hauled it to some friends' property where it couldn't be seen from the road. I looked at the pictures. It was awesome. And it had solved her problem of affordable housing.

But a mobile structure, no matter how lovely, is like a car: it loses value. Land, however, is permanent and, for the most part, gains value. I wondered how much of the tiny-house craze was simply a reaction to the historical forces that have made land impossibly expensive. Indeed, Shafer, Williams, and Zamudio were each parked on someone else's property, a situation offering fine lessons in building community, in our interdependence on our fellow human beings. But that doesn't achieve my own dream: to piss off the porch onto my own damn land and owe the bank nothing.

Which leads us to the movement's holy grail: legality. The hot Jam topic is changing code. Shafer has proposed using the zoning of an RV park to create a village of bungalows. Builders in Colorado have run with the concept, developing permanent, legal tiny villages in the towns of Salida, Walsenburg, and Fairplay. "This is not just a movement," said Darin Zaruba, owner of EcoCabins, organizer of the Jamboree, and developer of the Whispering Aspen Village in Fairplay, which is already taking $1,000 deposits for lots. "It's becoming an industry."

The cities of Fresno and Ojai, California, have permitted backyard tiny houses, often as rentals, to help homeowners pay their mortgages. If the movement is to have widespread impact, its adherents will have to master not just carpentry and wiring but the tedious jargon of planned unit developments and accessory dwelling units. They must step out of the shadows and into city hall. In November, a crew of Luminaries, including Zach Giffin, descended on Kansas City for the International Code Council hearings, where the nonprofit ICC writes building codes adopted across the country. They won preliminary approval for the first set of tiny-house building codes, covering everything from emergency egresses to low-overhead staircases. The changes don't apply to homes on wheels or affect local zoning rules—but proponents said they'd cleared a first major hurdle.

Nonetheless, the thrill of freedom reigns. Those who do first and ask forgiveness later seem to win as often as those who seek permission. "I didn't stress about zoning and code," Zamudio told me. "I wanted a tiny house and I didn't give a shit."

That night a series of thunderstorms soaked the Jam. I drove to the Drury, which jutted out of a shopping center with all the proportions and geometry of a ten-pound brick of government cheese. No vacancy. The closest room was in Denver, sixty miles away. I returned to the field at the base of Mount Apocalypse and stuffed my muddy feet into my damp sleeping bag.

My Midwestern van friends were gone. I checked their Facebook page. They'd posted a forty-second video, without commentary, shot from the window of a moving vehicle, of the landscape of the West, where so many have chased a dream of a better life: yellow flats framed by brown mountains, a dust devil swirling in the distance.

·+·

As for those AFGOs: After feuding with his partner, Shafer lost ownership of Tumbleweed Tiny Houses in 2012, before the company tapped its current bonanza of eighty plus employees building fifteen homes a month in its Colorado Springs factory. Jay left with a $30,000 debt that he has still not paid. Tumbleweed's lawyers accused him of willful trademark infringement and advertising "knockoffs" of Tumbleweed products that Shafer himself had designed. Then, in 2016, after seven years of marriage and two sons, Shafer and his wife split up. Despite what you might guess, the reason for divorce was not that all four were crammed into ninety-eight square feet. The family had bought a very small fixer-upper and planted Shafer's tiny house in the yard, which he used as an office. Until just a few months ago, when he hauled his home to an orchard, he'd been sleeping in a tent, crashing on friends' couches, pulling food from dumpsters. He told me he hadn't earned any income in the past year. "Some people set up social media accounts for me, but I stopped looking at them," he said. "I stopped responding to email."

Shafer's tale is the inverse of his acolytes': the tiny house came first, followed by debt, despair, an unhappy marriage. In keeping with his belief in the integrity of raw material, he was candid about his hardships. He would no more disguise heartbreak than he would structural columns.

I kept thinking of the story—perhaps a myth—of the Rolling Stones' 1964 visit to Chicago's Chess Records, the label that recorded Howlin' Wolf and Bo Diddley. By then, white boys had turned the blues into the booming industry of rock and roll. Keith Richards told a biographer that at the studio, perched on a ladder with a brush, was his hero, Muddy Waters. "He was painting the goddamn ceiling, dressed all in white, with white paint like tears on his face, 'cause he wasn't selling records at the time." I told this story to Jay Shafer, and he nodded and said, "I can understand that."

·+·

On the final morning, Williams spoke on stage. She said nothing about woodworking or circuit breakers. She talked about her limitations, all the things she didn't know how to do, how her friends had stepped up. She spoke of mortality, the passing of loved ones, the decay of her body, the acceptance of her ultimate death. She wanted to face it without artifice or delusion. She wept freely, and Shafer and the Luminaries camped in the front row wept with her.

Maybe the big isolated homes, long lonely commutes, stacks of bills, endless hours bound to a screen—they aren't the disease but the symptoms of something more pervasive. A sense that we don't belong; that our place in the world is without meaning; that we can't dissolve the boundaries of individuality and connect to the divine, to nature, to each other.

When the people's choice prize was announced, I inspected the winning house. The siding appeared to be wood, but when I ran my fingers across it, it was cool metal, stamped with fake grain.

The people had spoken. They preferred the comb-over.

Uprising at Standing Rock

In the summer of 2016, the Standing Rock Sioux Tribe in North Dakota emerged as climate change heroes when, with little political clout or media spotlight, they briefly halted construction of the $3.7 billion Dakota Access oil pipeline. As tribal chairman David Archambault II and others were arrested for pushing past barricades to block excavating machinery, the tribe sued the US Army Corps of Engineers to stop crews from burrowing beneath the Missouri River immediately upstream from their land, and the homely, hashtag #NoDAPL surged on Twitter—short for No Dakota Access Pipeline.

Meanwhile, the defiance evoked America's ugly racial past—and present. "It feels like 1875 because Natives are still fighting for our land," tweeted Native writer Sherman Alexie. Archambault could have been describing Ferguson or Baltimore when, in the *New York Times*, he decried racial profiling and claimed that "the state has militarized my reservation." In a touch of epic derp that would be funny if it didn't actually reveal how people of color are assumed to be violent, when the Lakotas invited relatives to pack their peace pipes and gather with them in solidarity, the white county sheriff thought they meant pipe bombs.

By August, several thousand Native Americans from around the country had arrived at Standing Rock, the 3,500-square-mile reservation with 8,250 residents. They were joined by a smattering of earthy white folk and a crew of Black Lives Matter activists from Minneapolis. The camp was just outside the boundary on land administered by the Army Corps. State troopers blocked the highway to Bismarck, allowing protesters—or "water protectors," as they called themselves—to leave but not return. In the US District Court for the District of Columbia, the tribe's lawyers argued that the pipeline would pollute their water and desecrate sacred burial grounds. Judge James E. Boasberg said he would decide in the coming weeks whether to issue an injunction against the corporation building the pipeline, Dakota Access, a subsidiary of Phillips 66 and a Texas company called Energy Transfer.

Sensing a conflagration of America's two most volatile issues—racism and climate change—I wrenched the back seats from my station wagon, loaded it with a mattress, five gallons of water, and five days' worth of provisions, and drove up to Standing Rock.

·+·

Just after sunset, I crested a hill above the Cannonball River, and there, in the flat, grassy bottom, beheld an iconic American sight: two dozen teepees and scores of tents lit by headlights and campfires, sheathed in a mist of tire dust and wood smoke, and riders galloping bareback on paint horses. At the central fire ring, I found circles of men pounding drums, surrounded by women who wailed with them in old Lakota song, singing well past midnight, fueled by cigarettes, coffee, and cough drops.

I parked alongside a towering teepee on the riverbank, slept in the car, and in the morning met my neighbors, a delegation of Pawnee elders who had driven eighteen hours from Broken Arrow, Oklahoma. The degree to which I didn't know what I was getting myself into was made clear when Chief Morgan LittleSun, fifty-eight, a warm and affable welder and teepee builder, told me that his biggest concern coming up here wasn't cops—it was the Sioux tribes.

"Pawnee and Sioux hated each other forever," he said. Even though the tribes had signed a peace treaty, LittleSun had seen hostility at powwows, and even fights.

I asked when the Pawnee and Sioux tribes had made this uneasy peace.

"A hundred and fifty years ago."

As far as LittleSun knew, this was the first time since then that Pawnee chiefs had traveled this far into Sioux territory. While dates of Indian wars and treaties are history-test minutiae that most white people (like me) tend to forget, LittleSun was one of many Native Americans I met for whom, as the saying goes, the past was not really dead, not even past. They rattled off these nineteenth-century events like they happened yesterday, and this gathering at

Standing Rock was occasion for a new round of history making. The site was called Seven Councils Camp, or Oceti Sakowin Camp, indicating the first time all bands of Lakotas had gathered in one place in more than a century. That afternoon, the Crow Nation marched into camp in war bonnets, waving flags, singing and whooping, bearing a peace pipe and a load of buffalo meat, offering the first real reconciliation since 1876, when Crows were scouts for Custer at Little Bighorn where the US Cavalry got its ass kicked by the Lakotas. At last count, representatives from more than 120 tribal nations had arrived from as far as Hawaii, Maine, California, and Mississippi.

But when I asked LittleSun—whose tribe historically had a proud tradition of stealing horses—if he'd felt uneasy here, he shook his head emphatically, and a smile spread over his face. "This is the greatest thing I've ever seen," he said. All day long, strangers walked into his camp and offered food and firewood and asked which tribe he belonged to, and when he told them, they didn't flinch but embraced him as a brother, an uncle, an elder. "But when I raised the Pawnee flag on a pole," LittleSun added with a laugh, "everyone moved their horses to the other side of camp!"

A series of kitchens were open around the clock to feed free meals to about 1,000 people. A microphone was open to just about anyone, and throughout the long, hot days, one wayfarer after another described how wonderful it was to be here, how much it meant to see Native Americans from all the nations gathered in common purpose. While I saw passion and anger and solemnity, the main thing I saw was joy. Travelers were reuniting with long-lost relatives. Parents brought small children, and an impromptu homeschool taught them to ride horses and make fry bread. t-shirts and banners with wry slogans like NATIVES WITH ATTITUDE and STRAIGHT OUTTA PINE RIDGE hinted at youth, pride, and immersion in political pop culture. A truckful of teenage boys rolled past a trio of pretty girls and hollered, hopefully, "What tribe are you from?" There was singing and dancing and praying, sweat lodges and kayaks and swimming—a regular Indigenous paradise.

Amid the evident pleasure they found in being not a minority but the overwhelming majority, as a white reporter I felt like a buzzkill at the thought of whipping out a pen and pad to ask questions. I hung out mostly at the Pawnee camp, each morning making coffee for my neighbors who'd forgotten to bring a pot. Unlike many tribal nations whose numbers have swelled in the past century, the Pawnees, who were forcibly marched from the Missouri River to Oklahoma, have just 3,482 enrolled members. The chiefs told me that going over the rolls after months when deaths outnumbered births was heartbreaking.

A few days before my arrival, state officials had removed a water truck that was in place for protesters. Perhaps they thought they were dealing with a band of starved hunters who might scare away easily instead of a sovereign nation with its own government, police, EMS, and radio station.

Within hours, the Standing Rock Sioux Tribe had hauled in its own infrastructure: banks of porta-potties, water tankers, a disaster response trailer, dumpsters, ambulances, a refrigerated semi-truck. Meanwhile, each delegation arrived with cash and food. Tons of food. I spent a day cooking meatball stew in the main kitchen and discovered, among other abundances, a four-person tent stacked to the ceiling with bags of flour. The tribe also had its own beef production enterprise. The Yakima Nation in Washington chartered a tractor trailer filled with pallets of fresh fruit and bottled water. Small donations were also received: somebody mailed four packets of Lipton noodles. When I asked how long they planned to stay, most said, "Till the end."

One day, it got so hot that I drove up the road to check email under the air conditioner of the Prairie Knights Casino and Resort, owned by the tribe. After days talking about spirit and justice under the big open skies, it came as a shock to hedgehog into the chilly dark cave of the casinos, ABBA tunes piped through the speakers, a television twice the size of my car. I watched fifty-eight senior citizens disembark from a motor coach from Bismarck, fifty-eight of them Caucasian, and as they plunked their pensions into the one-armed bandits, I wondered if they knew they were underwriting the civil disobedience down the road.

·✝·

The only note of standoffishness I detected at Seven Councils was a settlement in a grove of cottonwoods called Red Warrior Camp, which had erected a fence around itself and hung signs that read: NO MEDIA. NO TOURISTS. CHECK IN WITH SECURITY. An organizer told me the camp was trained in direct nonviolent action. "Whatever happens in Red Warrior Camp stays in Red Warrior Camp," she said. When they held an open mic outside the gate, their rhetoric included the same message of togetherness and spirit but with a more militant tone. Its people were younger, quite a few of them white, some wearing camo fatigues and bandannas over their faces. I was told that many of the activists came from Pine Ridge Indian Reservation in South Dakota, home to the Wounded Knee Massacre of 1890 and uprising in 1973, still bearing a stamp of badassery from the days of the American Indian Movement. Unlike the Standing Rock Tribe, which courted mainstream reporters, Red Warrior pumped out its own message on Facebook. I didn't attempt to penetrate the place but met some young Native guys staying there. "For a place calling itself Red Warrior Camp," one of them quipped, "there sure are a lot of white warriors."

Nonetheless, in five days I witnessed no violence, lawlessness, alcohol, or even hostility. A couple speakers even welcomed "European relatives" such as myself. The days were filled with peaceful marches and prayers at the idle construction site, ceremonial welcoming of newly arrived tribes, and as afternoon temps rose to the nineties, flinging ourselves into the cool waters of the once-mighty Cannonball. "River" is the incorrect word to describe this body of water. With its currentless murk and silty mud, the thing is a reservoir, an arm of the man-made lake impounded by the Oahe Dam.

I met Nick Estes, a Lower Brule Sioux from South Dakota who remembered that when he was a child, his grandparents told stories about the wonderful Missouri River. "But after the 1940s, the stories stopped." The Pick-Sloan Missouri Basin Program authorized nine dams—five on Indian land, displacing those who lived along the banks. Standing Rock lost 55,000 acres, while adjacent Cheyenne River Reservation lost 150,000 acres.

"If Dakota Access kills this river," said Estes, "it will be its second death."

According to historian Michael Lawson, author of *Dammed Indians*, "The Oahe Dam destroyed more Indian land than any other public works project in America." Estes said his elders "died of heartache."

Indian nations, with their ample resources and limited political power, have often borne the brunt of resource extraction. For the Lakotas, the "Black Snake," as many call the Dakota Pipeline, feels like just one more case of whittling away of their land—which is to say, breaking their treaties. And Indians can't help but notice that, although the reason they keep getting screwed is never acknowledged to be racism, the victims of the various ecological catastrophes through the decades are often members of their race. Between dams, toxic dumps, fracking, oil spills, and atomic bomb tests, the list of injustices against Native communities could fill pages.

In 2014, the proposed route of DAPL went through Bismarck, the capital of North Dakota, with roughly 61,000 residents, 92 percent of them white. After the Corps determined that the pipeline could contaminate drinking water, it was rerouted to pass by Standing Rock. "That's environmental racism," said Kandi Mossett, of the Mandan, Hidatsa, and Arikara Nation in North Dakota and an organizer with the Indigenous Environmental Network.

This type of outrage is not limited to activists. Jetting in from Arizona was Russell Begaye, president of the 360,000-member Navajo Nation, by far the country's largest. As the only man on the grounds in a coat and tie (a giant turquoise bolo, to be precise), he looked every bit like the most politically powerful American Indian in the country. When I asked if he thought the placement of projects like DAPL on Native land were evidence of racism, Begaye said, "Of course, because they could put this further north, but they are not going to do that because the population up there is not Indian." He cited the 2015 Gold King Mine wastewater spill on the Animas River in Colorado, which polluted Navajo water and farms.

Much of this debate hinges on a concept to which most non-Native Americans give little thought: sovereignty. According to the treaties, Indians were to be treated as autonomous nations and dealt with diplomatically, like foreign governments. That didn't happen. Reservations were ruled by unelected white agents from the Bureau of Indian Affairs, who outlawed Indigenous language and religion. But in past decades, reservations have established their own governments and, with bands of lawyers, have fought for—and, in many cases, won back—their treaty rights. The Standing Rock lawsuit would hinge on the definition of sovereignty. The law required the Army Corps of Engineers to consult with the tribe before it permitted the pipeline, but it didn't require that the tribe approve. So Standing Rock contends that its wishes were overruled.

"When we need help, they say we are sovereign," said Mossett. "But when it comes to development of our resources—oil, gas, coal, uranium, water—then they step in to see how much money the state can get."

The United Nations appears to agree. Its Permanent Forum on Indigenous Issues released a statement that the failure to consult with the Sioux on DAPL violated the Declaration on the Rights of Indigenous Peoples, a resolution President Obama signed in 2010.

·+·

For all their notoriety as climate crusaders, the Standing Rock Sioux Tribe did not ask for that mantle. Their lawsuit, in which they are represented by the environmental group Earthjustice, does not mention carbon or fossil fuels. For that matter, it doesn't mention racism. It focuses strictly on two issues: potential pollution of their water source in the event of a spill, and the disturbance of sacred sites. And yet their defiance has stirred the pot, and in this moment of galvanization, other indigenous Americans are bringing to the table ideas that combine the often-estranged progressive causes of ecology and racial justice.

"Climate change is inherently racist," said Nick Estes, co-founder of activist organization the Red Nation and a PhD candidate in American Studies at the University of New Mexico. "The Anthropocene began with fossil fuel extraction, which began with colonization. The rise of temperatures began with the industrial revolution. And the damage was done to 'expendable people,' exploiting the labor of Black people and the land of Indigenous people."

Gone is the nineteenth-century attempt to defeat Europeans or the twentieth-century attempt to assimilate. The strategy now is to marshal attorneys, money, land, and political clout to outlast them. "I call us the weebee people," said Brian Cladoosby, president of the National Congress of American Indians. "We be here when they came, we be here when they gone."

Perhaps the most startling idea to emerge is a full upending of the narrative of the benevolent—perhaps paternalistic—white liberal uplifting the oppressed minority. People I met here felt that white people had strayed so far from their spiritual core that it was the Indian who would have to rescue them. A Pawnee hip-hop artist who calls himself Quese IMC (born Marcus Frejo Little Eagle), with black beard, hoop earrings, thick-rimmed glasses, and a cocked ball cap, told me that both racism and exploitation of the earth came from the same sickness: a lack of spirituality, which breeds a lack of compassion for other beings. "The earth is a spirit, the water is a spirit, and if you have no spirit, and you have no connection to those things, it will be easy to destroy them and not even care."

When I asked Chief LittleSun what was so great about the gathering, he said, "The spiritual part of this movement. This ground is the holiest place on Earth right now." This was the first time in his entire life that he'd taken part in any sort of protest or movement. I asked if he considered himself an environmentalist. LittleSun shook his head. "I don't even know what that is." It was as if I'd asked him if he were a "skin-ist" or a "body-ist." He simply didn't think of himself as an entity separate from the earth.

Speaking to the main camp circle, Begaye compared the Navajo code talkers who helped defeat Hitler to Native Americans today leading the fight to protect land and water. "We have always saved the white people from themselves!" he declared, and the crowd roared its approval.

·+·

With so much celebration in Oceti Sakowin Camp, people hardly noticed that crews were still bulldozing away just miles from the site where they'd been turned back. But the Red Warriors noticed. Before dawn on August 31, two young Lakota men chained themselves to heavy machinery at a pipeline site about twenty-five miles from camp.

State and county police quickly arrived, blocked the highway, and began trying to extract the men. Dale American Horse Jr., twenty-six, of Sioux Falls, South Dakota, who went by the excellent nickname of Happy, was perched seven feet off the ground, his arms chained to a hydraulic rod that towered high above him. He was a big handsome guy, clean-shaven, with a thick red bandanna tied just above his eyes, covering his black braid. He said little as the firefighters attempted to remove him or as a crowd of about fifty supporters sang and drummed and taunted the baby-faced cops.

"Did you ever wear a uniform to defend that Constitution?" jeered an older Native man, a long gray braid beneath a headband. He sucked a cigarette and blew smoke into the wind, and when the police prevented supporters from smudging American Horse with burning sage, his voice rose. "That's a religious right we paid for with blood, with the red stripe on the flag! We all wore uniforms! We won wars for you!"

Happy American Horse was extracted and arrested after being locked to the excavator for six hours. Red Warrior spokesperson Clay Hall called the action a success, halting construction for a day and costing the company hundreds of thousands of dollars in delays. "In the Lakota way, we call that counting coup," he told me. "We took them with an action when they weren't expecting it." Hall said that his group wasn't merely interested in rerouting the project; they wanted to kill the Black Snake altogether.

The Red Warriors had staged a stunning bit of guerilla theater. Thirteen thousand people watched the action live on Facebook. The picture of Happy American Horse bear-hugging that steel boom went viral. Locked to the pole with a free country behind him, arms bound, eyes cast down serenely, a brown man being handled by white guards: the image that was beamed from America to the world looked all too much like a condemned warrior being led to the gallows. Or to the cross.

Last Days at Standing Rock

On Friday, December 2, Bobby Robedeaux and seven other members of the Pawnee Nation left Pawnee, Oklahoma, hauling a trailer full of firewood 900 miles north to the Standing Rock Sioux Reservation in North Dakota. From the highway, Adrian SpottedHorseChief posted on Facebook: "Pawnee war party on the move."

The weekend promised drama. After a four-month standoff between Native American protesters and law enforcement over the construction of the Dakota Access Pipeline, both the governor of North Dakota and the US Army Corps of Engineers ordered the water protectors to evacuate their camp by Monday, December 5. Meanwhile, thousands of US military veterans were slated to arrive on Sunday to serve as "human shields" for the Native Americans.

The Pawnees were not a literal war party. Although they were prepared to march the barricades, they were unarmed. Their primary mission was to pray. In early September, Robedeaux and SpottedHorseChief made their first journey to the Oceti Sakowin camp on the banks of the Cannonball River to hold a traditional all-night ceremony.

That was when I met them. Robedeaux is a former wildland firefighter with scarred fists and knuckles that hint of rough years behind him. Now thirty-five, he has settled down, raising two children with his fiancée in a Tulsa suburb while studying pre-law. He is over six feet tall, a block of muscle with hair pulled back in a ponytail. He is quick to laugh, quick to tears, and a complete ham. I once saw him walk up to a satellite news truck, take his place uninvited in front of the camera, and proceed to address the folks back home in his hill-country drawl: "Hi, I'm Bobby Robedeaux of the Pawnee Nation in Pawnee, Oklahoma."

SpottedHorseChief, forty-one, is a former high school football player who wears a mohawk and served as an adviser during the making of the film *The Revenant*. He sits on the Pawnee Business Council, the tribe's governing body. He was raised by his grandparents, who taught him traditional ways, and he now lives in the same small house on a dirt lane that he grew up in.

That day in September, I helped them set up the teepee that would house the ceremony, a process that began with a blessing of the poles in both English and Pawnee. When it was up, they looked for a stepladder so someone could fasten the flap above the door. A young Pawnee turned to me and said, "I'll have to climb on your shoulders."

I thought he was kidding. But he wasn't.

I squatted, he mounted my shoulders, and I straightened my legs, quivering a bit beneath the weight. He was the lightest of the group, and the older guys thought the sight of him sitting on this forty-five-year-old white dude was pretty funny. I soon learned that this was his first time performing the task of threading the dowel rods through the holes. It took some coaching from down below, and some practice.

One of the guys said, "Turn around."

"Yeah, turn around," another said. "Mark, stay how you are."

That cracked them all up.

We prayed all night, sitting cross-legged in a circle in the teepee, burning oak and walnut wood they'd hauled from Oklahoma. We prayed generally for family members and for cures to illnesses, and specifically that the creator and the Army Corps of Engineers would stop the Black Snake that might destroy the drinking water on what remained of the Great Sioux Nation, which had been drastically chipped away at since the treaties of the nineteenth century. At dawn, we ate corn paste and pinto beans, and oranges and candy bars. The mood was festive. That day, the local Lakota Sioux held two feasts for their ancient enemy, the Pawnees, in gratitude for the prayers.

But even then, signs were ominous. The same day of the ceremony, September 3, dogs attacked protesters as they tried to block bulldozers from destroying sacred burial sites. And back home in Pawnee, a 5.8-magnitude earthquake rattled the reservation, destroying historic sandstone buildings built in the early twentieth century. The earthquake epidemic in Oklahoma is thought to be linked to the proliferation of fracking, when wastewater is injected deep underground. Some fracking occurs on the Pawnee reservation, both on land owned by the tribe and land owned by individual members—all of which is administered by the federal Bureau of Indian Affairs. Seeing the mass resistance flowering in North Dakota, the Pawnees wanted to right the wrongs in their own home.

·+·

Traveling with the Pawnee party last weekend were two tribal elders. Andrew KnifeChief, a Marine Corps veteran, is the executive director of the Pawnee Nation. For three months, he had been approving expenditures and supplies to support the Pawnee camp in Standing Rock. Now he wanted to see it with his own eyes. Chief Morgan LittleSun, the welder and truck driver and teepee maker I'd met my first morning in the camp, was making his fourth visit to Standing Rock. In August, he set up a teepee at Pawnee camp on the banks of the river. In October, he brought and pitched the twenty-by-forty-foot canvas army tent, and in November, he outfitted it with a wood-burning stove and a chimney.

LittleSun's comings and goings were typical of many I met at Standing Rock. They established their camps, but then made trips home to tend to jobs and families. The Pawnee camp had been established in August by Marcus Frejo, the Oklahoma hip-hop artist who performs under the name Quese IMC. Frejo, thirty-eight, had been coming to Standing Rock for many years, serving as something like a motivational speaker to teenagers during an epidemic of youth suicide. Last summer, after a contingent of young Lakotas ran all the way from Standing Rock to Washington, DC, to protest the pipeline, Frejo arrived at Sacred Stone Camp, situated on private land on the reservation on the south bank of the Cannonball River. In August, when Dave Archambault, chairman of Standing Rock, was arrested for blocking construction crews, thousands of allies began to stream in, quickly overflowing Sacred Stone. The tribe established an overflow camp, Oceti Sakowin, on the north side of the river on Army Corps land. Frejo wanted a place for his relatives to stay, and he told me that after praying, he was led to the riverbank within Oceti Sakowin, where he pitched his tent. Four months later, it became home to dozens of Pawnees—and thousands of others—as they made the pilgrimage to North Dakota. I had made four trips and spent nearly five weeks in Pawnee camp.

This December, the Pawnees arrived late Friday night. On Saturday morning, they attended the Oceti Sakowin camp's daily meeting inside a vast white geodesic dome. Although the Standing Rock Tribe is nominally in charge of camp, it doesn't manage the overwhelming day-to-day tasks of feeding, housing, and providing medical care for thousands of visitors. Those tasks were left to a loose coalition of facilitators and volunteers—some Native, some white—and it was often unclear who was leading.

As they looked around, the Pawnees realized that Oceti Sakowin had changed. To begin with, despite the snowstorms and cold snap, the number of people in camp had substantially increased. In August, there were fewer than 5,000 people. Now, according to Desiree Kane, a volunteer media coordinator, since July the weekend crowd had swelled to about 11,000, including 4,000 veterans. Snow-covered yurts and wall tents and motorhomes and tipis and vehicles were packed across the bottomland as tightly as they would fit.

Next, the water protectors were no longer free to come and go north to Bismarck on Highway 1806, which was now blocked by armored military vehicles and spirals of razor wire to keep them off the construction site. On the bluffs above camp, pipeline workers had erected a row of stadium-style floodlights that shone down on camp all through the night to prevent anyone from climbing the hill to the drill pad. A helicopter and an airplane circled the camp at all hours. It felt like a prison or a demilitarized zone, especially after the summer's peace met autumn's pepper spray, batons, fire hoses, and rubber bullets, not to mention the nearly 600 arrests. The images of armored light-skinned police inflicting pain on unarmed dark-skinned citizens brought echoes of the Jim Crow South.

But what the Pawnees noticed most, inside the dome, were the white people. In a crowd of 200 attending the morning meeting, the Pawnees were among fewer than a dozen Natives. In August, Natives comprised about 80 percent of the camp, but now it seemed like it was closer to 20 percent. Natives still led the movement, but in calling for allies from around the world to join them, they had changed the makeup of camp. For the most part, the alliance was harmonious, with non-Natives assuming important roles, from building to cooking to getting arrested on the front lines. But some racial tensions had flared up, and on social media, Natives accused whites of ignoring tribal protocols, disrespecting elders, treating the experience like Burning Man or some other way station on their own "spiritual journey," or even "colonizing" camp by helping themselves to space, food, and firewood without giving back.

I had witnessed the full spectrum. One white friend arrived with a four-wheel-drive truck and chainsaws and expertise, and was essential to keeping things running. On the other hand, I'd picked up a white couple who'd hitchhiked from California with ten cardboard boxes of acorns and leather, intending to teach the Natives to make flour and moccasins. Just last weekend, I rescued a white guy who was sitting on the snow in a blizzard, too tired and hypothermic to keep walking. As the Pawnees fed him soup and warmed him by the fire in their tent, he lectured us about the philosophy of anarchism.

LittleSun, Robedeaux, and KnifeChief volunteered to help around camp. They spent the morning unloading a trailer of lumber that was used to build winter structures. It wasn't clear who was in charge. Then they were asked to haul forty bags of clothing to the thrift store in Bismarck. Normally this would be a forty-mile drive, but because of the road closure, it was seventy. They were also handed $2,100 to buy supplies. The men completed the tasks but not without qualms. Robedeaux couldn't help but notice that all these clothes donated to Standing Rock protesters would now be given to a community that has been hostile to Native Americans. He voiced this to the people giving orders but was informed that the camp had received more donations than it could possibly use. By the time the Pawnees returned to camp it was dusk, and they had trouble finding someone to give the change and receipts. As they unloaded supplies, someone barked at them to move their truck.

When the men finally pushed through the canvas doors of their tent, where I was sitting, they were frustrated. They pulled up chairs to the woodstove to warm themselves. The green canvas roof was dry above the fire but frosted everywhere else. Battery-powered lanterns swung overhead. An entire wall was stacked with shelves of food, propane stoves, pots, and pans. Cots and air mattresses covered most of the floor, which was lined with plastic tarps. A small summer tent in the corner provided one private bedroom. Mounted on a propane tank was a rickety device called Mr. Heater that looked capable of emitting a fatal dose of carbon monoxide.

Just then, a bearded guy with long blond hair poked his head in and said that so-and-so had a question about the receipts and wanted them to come back and discuss them. Bobby told him to send so-and-so over here if they wanted to talk, that he was done running errands for the day.

Andrew KnifeChief called a meeting of his relatives. (Pawnees consider all members of the tribe relative, even if they are not closely related by blood.) He described what he'd seen as a circus. Standing Rock wasn't at all what he'd expected. Instead of a well-run Native organization, he'd seen a chaotic festival run by hippies. They'd heard more talk about yoga and meditation and the wellness tent than they had about stopping the pipeline. KnifeChief was worried that if police were to raid the camp, neither the unarmed band of volunteer camp security forces nor these well-meaning white folks could ensure the safety of the Pawnees. What's more, he said, the Pawnees needed to concentrate their efforts on the fight at home. Just a week earlier, the tribe had filed a lawsuit against the Bureau of Indian Affairs and the Bureau of Land Management, alleging that the fracking leases on Pawnee soil were illegal. While Standing Rock had emboldened them to fight their own battle, maybe it was time to return home.

Just then, the flaps of the tent parted. Buoyed by an icy wind, two people pushed through: the blond dude and a stylish young white woman in a scarf, wool hat, and designer eyeglasses.

"I have serious issues," said the woman.

She marched toward the woodstove where we were huddled and pulled an envelope from her parka, revealing a pile of cash and a stack of receipts.

"We gave you over $2,100," she said. "But there's more than one thousand missing."

The men jumped to their feet in protest.

"We spent $1,700," said Bobby. "And we brought back $400."

"You only spent $800," said the woman.

Howls of anger rose up. Bobby demanded to see the receipts. Rifling through them, he said, "See? Here. We spent $1,253 and 74 cents at Home Depot!"

But the woman didn't believe it. "I just had three other people look these over. We're missing more than $1,000."

"It says so right here."

The woman peered at the receipts. Someone jeered, "Maybe your glasses are foggy."

The woman saw that she'd make a mistake.

"How dare you come in here and accuse us of stealing," said Robedeaux, his voice rising.

"I didn't accuse," she insisted. "I said it's a serious matter—"

"It's serious now!" bellowed Chief LittleSun. "Count that money in front of us! You're about to get me riled up."

Andrew KnifeChief stepped in and extended his business card. "I'm the executive director of the Pawnee Nation."

"Do I get to speak?" she said.

"No, not right now," said KnifeChief. "We're all tired. We didn't expect to spend nine hours today delivering stuff. I am the guy in charge of our nation's government. We don't steal from people. Especially not on my watch. So, now you can speak."

"Thanks." The defiance was gone. "I didn't actually accuse anyone of anything. And I have been working sixteen hours a day for the past three months. A whole bunch of stuff actually did get stolen from us, like, within the past two hours. So I am very stressed out because I'm working on a very serious thing right now, a number of very serious things that involve people's lives."

"Can we shake hands?" said KnifeChief.

"Yeah, I got no beef with you. But I also feel a lot of anger and accusation that I've accused you of something, which is not what I was doing."

Robedeaux said, "What angers me is that we have ways of doing things. These Sioux people have ways. So you guys need to learn these ways. Because this is their land."

"Respect Indian ways," said SpottedHorseChief, jabbing the air with a finger, "of how to treat and talk to people. It's respect."

"Yeah, you're working sixteen hours," said Marcus Frejo. "I've been here since day one. I got a felony. I've been through the hardships of all these battles. Now I see all these white people all around us. And as Indian people, we're thinking about heading out because it's been taken over. And then you come in. All my relatives here. We have chiefs here. Elders, veterans here. It hurts my heart. Because this is what this camp has become."

"When your stuff gets stolen," said Robedeaux, "know this: when it was all Natives, nothing got stolen. Now, things being stolen: look at your people."

"I apologize to come in to you guys in what felt like a bad way," she said.

She asked to shake Robedeaux's hand. He refused. And with that she left. Robedeaux found himself weeping. The chief threw his arms around him.

To heal the bad energy, Chief LittleSun pulled a pile of embers from the stove with a shovel, then sprinkled on sprigs of cedar. They blessed themselves in the fragrant smoke. Many of the men here, in middle age, had begun taking classes to learn their language, and they prayed in Pawnee. They decided that the incident was part of the creator's plan. It had happened for a reason. They hoped the woman had learned something from it. For them, it confirmed their fears about what the camp had become. They decided to go home.

"We came in a good way, and we'll leave in a good way," said LittleSun.

In the nineteenth century, as many as 45,000 Pawnees peopled the Great Plains along the Missouri River. But by the time of their forced removal from Nebraska to Oklahoma in 1875, there were fewer than 1,000. Today, the tribe's numbers have rebounded to more than 3,000. They couldn't afford to lose any up here in North Dakota if a police confrontation grew violent. So Andrew KnifeChief finalized the decision to head home. He shook his head gravely. "There's just so few of us."

This sacred camp, a beacon for tribal sovereignty, had eroded into a place where Indians were bossed by whites and presumed to be criminals. It had become like the rest of America.

·+·

Bobby Robedeaux felt moved to speak. Not just to his relatives. He wanted to address the entire camp. His elders granted permission. About an hour after the confrontation, he wrapped himself in a Pendleton blanket that showed the Pawnee flag: a red wolf's head on a blue background. He removed a fan of eagle feathers from a case. Then he and LittleSun set out into the snowy night.

Instead of following the well-traveled paths, Robedeaux picked a route between tents and cars. I asked why. "People been walking these same paths, but they been in the wrong," he said. "I don't want to follow them."

When we arrived at the sacred fire in the heart of the camp, we found a large crowd around a circle of drummers and singers. A few people were dancing. But what struck me was that there was hardly a Native American face in the crowd. Robedeaux asked around but could not find out who was in charge. He convinced one of the drummers to give him the microphone. The music stopped. The crowd looked on at Robedeaux in his wolf blanket, mic in one hand, eagle feathers in the other.

"I'm looking for a Lakota elder," he said.

No response.

"I need to speak with an elder from this camp, a Lakota or Nakota or Dakota."

After what seemed like a long time, a small gray-haired woman approached. He bent down and consulted with her, the microphone not capturing their words. It lasted a few minutes. Still the crowd looked on curiously.

The woman took the mic. She greeted us in the Lakota language, and then spoke Lakota for five minutes. Then she translated, saying that it was important that the camp respect Native ways, and that the Pawnee people had been treated unfairly. She wanted them to speak. She invited the whole Pawnee delegation to the front, and as snowflakes fluttered in the night sky, the eight men and one woman lined up alongside Robedeaux.

A lot was riding on this. After all, the Lakota Sioux and the Pawnees have been enemies for centuries, and the unity at Standing Rock to fight the Black Snake brought a historic truce. The Lakotas didn't want their guests mistreated, and the Pawnees were careful not to come across as ungrateful.

Bobby took the mic and, holding the eagle plume, began to speak. He said that back in September, a stream of Native people would walk past camp and introduce themselves, but now white people didn't even say hello. He spoke of how powerful it had been, and how it now seemed fractured. He kept his words gentle, though, never mentioning the alleged theft. He announced that the Pawnees would be breaking camp and heading back to Oklahoma. Then Adrian SpottedHorseChief took the mic and recounted the accusation by the white woman. I looked behind me and saw that dozens of Native Americans had moved to the front. "Don't come here and try to change things," he said. "If you come here, join in and learn from us."

Marcus Frejo took the mic, and after praising the white allies he'd met, he spoke bluntly. "Some of you white folks don't even acknowledge us here. So why did you come? If all you ever said was I'm here to stop a pipeline and not once said I'm here to pray with this water, acknowledging the power and spirit of the water, then you have no right coming to stop the Black Snake, because you are the Black Snake."

When they were done, the Lakota elder asked everyone in the crowd to shake their hands. A long line formed, and we approached and shook each hand. A lot of people—both white and Native—thanked Bobby for what he'd said. These kinds of things had been going on for weeks, they said, and it was time someone finally brought it up.

That night, the cold front arrived. I slept in the back of my car in heavy down sleeping bags. Bobby hardly slept. He spent most of the night wandering camp, waking the chief to pray and smoke tobacco on the riverbank before dawn. I asked what he'd seen in the night. "A lot of teepees with no fire in them," he said. "A lot of people who didn't know why they were here."

·+·

As the morning sun emerged clear and cold, we walked to the sacred fire. Thousands of veterans were streaming into camp, a line of traffic backed up a mile, as far as we could see. We walked to the front line, the barricade across Backwater Bridge that for the past six weeks had prevented protesters from marching to the construction site. Earlier that morning, US Congresswoman Tulsi Gabbard, a Democrat from Hawaii, walked to the barricade. The police agreed to remove their armored vehicles and personnel from the bridge as long as the protesters agreed to stay off it. Something like a de-escalation had occurred.

Nonetheless, the vets—and the water protectors—were fired up. With their numbers higher than ever, many wanted to overrun the hated barricade and the cops once and for all. But the Standing Rock elders had other ideas. They gave orders for camp security to send all marchers back from the bridge to camp. When we arrived back at the fire, the plan was announced. We were going to pray. We were going to form a circle, hands held, around the entire camp, and we would pray. I heard at least one groan, and one guy wrapped in camo fatigues muttered, "You mean we're not going to stop the pipeline?"

A team of riders was dispatched to circle the camp on horseback and spread the word. Robedeaux, with his Pawnee flag, joined the procession. An hour later, the circle was not quite complete. Many in camp either didn't get the memo or didn't care, and just went about their business. Chief LittleSun and I headed for the mess hall to get some lunch. We could see the prayer circle forming all around us. Just as we reached the buffet, I heard two reporters behind me in line: they'd heard word that the Army Corps had denied the easement.

The United States had blocked the pipeline.

With my plate of stir-fry, I hurried to the sacred fire, arriving just in time to hear whoops from the crowd. The prayer circle was disbanding as everyone rushed to the fire. Standing Rock Chairman Dave Archambault was jubilant. "We won!" he said. "You can go home and spend the winter with your families!" Drums pounded, and the high wails of a victory song rang into the cold sunshine. Hundreds stomped their feet in a victory dance. Another elder, Phyllis Young, announced, "We are making peace with the United States of America!" LittleSun and I pushed to the front, where we saw the blue-and-red Pawnee flag bouncing at the center of the circle. There were SpottedHorseChief and Robedeaux, tear-stained cheeks, crying with joy.

That night, the Pawnees tied a traditional drum by spreading rawhide across a ceramic bowl filled with water. They burned sage and cedar and sang songs of thanks—victory songs. By the next morning, they'd be on the highway to Oklahoma, where they'd get the news that yet another earthquake had shaken their homeland. I stuck around another day, only to find that the celebration was short-lived.

Even as the Standing Rock Sioux Tribe asked all protesters to leave the camp and go home, a white guy wearing a serape walked through camp with a bullhorn, entreating people to stay, claiming that DAPL planned to continue drilling despite the Army decision. This could not be confirmed, partly because the drill pad is closed to reporters. But that same day, its parent company, Energy Transfer Partners, pressed a US District Court to reverse the decision and issue the easement. A spokesperson for President-Elect Trump said that he supported the pipeline—indeed, Trump owned stocks in several of the parent companies, and Kelcy Warren, the CEO of Energy Transfer Partners, had contributed $100,000 to the Trump Victory Fund. It's unclear if a president can legally overrule a decision by the Army Corps of Engineers.

Meanwhile, a blizzard tore through with fifty-mile-per-hour winds and subzero temperatures. On the morning I left, the last holdouts in the Pawnee tent awakened to find a thin layer of snow had whipped inside a gap in the flap. As roads iced and visibility dropped to zero, dozens of vehicles slid into ditches, and thousands of vets and water protectors were stranded, either bracing against the bitter cold in camp or taking refuge on the floor of the nearby casino. Leaders from Sacred Stone Camp and several other Native-run activist groups ended the call for new recruits to join the camps.

In the end, the Pawnees went home satisfied. They had traveled north to pray. And their prayers—at least for the moment—had been answered.

How the Mighty Have Fallen

Utah had a problem. Shown a photo of Delicate Arch, people guessed it was in Arizona. Asked to describe states in two adjectives, they called Colorado green and mountainous but Utah brown and Mormon. It was 2012. Up in the governor's Office of Tourism, hands were wrung. Anyone who had poked around canyon country's mind-melting spires and gurgling green springs knew it was the most spectacular place on the continent—maybe the world—so why did other states get the good rep?

The office hired a Salt Lake City ad firm called Struck. The creatives came up with a rebrand labeled the Mighty Five, a multimedia campaign to extol the state's national parks: Zion, Bryce Canyon, Capitol Reef, Canyonlands, and Arches. By 2013, a twenty-story mashup of red rock icons towered as a billboard over Wilshire Boulevard in Los Angeles. A San Francisco subway station morphed into a molten ocher slot. Delicate Arch bopped around London on the sides of taxicabs. The pinnacle was a thirty-second commercial that was—let's face it—a masterpiece.

An attractive, young, and somewhat cool family of four—Dad sports shaggy hair to the chin, stubble, and wraparound sunglasses—takes a road trip for the ages. They splash through the trippy slo-mo waterdrops of a slot canyon seep, spin beneath psychedelic pillars the voice-over calls "giant orange drip castles," behold a rapturous explosion of Milky Way stars framed by rock walls, and punch their J-rig through a gargantuan wave in Cataract Canyon. Then finally—and this is the shot I'm sort of embarrassed to admit still fills my eyes with tears—the little girl, who's about ten years old, scrambles along a slickrock bench with a headlamp in the dark until she catches a heart-stopping sunrise glimpse of daybreak clouds rushing over a red rock wedding ring.

"I was like, holy crap," says Lance Syrett, chairman of the state's Board of Tourism Development, remembering his first viewing. "You get that feeling—like hair standing on end—this is lightning in a bottle!"

I've lived and guided in these canyons for over a decade, and the ad plucked all my heartstrings. It evoked the hardscrabble seclusion of Ed Abbey and the mad descent of Everett Ruess and the soul serenity of Terry Tempest Williams, yet it promised that you don't have to be a hermit or daredevil: the Cool Family Robinson managed to follow their bliss, apparently, in a Subaru.

"It was laughably simple," says Alexandra Fuller, the former creative director of Struck. "Taking natural features that have been there forever and parks that have been there for decades and putting it together with a new brand."

The campaign introduced to the mainstream a type of adventure that for decades had only a cult following. Unlike traditional park fare—peaks, woods, wild animals—canyons are an acquired taste, less achievement and more mystery, an immersion into the stone innards of creation that can be at once sensual, hallucinatory, and religious.

The Mighty Five campaign was a smash. The number of visitors to the five parks jumped 12 percent in 2014, 14 percent in 2015, and 20 percent in 2016, leaping from 6.3 million to over 10 million in just three years. The state coffers filled with sales taxes paid on hotels and rental cars and restaurants. The Struck agency brags that the state got a return on its investment of 338 to 1. The clink of crystal flutes bubbling with Mountain Dew echoed across the land.

And then, on Memorial Day weekend of 2015, nearly 3,000 cars descended on Arches National Park for their dose of Whoa. Inside, all 875 parking places were taken, with scores more vehicles scattered catch-as-catch-can. The line to the entrance booth spilled back half a mile, blocking Highway 191. The state highway patrol took the unprecedented step of closing it, effectively shutting down the park. Hundreds of rebuffed visitors drove thirty miles to Canyonlands, where they waited an hour in a two-mile line of cars.

Since then, Arches has been swamped often enough to shut its gate at least nine times. Meanwhile, in Zion, hikers wait ninety minutes to board a shuttle and an additional two to four hours to climb the switchbacks of Angels Landing. There, visitors sometimes find outhouses shuttered with a sign that, although specific to excrement, might well express the condition of the Utah parks as a whole:

Due to extreme use, these toilets have reached capacity.

A. B. Guthrie Jr.'s novel *The Big Sky* tells of a young man who heads west from Kentucky, hoping to track down his mountain-man uncle. But when he reaches Montana, Uncle Zeb has soured.

"The whole shitaree! Gone, by God," laments Zeb. "This was man's country onc't. Every water full of beaver and a galore of buffler any ways a man looked, and no crampin' and crowdin,' Christ sake!"

"It ain't spoilt, Zeb," someone dissents. "Depends on who's lookin'."

"Greenhorns on every boat, hornin' in and sp'ilin' the fun. Christ sake!" Zeb says. "Why'n't they stay to home? Why'n't they leave it to us as found it? God she was purty onc't. Purty and new."

The year was 1830.

I've heard Uncle Zeb in my own rants over the past thirty years, lamenting the ruination of my personal West: the canyons around Moab circa 1993. They remain in my memory purty and new: a craggy outpost where just about any dirtbag could roll into town, get a job washing dishes or rowing rafts, park a rig on dirt roads galore and live rent-free, no crampin' and no crowdin'.

It's no longer the same place. Moab is the gateway to Arches—the second smallest of the Mighty Five, where famous landmarks like Delicate Arch, Fiery Furnace, and the Windows are reached by a single dead-end road. More than any other town, it has borne the brunt of the tourism spike. While the county population has grown slowly in thirty years, from roughly 6,500 to 9,500, where there was once a dozen or so low-rise, low-rent, mom-and-pop inns with names like the Prospector Lodge and the Apache Motel ("Stay where John Wayne stayed!"), there's been a flabbergasting growth in lodging: there are now thirty-six hotels and 2,600 rooms, plus 600 overnight rentals and 1,987 campsites. There's no way to track how many people occupy each, but on a fully booked holiday, with a moderate estimate of three tourists per unit, that's at least 15,000 people, vastly outnumbering the locals. Traffic jams extend from tip to tail, and the two-mile drag down Main Street is a thirty-minute morass.

Rents have skyrocketed because hundreds of homes are now used as overnight lodging. Camping now costs twenty bucks a night, and workers pay upward of $800 a month to share rooms in "bunkhouses" converted by employers.

I still own my little piece of the past, a singlewide on an acre of thistle on a dirt lane by a creek, and each time I return, my heart cracks a little at yet another plywood box stuccoed into a ComfortSleepDaysExpressSuites, at the jacked-up dune buggies revving down Main Street like the Shriners of the Apocalypse, and at the once-secret swimming hole overflowing with greenhorns.

And so it was with a blossom of dread that I planned a Labor Day excursion to investigate this story. I lived in Albuquerque at the time, and my trailer was rented, so I approached Moab as a regular tourist. Five weeks in advance, I snagged the last available ticket online for a guided hike through Fiery Furnace in Arches. The receipt said, "Expect possible delays at park entrance booth and on park roads." In a town where I used to pay a hundred bucks a month in rent, even the middling motels now cost two hundred a night. My visit coincided with the opening of a new Hilton called the Hoodoo, which that weekend was charging a cool $330. Per night.

Hoo gonna doo that?

On Friday evening, I checked into a decades-old motor lodge instead, where my room was neither a cave nor a basement but resembled both. The lot was full. The place used to be a Ramada Inn, generally vacant enough that river guides and cocktail waitresses could easily sneak into the swimming pool after last call for moonlight skinny-dipping. Now there was a tall fence and you needed a key.

My curiosity beckoned me over a footbridge on a creek and down the hot streets to the Hoodoo, built over an old trailer park where I once responded to a roommate-wanted ad and was greeted by an old-timer with a plastic tube snaking from his nose to an oxygen canister that he toted on a small trolley. I assumed, rightly or wrongly, that he'd been a uranium miner and his days were numbered. I was moved by his immediate adoption of "we" statements. "Here's our radar oven for popping corn," he said, pointing at the microwave. "And here's the couch where we'll watch the VHS."

Nostalgia comes easy. We don't just yearn for a place that's gone, we long for our youth, when we had the freedom and wherewithal to bask in it. When I first moved here, the local alternative paper, *Canyon Country Zephyr*, proudly boasted that it was "Desperately Clinging to the Past Since 1989." Searching its archives last month, I found this: "More people are pouring into town than ever before. The record-breaking visitation numbers at Arches National

Park in 1991 now look puny compared to this spring so far. There were groups camping in parking lots, lining up at City Market, pitching their tents in back and front yards, occasionally without the permission of the homeowners."

That was 1992. Those record-breaking visits to Arches back then totaled nearly 800,000 a year, half of what came last year.

We are stuck between two metaphors. Are we the boy who cried wolf, always convinced the whole shitaree is spoil't, or the frog in hot water, who claims things are just slightly worse, but still OK, until it's too late and we're cooked?

I ended up getting free rent in a garage that season, so I never watched *Titanic* with the old miner. I remembered him as I approached the shimmering glass and modernist cubes of flagstone at the Hoodoo. Audis and 4Runners glimmered in the lot. A variation of a Joni Mitchell melody sang in my head: They paved a trailer park, and put in a paradise.

Peering through the glass into the foyer, I saw only one person, a uniformed maid, bent low in the mood lighting, polishing with a white towel a pair of steel pigs.

Maybe we can think of the Utah Office of Tourism as Dr. Frankenstein, and its Mighty Five campaign as the glorious creature run amok. "It has been said by others that it's almost like some type of nuclear weapon," says Lance Syrett, chairman of the tourism-development board that oversees the office. He's the fourth-generation owner of a cluster of hotels perched on the rim of Bryce Canyon, and he speaks with a likeable country frankness. "They say it works too well. We need to lock it away and not use it anymore."

I watched a video from this past spring, when Vicki Varela, director of the office, addressed a travel industry conference in Cedar City, Utah. She wore a camel-colored blazer and an earth-tone scarf, exuding a can-do casualness that made her seem as approachable as a PTA mom and as capable as a Fortune 500 boss. She has proven a great bridge builder: when the federal government shutdown of 2018 caused many parks to close for thirty-five days, Varela's office brokered a deal between two hostile factions—the State of Utah and the National Park Service—to keep the Mighty Five open for Christmas. From the podium, she boasted that tourists spent $9.75 billion in Utah in 2018, which translated to $1.28 billion in tax revenue, or between $1,200 and

$1,300 in "tax relief" for each household in the state. Tourism accounts for 136,000 jobs, putting it in Utah's top ten business sectors.

Of course, neither Varela's office nor the Mighty Five campaign can take full credit for these booming figures or for the onslaught of tourists. Other factors helped. In 2016, the Park Service celebrated its hundredth birthday, launching its own ad campaign; between 2013 and 2016, park visits jumped 21 percent nationwide. The past five years have seen a recovery from the Great Recession, low gas prices, and a continued reluctance by Americans to travel overseas. The populations of the nearest big cities—Denver, Salt Lake, and Las Vegas—are booming. And social media creates its own viral marketing. Southern Utah is a victim—or beneficiary—of the global phenomenon of overtourism that has wreaked havoc from Phuket to Venice to Tulum, caused by factors far beyond the purview of state officials: a rise in disposable income, the advent of rock-bottom discount airlines, and innovations like Airbnb and Tripadvisor that have made travel easier and cheaper. Nonetheless, a study by Utah State University economists attributed half a million yearly visitors directly to the Mighty Five ads. Those additional visitors represent a modest, but not insignificant, 5 percent of the ten million annual visitors to the five parks.

When word trickled back in that the ads had worked too well, the Office of Tourism responded. In 2016, it tweaked the campaign, calling it the "Road to Mighty" and highlighting lesser-known state parks and Grand Staircase–Escalante National Monument, aiming to disperse crowds and spread revenue to other towns. The strategy appeared to work. Visits to the Mighty Five flattened, growing only 4 percent in 2017 and a little more than 1 percent in 2018, while the state parks saw double-digit jumps. (Visits to Grand Staircase grew over the years, but its jump and dips didn't correspond neatly to the ads.)

Just as Road to Mighty hit the airwaves, President Obama, in January 2017, designated the Bears Ears National Monument, with the support of five Indian tribes. Later, Utah governor Gary Herbert and the state legislature asked President Trump to cancel the monument. Trump slashed Bears Ears by 85 percent and Grand Staircase by half in December 2017.

Still, in 2018, Governor Herbert's Office of Tourism massaged the campaign again, calling it "Between the Mighty" and adding Bears Ears to its destinations. At the 2019 conference, Varela said this new iteration of the

Mighty Five ads would increase visitor spending, but not the total number of visitors, by targeting a subset that's more likely to hire a guide than go it alone, glamp instead of camp, and dine on grass-fed leg of lamb drizzled with a balsamic reduction instead of roast weenies on the campfire. What's more, some resources would be diverted away from advertising into what she called "destination management" and "destination development"—for example, increased signage and trails in the state parks, which she says will reduce visitor impact. Varela also cooed about a new strategy for "addressable TV," which could target specific customers based on data collected by their cable companies. While one person watching CNN might see a commercial for Oreos, another might see Bears Ears.

Many questioned if crowding could be addressed by sending tourists elsewhere. "National parks are designed to handle these big crowds," says Kevin Walker, chairman of the Democratic party in Grand County (which includes Moab) and a member of the planning commission. "They put so many people in them that they basically broke them. Now they're saying, 'Let's send them to these places that can't handle it.' It's insane." As one salty Moabite summed up the new campaign: "They ruined the parks, and now they want to ruin the places in between."

In Garfield County, which is home to Bryce Canyon National Park and much of Grand Staircase, many locals have resisted their placement on the Road to Mighty. Blake Spalding is co-owner of Hell's Backbone Grill and Farm in Boulder, population 240. One of the largest employers in the county, and the state's only restaurant honored as a semifinalist for the James Beard Award, the place is a perfect fit for well-heeled tourists. But when Spalding was approached by the Office of Tourism to appear in its ad campaign, she declined.

"I'm not your good poster girl anymore," she told me. "Furthermore, I'm furious with the governor. He's being disingenuous, putting all this money into promoting tourism on the one hand and then actively supporting the diminished funding and protection of the monument."

When I asked Varela why her office still advertised Lower Calf Creek Falls in Grand Staircase after the cuts to the monument and reports of overcrowding on this trail, she said, "We don't have written guiding principles about how that was done. We chose what we thought were iconic locations. We have considered if it was problematic to run that ad. We did some due diligence. But that area still has capacity."

Still, it's hard not to think the monuments have gotten a double punch: just as visitation jumps, the capacity to handle the visitors with rangers, law enforcement, and toilets has been cut. With jargon like "infrastructure" and "resource management," the layperson might not understand what it means for a place to be overrun. What it often comes down to is poop. With Escalante's newfound fame and shrinking budget, cleanup is left to locals. Spalding says, "We all hike with lighters so we can light other people's toilet paper on fire."

It was 8:20 a.m., and I was cruising the Delicate Arch parking lot, which had already reached capacity. It did my heart good to see the hordes of Type A bucket-listers, zipping off their pant legs, haloed in the sunrise mist of aerosol sunscreen. Even as I chafe against crowds, I believe these people will go home improved, rejuvenated, inspired, and perhaps even willing to vote for congresspeople who might increase funding for the parks.

But also: this mob scene was nothing like the Mighty Five commercial.

I headed on to the Fiery Furnace for my guided ranger hike. Amid the chaos, the park has managed to maintain a sense of quiet. We wound through fins and alcoves, taking time to view fox tracks and a black widow tucked into a crack. It was lovely. A part of me hated making a sixteen-dollar reservation, when twenty-five years ago my friends and I clambered through here unregulated and inebriated in the middle of the night. But it's like rafting the Grand Canyon: so precious that you may only get to do it once or twice in your life, and the planning and red tape is worth it.

My group contained a trio of Utahns from the suburbs of Salt Lake, an older man and his grown sons. They own a home in Saint George and have been hiking the Zion Narrows and other classics in the Mighty Five all their lives. One of the sons thought Zion had been overrun. "The state should stop advertising," he said, "or at least give some truth in advertising." The magical thing the Mighty Five advertises is solitude, but unless you're able to visit midweek during the school year or in the dead of winter, you won't find that in the parks. When we emerged from the Furnace, a ranger informed us that because every parking place was full, the park's entrance was closed.

Although the Mighty Five parks are too crowded, I wouldn't say they're ruined. Recently I was in Zion on a busy weekend. With 4.5 million annual visitors, Zion is by far the most packed of the Utah parks (and was the fourth most visited US national park in 2018). This is largely because it sits within a seven-hour drive of 20 million Southern Californians. The horror stories about the lines and the crowds are all true.

But I had a blast.

Twenty years ago, the park made the visionary decision to shut Zion Canyon to cars. Everyone leaves their vehicles at the visitor center, the campgrounds, or the town of Springdale, and takes a shuttle to the trailheads for Angels Landing and the Narrows. So there are no traffic jams, no motor homes circling for a space. From the tops of the sandstone cliffs, the valley below is silent.

Better than any front-country park in the entire nation, Zion has realized Ed Abbey's dream of carlessness: "You've got to get out of the goddamned contraption and walk," he pleaded, "better yet crawl, on hands and knees, over the sandstone and through the thornbush and cactus." At Zion, though I was rarely less than ten feet from another human, I didn't have that soul-sucking "park experience" endemic to Old Faithful in Yellowstone or the South Rim of the Grand Canyon, the feeling of inching forward on asphalt, then shuffling in a herd a few hundred yards to a vista, only to return to the confines of the car. I never saw so many fit Americans concentrated in one place, bedecked with hydro packs and hiking poles and amphibious footwear, hustling at the crack of dawn to hike ten miles with steep exposure, risking heatstroke and hypothermia in the same day. Despite the crowds—no, because of the crowds—Zion still feels like a celebration.

As Grand County's Kevin Walker pointed out, national parks are built and managed to handle people, and despite the continuous budget cuts over the past two decades, they've done a good job of it, even if the only solution at Arches, for now, is to simply shut the gate. What's more concerning about Utah's ad blitz is the effect on the Insta-famous canyons—and their surrounding communities—that don't have a gate rangers can shut.

When I asked Varela about the accusations that advertising is ruining canyon country, she said, "That is contrary to everything I stand for as a resident of this state and one who also wants to build a tourism economy. If you contrast the tourism economy with other ways to make a living in Utah, it is more sustainable."

To be fair, Moab's growth has its upsides. The schools and public pools and bike paths are better now. The new housing stock is an improvement over the dilapidated trailers left from the mining era. Dine-out options used to be mostly burgers, but you can now get sushi, pho, and pad Thai—all on the same block.

And just as Moab has been hit hardest by the advertising, it has been the most assertive in fighting to preserve itself. Last year both the city and county passed moratoriums on construction of new hotels or overnight rentals. The city banned single-use plastic bags, which had begun to litter the scenic drive to the landfill. In what could serve as an example to the state Office of Tourism, the county's tourism board has tried to shift the money raised by its local hotel tax away from advertising and into building infrastructure and educating visitors with its new Do It Like a Local campaign, which teaches etiquette like "don't bust the crust" (when hiking or biking, stay on marked trails to avoid destroying microbiotic soils) and "respect the rocks" (stay off rock formations and don't touch Native American rock art, which can be ruined by oils from your skin). In 2017, Moab elected a new mayor, Emily Niehaus, who was previously a ranger at Bryce Canyon and founded a nonprofit that helped low-income people build and own straw-bale, solar-powered homes.

But the town's attempts to turn back the state's pro-business agenda are in limbo. One of Niehaus's first duties as mayor was to travel to Salt Lake City and defend Moab's new laws from an at times skeptical, if not downright hostile, legislature. When Moab banned plastic bags, a legislator introduced a bill that banned cities from banning bags. A state law demands that the county spend 47 percent of its hotel tax to promote tourism. Meanwhile, the ban on new hotels is under scrutiny. The governor has warned of the rise of "socialism" in places like Grand County.

This same pro-business view seems built into the Office of Tourism, too. The governor's Board of Tourism Development, which oversees it, consists of reps from the lodging, restaurant, car-rental, and ski-resort industries; notably absent are federal land managers, environmentalists, or advocates for affordable housing. Lance Syrett, the chairman of the board, owns hotels that have boomed since the days of the Mighty Five campaign. The budget for the Office of Tourism is incentive based, too: if tourist-related tax revenue increases 3 percent in a year, the office can receive an additional $3 million from the legislature. (However, Syrett told *Outside* that the incentive agreement is nonbinding for the state; there have been years when his office did not receive additional funds, even when taxes from tourist-oriented goods and services increased by more than 3 percent.)

But who in southern Utah benefits from this growth? Clearly, the owners of restaurants and hotels and rental cars, some of whom are local residents while others are out-of-state corporations. Workers get jobs, but these tend to involve seasonal service work, with low wages that are eaten up by exorbitant rent. Return visitors and residents alike find their favorite places teeming with crowds. As for the office's claim that each household gets a $1,200 tax break from tourism revenue, that's mostly true but also misleading. It assumes that if tourism suddenly evaporated, the state would not trim its budget to fit the dried-up revenue stream. Syrett surprised me with this little-known fact: in terms of gross revenue, the city that has profited most from the Mighty Five campaign is not Moab or Saint George or Escalante. With its international airport, car-rental companies, and airport hotels, it's Salt Lake City.

For such a petite person, Mayor Niehaus commanded a withering glare. During my Labor Day visit, I met her and her ten-year-old son, Oscar, at their house for breakfast, where she scrambled eggs with onions, garlic, and herbs. "Everything you're eating was grown in the yard," she told me. As I was finishing my eggs, she peered over and said, "Does *Outside* magazine understand the irony of looking for the villain of the degradation of red rock country? *Outside* magazine, along with Instagram and the Mighty Five ads, are the top reasons this place is crowded."

"Did you put hot sauce in this?" I sputtered. When I first started writing for outdoor magazines, my Moab friends threatened me with banishment and beatings if I ever revealed secret spots. A few years later, when I lived in New York, a publication similar to *Outside* solicited a few Moab tips. I'd like to say that I stood tall and refused it—or at least that the price for my soul was high. But I really needed the $600. I resolved to write the thing but to only send people to the national parks and locally owned businesses. I called one of the local bike-tour operators, and before I had a chance to explain my good intentions, he hissed, just before hanging up, "Your magazine sucks."

A tour operator may lack claim to the moral high ground, but nearly everyone who lives in southern Utah loves it as it is—and also wants to earn a living. Whether your job here is cook, waiter, miner, rancher, ranger, or telecommuter, your very existence will in some way change the thing you love. We all bear some responsibility in changing this place.

Yet we don't bear it quite evenly. Market forces and shifting demographics and social media don't deserve the same sort of scrutiny as taxpayer-funded programs like the Office of Tourism. And the more I learned, the more I became convinced that these initiatives may actually hurt the taxpayers who are paying for them.

Syrett likened what was happening in Garfield County to an oil boom, with 47 percent of jobs related to tourism, more than any other sector. And most booms are followed by bust. Early numbers indicated that 2019 was another flat year for Utah national-park visitation, or maybe even a decline.

"All these businesses have popped up now because of the Mighty Five, and there's a bit of a panic," said Syrett. "We're in a free fall." According to him, small towns in Utah are clamoring for more ad money for their areas. It's easy to see how a cycle of taxpayer dependence is born. The state advertises, the hoteliers build, the rooms aren't filled, the owners demand more advertising, and so on.

I asked Syrett, "Is it government's role to bail out these entrepreneurs who made risky investments?"

He let out a patient laugh. "Well, we can debate that all day long. The small rural communities that surround the Mighty Five destinations have been desperate for economic development for so long, that you can't judge them for being excited for the investment in their communities. Were there some planning mistakes made? Sure, but the investment has been welcome."

I was fascinated by the Office of Tourism's "addressable" TV strategy. After years of crunching data, Varela's team has divided her audience into four personas. Achievers, who favor personal challenge, are served images of mountain biking and rockclimbing on television and social media ads; Explorers, who seek unique personal experience, see slot canyoneering; Families, who wish to give their children an unforgettable journey, see a child trout fishing with dad; and Repeat Visitors, who want the off-the-beaten-path experiences and locations they missed the last time, see Navajo weavers.

While this sort of opus analytica represents the pinnacle of travel marketing in the era of Big Data, it also turns my marrow to ice. At the risk of revealing my age, I'll say that, in the old days, if you wanted red rock magic, you followed these steps:

- Engage in hitchhiking.
- Insert intoxicants in your mouth.
- Misplace the map.
- Break down on a dirt road.
- Start walking.

Now, when the recipients of these addressable ads ride that sandstone rim on their mountain bikes, or squeeze through sheer red narrows, it might be because marketeers collected their clicks and coded that dream for them.

It's a well-worn chestnut here that wilderness isn't just a cool trip but a type of freedom, essential to democracy and the soul. In nature, we free ourselves from the world's day-to-day moneygrubbing and conformity. In creation we find Creator. But what if freedom is a commodity packaged by advertisers? When our dreams are concocted by focus groups to maximize what we spend on VRBOs and craft brews, that old Guided by Voices anthem rings in my head: You can be anyone they told you to.

It may be tempting to blame the marketeers, but they are simply carrying out orders from a governor who has a history of pushing to develop public lands for revenue. In 2012, Governor Herbert demanded that the federal government hand over 30 million acres of public land to the state. He excluded the five national parks from his scheme but included the monuments, Glen Canyon National Recreation Area, the national forests, and millions of acres administered by the Bureau of Land Management. Herbert hasn't explicitly stated what he would do with those lands—he frames it as a states' rights issue—but precedence hints at how Utah might manage them, given the chance. The state already owns 3.4 million acres of trust lands, which it has decided not to "preserve and protect," as with the national parks, but commercialize. These lands were deeded to Utah when it entered the union in 1896 but were generally left undeveloped until 1994, when the legislature created an agency that would assertively raise revenue on them. Projects include a 40,000-person artificial-lake subdivision in the desert near Zion. Outside Moab, over the howls of locals, the state is developing a twenty-four-hour truck stop and, at the base of the Slickrock Trail, a 150-room four-star hotel with a convention center, 150 rental "casitas," and forty-three homes.

In 2008, the Utah legislature passed a law allowing off-road vehicles on all dirt roads, including those in the Mighty Five. This was another effort to buck federal control over state lands—ATVs have typically been prohibited by the National Park Service. The NPS resisted for more than a decade, but after rounds of pressure from Utah lawmakers, it finally caved. The advertised epiphany of biking under the vast skies of Canyonlands' White Rim Trail would be updated with the high whine of ATVs.

I drove south from Moab into San Juan County, which contains a portion of Canyonlands as well as three of the campaign's "in between" spots: Bears Ears, Goosenecks State Park, and Monument Valley Tribal Park on the Navajo Nation. I crossed the Ute Mountain Ute Reservation at White Mesa. Until a 2016 federal court action, a white minority ruled over the Native majority here. The county officials despised Bears Ears, while the tribes supported it. Before being voted out in 2018, the county commission stuck its citizens with a half-million-dollar legal tab, paying an out-of-state attorney $500 an hour to thwart Obama and the tribes.

Maybe complaints like mine are just a lot of pissing in the wind by white people who, if we really want to know what it's like to be pushed off the land by newcomers, should go talk to an Indian. True. Yet the forces of history that stole the continent from Natives are similar to those that now sell it. The machinery of civilization churned across the West, slayed the buffalo, dammed the Missouri and the Colorado and the Rio Grande and the Columbia—and will next gobble up our world's most precious commodity: solitude. What society needed then was land and timber and buffalo hides, and it took them. In the twentieth century, it needed water and electricity, so it stopped the rivers. Now it needs Mystery and Mystical, and it will advertise and sell them until they're gone.

So which are we: The boy crying wolf about a land that will nurture us no matter what? Or the frog in the pot, unable to sense how bad it already is? I don't want to just be a curmudgeon who mourns the passage of time, who fights any change to the landscape because conceding change concedes my own mortality. I will never be young again, I get that. But maybe, if the sorrow of human life is our inevitable death, then one way we tap into the eternal is to see how that which is not made by our hand will outlast us all, just as it preceded us.

Shortly before crossing into the Navajo Nation, I stopped at Goosenecks State Park, which pretty much defines being in the middle of nowhere: the places it's in between are Bluff, population 320, and Mexican Hat, population thirty-one. I hadn't been here since 1990, my very first trip to Utah, five of us longhairs in a VW camper van emitting puffs of "wow" and "holy shit" as it bounced over red washboard roads. Now I bumped along that plateau of sagebrush and juniper, paid five dollars at a booth, and there, amid a smattering of picnic tables and outhouses, peered over the rim into the staggering canyons of the San Juan River.

The place looked unchanged. A Native woman sold silver jewelry beneath a tarp. It was Labor Day and—ad blitz notwithstanding—only nine cars had found their way here. A child gazed down at the green river meandering a thousand feet below, a million years away, and said, "I want to go swimming in that pool."

By doing just about nothing here, the state appears to have done it right.

The Office of Tourism likes to brag that, anywhere else, its state parks would be national parks. Maybe. But as I looked around and found no trails, no rangers, nowhere to go other than this dirt lot, I wondered if this "park" might more accurately be called a scenic overlook or a campsite. The Goosenecks were briefly enveloped by Bears Ears, and after the cuts to the monument, the state has proposed to construct mountain-bike trails on the no-longer-protected desert. Do humans need to change this landscape, to make it more attractive, more fun?

With talk of "destination development" and "destination management," civilization forges ahead, until one day this chest-clenching slab of infinity, this windswept monument to nature's indifference, these eternal deep twists of snowmelt in dubious search of the sea, will cease to be sacred—and will become a Brand.

I hope to God it fails.

The Shinglewide

In 1993, while squandering a perfectly good college degree, I washed up on the shores of the Colorado River in the sweltering hamlet of Moab, Utah, and found work as a river guide and dishwasher. I was twenty-two. I'd left San Francisco, where, like other English majors, I had hoped to find the writer's life but instead worked bad jobs to pay rent, which back then was $350. Exorbitant, I thought. In the desert, I fell in with a circle of rock climbers, Jack Mormons, Navy vets, survivalists, earthen-home builders, truant teenagers, cowboys, a Broadway dancer, a Bryn Mawr art history major, and a petite international relations PhD rowing rafts for fifty dollars a day. Most of the people I knew drifted in for a season, hustled tips on the river or in diners, shacked up in tents and buses, then drifted off again.

I'd been invited to dinner at the home of one of my fellow guides, and when I stepped onto the creaky floorboards of the old cottage, I discovered a woman in jeans and sandals and a sleeveless shirt stirring soup on the stove. Her shoulders and hair were bronzed by the sun. She was tall and lean, with chiseled cheekbones, a square jaw, and flinty green eyes. She offered me a bowl of miso soup, and though I'd been raised in Los Angeles—I was no rube—I didn't know what it was.

"Fermented soybean paste," she said with a kind of irony, perhaps embarrassed to possess this knowledge.

It was delicious. To this day, whenever I have a bowl, I think it was she who invented it.

Wendy was a decade older than me and, unlike the rest of us, presented as an actual adult. She owned a business and a Toyota 4Runner, and had worked on fishing boats in Alaska. I, meanwhile, lived in my station wagon and dated a seventeen-year-old. For most of the year, Wendy stayed a few hours away, near Telluride, living with a full-grown man named Buck, who had a beard and a braid down his back. Buck was an artist. Together, they had opened a shop on Main Street in Moab to sell his screen-printed shirts.

Wendy and I took a walk together one afternoon, high on a windswept red mesa studded with piñon and juniper. With the given name of Frances Wendell, she had a pedigree particular to the American West, unlike anyone I'd met in the suburbs of LA. Her mother was a Seven Sisters blue blood who'd gone to a Montana dude ranch one summer in the 1950s and fallen in love with a strapping son of the owners. She married and stayed there on a ranch on Hanging Woman Creek, a name so arch-western that not only could I not make it up, but Louis L'Amour chose it as a novel title. Wendy and her brothers moved from ranch to ranch, and she came of age in a settlement called Emigrant, in Montana's Paradise Valley, where she rode her horse to school and was crowned rodeo queen. After getting a college education nearby, she found herself engaged to the scion of a cattle empire who listened to Bach in his Mercedes. Wendy spent the engagement clinically inseminating prize heifers and anticipating an entire life of the same.

Then the rodeo came to town.

Wendy met a clown. She described him to me as the desert breeze blew in her hair, her eyes glossy. "He had a Fu Manchu mustache and an eight ball of coke. We took off in a Porsche," she said. "The next day, we were in Canada."

In the summer of 1994, Wendy moved to Moab and bought an acre of land along a dirt road where a lazy creek twisted through a shallow valley. It was shaded by ancient cottonwoods and thick with fresh tumbleweeds, though at the time I couldn't have said which was which. From a used trailer lot, she purchased a 1961 Artcraft mobile home for $2,500 that was ten feet wide and fifty-seven feet long, a hull of sun-battered white aluminum. She placed it upon the land with its two doors opening to the creek and the tall, crooked trees.

Wendy embarked on a total renovation, pouring far more money into the trailer than its price. She hired a friend with a backhoe to lay a water main and a sewage line. She ran an underground gas line and electrical wire. I was hired to do odd jobs at ten dollars an hour.

To help with the construction—and also for style—she bought a 1965 Chevy pickup with a classic domed hood. Its original color was something like turquoise, but the decades had faded it to rust. Two bumper stickers read "Boulder Gun and Stock Shop" and "Try Love and Happiness." A gun rack spanned the back window; Wendy stored a rifle there.

I remember in those days, among Wendy and the guys she hired, robust debate about where to put your gun. One guy mounted his handgun on the gas tank of his motorcycle, where it could be seen by a cop. "They treat you with respect when they see you're packing," he said. Wendy announced that she was going to end her illegal practice of stashing her handgun under the seat or in the glove box and instead latch a holster to the gearshift.

Now and then, Buck came to town. They'd go camping—he behind the wheel of the Chevy, Wendy sitting middle with her arm around him, his braid visible through the rear window, obscured only partly by the rifle.

As for me, I didn't own a gun or a motorcycle. I was afraid of both. I had a truck, but it was just a little Toyota—low clearance, two-wheel drive. My parents had given me $7,000 to buy it after I'd wrecked my station wagon the year before, and it had put me in a cycle of humiliation and never-ending adolescence. I needed the truck to be independent—I often slept in it, reading the fat hardbacks of Leo Tolstoy and George Eliot by headlamp—but felt like a spoiled shit because my parents had bought it for me, even as I justified this with the fact that they had just inherited some money after the deaths of three grandparents. Driving the truck to Utah after buying it in LA, I bought snow chains at a gas station at the base of a pass. I wanted to be the sort of man who is competent with chains and repairs, rough roads and icy curves, but I still saw myself as a child riding a skateboard on the smooth asphalt of sunny subdivisions. I considered hiring a mechanic to put them on. My pride forbade it. Reading the instructions in the blowing blizzard, I managed to affix the chains to the front tires. It wasn't until months later that I learned they needed to be on the rear tires. Even though the California tags were good for six more months, I got Utah license plates as soon as I landed in Moab. I could just roll into town and become someone else.

The mechanical incompetence was just the start: there was a lot to dislike about myself. I had a downturned mouth and watery eyes, and people always asked what was wrong, was I sad about something? Having skipped first grade,

I may have been the smartest kid in my class, but I was also the smallest, and I rode the bench during soccer and baseball games. My older brother, Richard, could knock a baseball out of the pony league park and the teeth out of a bully, while all I could do was swat junior varsity tennis balls and win first prize in an essay contest about the Sandinista conflict.

The girls loved Richard. They snuck into the backyard, giggling, nursing bottles of Boone's Farm, rapping on his glass door. When I got to high school, standing a spindly five foot four, the girls in my grade, who were partying with him, began to call me, with real affection, Little Richard.

Wendy's trailer came from an era before plastic, when the boatbuilders of World War II had been redeployed to build these land yachts. While the exterior looked like basic trailer park junk, the interior maintained a certain shipliness. In the front room—farthest forward if it were being hauled down the highway—large windows faced north, east, and south, making the tiny chamber feel airy. Miniature aluminum handles cranked the panes outward. Walls and ceiling were paneled with lacquered plywood, aged to a golden honey, the brass screws spaced every few feet, each emitting the slightest black stain. The corners housed built-in bookshelves of the same wood grain, trimmed with scallop-cut molding, adding to the beached-nautical sensation. Mounted on the ceiling was an antiquey copper-shade lamp with a cut-glass globe. The cabinet handles and hinges were hammered copper, die-cut into the shape of spades. Even tiny details—the square-headed copper screws—exuded a sense of craftsmanship, or at least a type of factory excellence that has long since been lost. I felt pleasantly trapped at the captain's table in the cabin of a rickety sloop.

The captain's chambers opened through sliding doors into a kitchen that featured the same cabinets, but the room had been defaced with stained yellow linoleum and decrepit countertops. The other rooms had disintegrated to what you'd expect for a $2,500 home.

With Buck not around to help, Wendy hired a friend and me to lay Mexican Saltillos on the bathroom floor, each corner trimmed to make space for diamond-shaped tiles of hand-painted wildflowers. Despite my bookishness, I had grown to be six feet tall and worked summers as a house painter, and gained enough aptitude around tools to not be totally useless. After a season rowing rafts on the Colorado River, my shoulders had grown broad and brown, and after two seasons I had finally learned to stand up straight. As for my stupid face, I hid it with a sun-bleached beard and wraparound sunglasses, and a baseball hat that said GOODYEAR.

We installed a porcelain pedestal sink, a shiny white toilet, and a sleek corner shower with a swinging glass door. Wendy laid wood floors in the kitchen and captain's room, tiling the counters and backsplashes with earth-toned squares. But her pièce de résistance was the humble living room, which she transformed into something like a Wild West bordello. Wendy covered the walls with fabric—not wallpaper, but actual cloth—an old-timey pattern of dusty pink roses on sandy linen, offset with a wainscoting of rough-cut boards. She trimmed the windows and door with the same rustic lumber, textured the ceiling with white plaster, and paneled an accent wall with tongue-in-groove pine.

I never asked where the money came from. Wendy didn't live high, but she never seemed to run out of cash. It would be many years before I realized that a person running a t-shirt shop in Moab was not making money so much as losing it. I wondered if there was a money nest in her family tree, but I never asked.

As the summer cooled, I landed an off-season job managing campsites at the Slickrock bike trail. Wendy moved into the trailer, and I moved from a garage into a house. I fell for a local woman I'll call Z, who was raising a two-year-old daughter. The dad was long gone. One night, early on, lounging in bed, she asked what kind of woman I wanted to marry. Either because we had real candor or because I was a jerk, I blurted out Wendy's name.

"But she's already taken," I added. "And probably too old for me anyway."

What I meant by old was that she would only choose real men like Buck or the rodeo clown. Despite my Utah license plates and emerging triceps, I was still a sensitive bookworm. While getting a literature degree at Stanford in the early nineties, I had wanted to be a writer, but now I renounced the idea, or at least wouldn't admit to it, intent on mastering the manual arts instead. If my own story felt phony, the second-best way to be authentic was to be close to people whose stories felt real. Wendy had such a story.

In Moab, Halloween marked the end of the tourist season, a big blowout for all the guides and waiters leaving for work in ski towns or launching treks to Mexican beaches and a pivot toward domesticity for those of us staying the winter. There were outrageous parties with elaborate costumes. Z and I dressed as a priest and a nun, she in heels and fishnets and a tight black skirt below her habit, me with eyeliner and lipstick and a flask with which I'd offer communion. We stopped at the trailer to pick up Wendy, and I introduced them. Wendy was dressed as a builder: work boots, jeans, tool belt, flannel shirt. She poured wine and showed us around. It was the first time there weren't power tools buzzing and sawdust drifting. In the living room she had hung an oil painting of cowboys roping cattle. She said the name of the artist, but I didn't know it.

"Well, according to my mother, he's very famous," she said with a laugh. "It's worth a whole lot more than this trailer."

A broken dinner plate sat on the counter. Wendy picked up two jagged pieces, held them together, set them down. "I'm saving these for when Buck gets here so he can feel useful."

She turned to Z. "You're even more gorgeous than Mark told me."

Z took a long pull of wine, her face flushed. "Mark said if he ever got married, it would be to someone like you."

"Oh!" Wendy said. We drank quickly from our glasses. Wendy looked at Z and Z looked at me and I looked at Wendy.

"Should we get going?" I said.

As the snow fell, Z and I had midnight fights where she stormed out of my house, screen door rattling, and walked home barefoot on empty streets while I idled the truck beside her, begging her to get in. She never did.

That winter, Wendy told me she was selling the t-shirt shop and going back to Alaska for her old job on the fishing boat. We were sitting on a couch on the porch of my house, rolling cigarettes and passing them back and forth, watching the Milky Way brighten in the black sky, when she leaned over and planted a kiss on my lips. I pulled her toward me. She popped open a shirt button and ran a hot hand across my chest. And then. She drove off in her truck.

She went back to Colorado the next day. A few months later, she broke up with Buck and made her way to Alaska, alone. I didn't fight for her to stay. I was too shallow to understand that, mixed in with all the desire, were the feelings that I now recognize as love.

I didn't hear from her. I had flings with other women, but nobody equaled her. Unable to maintain a relationship, I got a dog, a heeler mutt puppy I saw in a cardboard box at the supermarket. I named her Sadie. When Wendy returned a year or so later, she was with a new guy, a fisherman, long hair and a beard, engaged to marry. He was the same age as me.

Wendy bought her land from a guy who had scooped up fifteen acres and built a home with a swimming pool and an orchard. He stipulated in Wendy's deed that she build a permanent home and not accumulate a compound of houses on wheels.

And this had been Wendy's intention. But now she and her husband, Jason, bought a house in Alaska. They planned to spend winters in Moab and devised a solution that would follow the spirit if not the letter of the covenant. Instead of building an actual house, she would make the trailer look like one.

In the winter of 1996, she and Jason installed a pitched roof of green tin on top of the existing flat tar roof. They built a wooden porch with a rough-cut pergola, where on mild days they could gaze at the towering old trees. But the element that was architecturally significant: they clad all four sides with cedar shake shingles, transforming the dusty white aluminum into something both rustic and avant-garde.

I received an invitation to Wendy's wedding in Alaska, but I didn't go. The flight was too expensive, I told myself. We fell out of touch. Now twenty-six, I moved back to Los Angeles to publish a magazine and go to grad school and write a book, a series of desert sketches, about which I kept silent as I spent summers in Moab working for Outward Bound, leading expeditions through rivers, canyons, and mountains. One night at the Rio Cantina, I found myself dancing with a girl I'll call Q, who knew Wendy and who was spending the weekend at her place. She blew hot encouragement into my ear and invited me up for breakfast the next day. The trailer was pulling me into its orbit.

Sitting out on the porch, Q told me about a time she'd been waiting tables in New Orleans, serving a group of college kids. One of the boys had said something lewd and then stiffed her, so she chased them to the street and pelted their car with wine glasses. She had grown up poor in a crumbling city where all the white families had long since fled, and after quitting high school she'd drifted around ski towns and the desert, pouring cocktails and falling in love. Here was someone who lived with the passion and risk I knew only from Kristofferson records and *The Sun Also Rises*. I saw in her a kind of redemption for my cushioned upbringing. She went home to Salt Lake City that day, commencing a volley of flirty postcards between us.

A few months later, Christmas of 1998, Q flew out to see me in California; I tied a red ribbon around Sadie's neck and sneaked the dog into the airport to greet her. I had just finished writing my book in my garage-top apartment by the beach. Back at my place, she announced that she had decided to have sex with only one more man. She didn't believe in birth control. I'd better be serious. I told her we'd wait until we were sure. For now, we laid a cotton blanket on the living room floor to see how our skin felt on it.

"What about this," I said. "Allowed?"

"Yes, but me on top."

We moved to the bed and drank red wine and blew cigarette smoke out louvered windows that even in winter didn't have to be closed. She pounded little fists on my bare chest.

"What's inside there? Why are you holding it in?"

"I've never been in love," I said. "I want to." I was afraid of falling for someone as conventional as me, waiting to forge some classless path of the rough-hewn romantic. Now I leaped.

For what seemed like weeks, I read her the entire desert manuscript as we lay there. "You got dust in my mouth," she murmured.

Q was not much of a reader, but the praise from this reckless woman and her pounding heart was all I'd ever sought. I wanted to be a writer without ever admitting that I wanted to be a writer, and now I'd won a wild soul who didn't give a shit about books, proof to me that my book transcended the embarrassing bookish parts of books.

If our peculiar abstinence was supposed to slow our free fall, it did the opposite, like snipping a flowering vine only to cause its lesser stems to shoot out a thousand new blossoms.

Still, Wendy was on my mind. I wrote to her: "You're off the hook. For so long, when I made a list in my head of women I wanted to marry, you were on top, but now you don't have to worry, because I've met someone else who has displaced you."

She replied in a hasty scrawl on five pages of scratch paper stuffed into an envelope, wishing me the best: "When I got married, the only hesitation was wondering what might have happened between you and me."

As soon as Q left, I drove out to Salt Lake City to see her. At a party with her friends, we were the only ones dancing. She led me in a smoky tango through the kitchen, nuzzled against my cheek, then took me across the living room, where we collapsed on the sofa and howled for another song and sucked from the same bottle of beer.

One night, she left me waiting alone for hours at her cottage. I almost called the police to ask about car accidents. I furiously packed my truck, only to quickly unpack it. She stumbled home from drinking with her boss from the diner who wanted to leave his wife for her and also lend her a couple thousand dollars. I told nobody. I felt a chunk of lead hardening in my chest.

Another night, when she whispered that it was time to end our prohibition, I told her I didn't want her to break the promise she'd made to herself. It sounded true. We flew back and forth for the next few months. During a visit to Salt Lake, the day before I was supposed to go home, she dumped me. She didn't want to be tied up, she said, she wanted to be single, but that was impossible, because she loved me.

In a moment of inopportune timing, Wendy was passing through town on the same day. Q insisted that she stay the night. Wendy said she'd call from a pay phone when she got close.

Q and I were naked and watery-eyed when the phone rang. If we missed Wendy's call, she would simply keep driving. On the fifth ring, Q leaped out of bed and picked up.

But it wasn't Wendy. It was some guy Q had met snowboarding the week before. She took the phone into the living room.

Wendy finally did arrive. Q and I made her dinner, saying nothing about our breakup hours before. In the morning, Q went to work and Wendy drove me to the airport to catch my flight home. I filled her in, the part about Q loving me too much to be with me. I didn't tell her about the night she had stood me up. Or about the snowboarder.

"Well, if you miss your flight," she said, "I could just drive you back to California."

I got on the plane.

The upshot of seeing Wendy was that when I moved back to Moab in that summer of 1999, age twenty-eight, she rented me the trailer for $300 a month. I wouldn't trouble her with complaints but would do any repairs myself.

I woke each night at 3:00 a.m. with my lungs clenched and visions of Q in my head. She'd been seen in Moab with that snowboarder. Now and then I'd call and tell her how she had betrayed me. I wallowed in the fantasy of my unrequited longing.

The story I told myself eventually unraveled. I replayed the memories. That night she offered herself to me: I hadn't declined out of some sense of chivalry. It was because, even as every molecule burned to make a child with her, I couldn't envision us raising the thing. All I could see us doing was smoking in bed and engineering increasingly innovative paroxysms. Which was what I thought love was.

Q already saw me more clearly than I did. I had shown her my heart, and she'd seen the cautious vanity I couldn't hide. In the future I wouldn't be so embarrassed to be a delicate writer, and I would treasure the exchange of ideas about literature and writing with a woman. But not yet. I still couldn't see past my own delusion.

Now the trailer was my home. When the river season ended, I woke each morning and made a cup of tea and hurried to the captain's cabin, where, usually clad in a down parka because the laborious furnace didn't push hot air all the way to that end of the trailer, I sat down and wrote.

Out the window, I watched fresh green tumbleweeds grow up and over the hood of Wendy's 1965 Chevy, abandoned in the deep sand that served as a driveway. They covered most of the acre. Also known as Russian thistles, the invasive weeds thrive in the desert during summer monsoons and fall storms.

At first they're beautiful: the green ribs of an enormous kettle; spindly lattices woven together; two, three, even five feet tall. But as they sit unharvested over winter, they grow brown and brittle, sharp to the touch, and as the spring winds howl, the minuscule root is dislodged and the husk rolls away, just like you see in the movies. On the open range, they just keep rolling to the horizon, but at my place, they rolled only as far as the neighbor's wire fence, where they piled up in impenetrable drifts, not before dropping thousands of seeds that lay in wait for the next rains.

As for that truck sunk in sand to the axle: Wendy said if I could get it to run, I could keep it. Wild Man Jimmy helped me install a new starter, and now I had a rig that could fit seven kayaks for a hot summer's day jaunt to the river.

I took up with a six-foot-one river guide named Slim, who drove a 1972 Ford truck and sang like Tammy Wynette. I told her I was too wounded for love. She said that was OK because she preferred to be single, and we drove across the creek to the Branding Iron to karaoke, where she sang "Your Good Girl's Gonna Go Bad" and I sang "I'm Gonna Break Every Heart I Can." Although, like me, she came from the California suburbs, Slim equally embraced the scuffed boots and sheepskin coats. Our romance could find no more glorious set than a rickety trailer.

Like so many insecure twenty-nine-year-olds, I had thought falling in love with some volatile sprite of a woman might make me more of who I wanted to be. But with Slim, neither of us was the other's fantasy. We adopted a Merle Haggard number as our anthem:

> And I don't have to wonder who she's had.
> No, it's not love, but it's not bad.

Each morning, as I lay half-awake, the lines and paragraphs filled my head. When I reached a page or so, I rushed to the captain's cabin, where I flipped on the old desktop and transcribed what had arrived, stopping only to brew a bag of Lipton, which were always free for the taking at the end of my Outward Bound courses.

Slim observed this behavior, kissing me on the cheek on her way out the door, then one morning made a proposal. "One day you're going to have an actual girlfriend," she said, "and you're going to want to impress her with your manners after she's spent the night with you. What if you were to offer her a cup of tea, too?"

I was a quick study. The next morning, as the Mac whirred to life, I brewed two cups with my special blend of cream and honey. I presented them on the counter as proud as a schoolboy. Slim could only laugh. My cup was ceramic. Hers was plastic. To go.

I spent that winter managing an Outward Bound base camp in Baja California and returned to Moab just in time for publication of my book. I took my first book tour through the Southwest and continued to work twenty-three-day expeditions. Meanwhile, Slim worked three months at a time, in the Utah canyons, the Arizona crags, the Sea of Cortez. The next winter, I returned to Mexico to research my second book. We always found one another back in the trailer. With scraps of rough lumber, I had assembled a sturdy bed frame, topped with a mattress and box spring from the going-out-of-business sale at the Prospector's Lodge. When our entanglements atop it caused Slim's head to bang on the ceiling light fixture, I industriously dragged the frame out to the dirt and sawed eight inches from each leg.

One day on the phone, we lamented that we couldn't see each other, because she was marooned at a base camp 200 miles away with no car. I went out to the bar and came home to find that Slim had hitchhiked to the trailer, let herself in, and gone to bed.

With the old trucks and the dusty Wranglers and the creaky mobile home, I could continue to fancy myself as something other than a private college English major, but now I fine-tuned my image to that of a windblown loner without roots, a tumbleweed, the type of guy in a Sam Shepard movie where outcasts loved and fought in low-rent motels at desert's edge. I'd damn near memorized the monologue from *Paris, Texas*, which Shepard cowrote with L. M. Kit Carson. In the film, Harry Dean Stanton's character, who has wandered for years alone across the badlands and forgotten how to talk, tracks down his lost lover—played by Nastassja Kinski, wow—who's now working behind mirrored glass in some grim Houston peep show. Having relearned to speak, he tells her a story:

"I knew these people. These two people. They were in love with each other." He can see her, but she can't see him, and it's been so many years that she doesn't know his voice. After a few minutes of hard-boiled Americana verse in which he recounts their torrid flame, Stanton drops a telling detail: "He'd yell at her and break things in the trailer."

"In the trailer?" she says, a note of recognition.

"Yes, they lived in a trailer home."

I was coming to learn that I couldn't handle the damn-the-consequence way that a Shepard character lived and fell in love. What I wanted was to be Sam Shepard himself, to write about smashed hearts from the stable view of relative sanity.

The trailer was shaded by cottonwoods, accessed by a single dirt road that required forging the creek since there was no bridge. The bottomland was a patch of Old Moab bypassed by New Moab. In the decade I'd been there, the mom-and-pop motels and diners and crusty old miners were replaced by bistros and subdivisions and a corridor of soulless chain hotels. On either side of me, new homes and condos rose out of the sagebrush. But down here were only a dozen homes, most of them dilapidated doublewides flanked by junk cars, sheds, and motor homes with extension cords snaking into the windows. I turned thirty at the bottom of the Grand Canyon, and when I came home, the tumbleweeds around the trailer were thick and tall enough to swallow a man. Like my romantic fantasies, they were pretty at first and quick to multiply. And while they thrived, nothing permanent could take root.

I set out to clear the weeds.

Tumbleweeds are best pulled when green, before they shed seeds and stickers, but it takes muscle, kneeling in the thorns and gripping the base of the stem. They inflict welts. I learned to wear long pants and long sleeves, and a hat and sunglasses. Weeding became an essential component of writing. I would write all morning, step outside and pull for an hour, then return to my desk, refreshed. But there's only a short time window when they're green. Mostly I wouldn't get around to it until they were brown and brittle and had to be dislodged with a rake. I invested in a propane weed torch, starting ferocious wildfires fifteen feet tall, greasy black clouds belching embers toward the uninsured tinderbox of the cedar-shingled trailer.

Having beaten back the wall of tumbleweeds, I began to plant. Two shrubs: an Apache plume and a New Mexico privet. Two vines: a clematis and wisteria, which I imagined would one day crawl over the pergola and shade the window.

I drove around town to friends' houses and dug up volunteer trees and loaded them into the back of the Chevy and brought them home. A cottonwood, a mimosa, a catalpa, and a reed of a sycamore, which I'd paid ten dollars for in a splurge. I ran a drip line on a timer.

During those years, the second book was written, as well as my first glossy magazine stories. I worked and reworked a story about a rudderless young man inhabiting a desert trailer who misspent his days in a mystical hunt for fossilized dinosaur bones and was rather hopelessly in love with an unavailable older woman who had once broken her engagement to an aristocrat by running off with a rodeo clown. It swelled from short story to novella to a full-blown novel, never to be published. What it lacked in merit it made up for in lessons.

To me, that is. Reading it years later would reveal my tendency to dwell in daydreams, to idealize one woman on the page while she carried on life with her husband, all the while diminishing the love I was actually in. It's not love, but it's not bad. I was now past thirty and had never really had a girlfriend, never been monogamous for more than a few months.

Slim and I had fallen hard and unexpectedly for one other. At the Branding Iron, she sang "Stand by Your Man" and led me in a duet of "You're the Reason God Made Oklahoma." But this didn't stop me from pining for others, only now we'd changed the rules so that we had to tell each other. So, when I met a girl who'd graduated from the same fancy college as Wendy's mother and was a mountain guide who wove her rough cloth with a literary lace (she wrote in her diary in French), I told Slim of my plan to pursue her. And I saw that, for the first time, I'd hurt her. We never recovered.

My third summer in the trailer, 2002, Outward Bound shipped me to Alaska to lead glacial mountaineering and whitewater trips. Slim sent me a Dear John inside a poster tube, along with a cottonwood stick she had collected from my place, complete with a set of bite marks left there by my dog. She had met someone else.

When I came back from Alaska, all my trees but the catalpa were dead. I threw myself a thirty-second birthday party and invited Slim, but she didn't show. Tumbleweeds rioted where the emitters dripped. I pulled them again, and in their place planted spirea and forsythia, a silver maple, and a purple leaf plum.

During a break from guiding that summer, I set out to visit Wendy. She was eight months pregnant. I got a ride to Anchorage, then flew to Juneau, where I boarded the ferry to Sitka, a ten-hour cruise. The galleys for my second book had just arrived, and as I sat out on the deck, mist rose from the banks of spruce while I pored over the pages with a red pen.

Over the years, Wendy and I had spoken regularly on the phone. Usually it had to do with some property issue: where to place the ready-made shed, how to winterize the pipes, or who would sublet when I was in Mexico. Every month, I slid my check for $300 minus repairs into an envelope and mailed it to Sitka.

During the ferry trip, what I should have been contemplating was how our friendship had come to resemble a kind of marriage. I didn't yet know that a marriage is, in addition to a romantic and carnal match, an economic relationship built on trust. One partner might contribute more of the money; the other might do more of the labor. In our case, I was doing countless hours of unpaid work on the trailer, while Wendy was undercharging on the rent and letting me sublet at will as I jetted around the continent. She had become my patroness, enabling my writer's life, letting me live alone in a secluded spot where I didn't have to work half the year. Our arrangement required that neither or us lie or cheat or get greedy. And it worked.

But that sense of trust was not what I contemplated as the ferry approached Sitka. She had mentioned that her husband would be out on the boat, fishing for a few days. And it struck me, less as a desire and more as a worry, that I'd never been the home-wrecking type.

After the ferry docked, I walked down the gangplank. Wendy was waiting there on the dock, full-bellied, trailing two dogs, waddling toward me. She looked radiant in the rare swath of sunlight that escaped the day's sea clouds. She drove us to their cottage, where I recognized her handiwork as decorator.

The pregnancy had only burnished her beauty. I felt a stirring of a kind of love that I can best describe as magical. We would not be together during this life. There was a glow between us that would glow into the next world. What surprised me about this feeling was that I had never believed in another world. I've since learned of a Buddhist cosmology that sees the universe as an infinite number of alternate realms, stacked like dinner plates, each containing a world slightly different than the one we know, each a result of our different choices. Although these theories were devised centuries ago, they seem to explain why the universe is constantly expanding.

There in Sitka, I imagined my life with Wendy on one of those cosmic plates. I didn't feel heartbroken. I was happy she was married and living in an Alaskan fishing village, about to have a baby girl. I was happy, too, that in some other corner of the galaxy, she and I were passionately betrothed in our trailer.

Trailer?

Yes, they live in a trailer home.

Early in 2003, Wendy sold me the land and trailer. I had always thought of home ownership as an activity for husbands and wives with children. But I'd come this far alone, and who knew what came next? I was a bachelor in a town of 5,000 people, with just a handful of single women, many of whom I had already burned a bridge with. The trailer's surviving trees were slim reeds, and I would be fifty by the time they cast any shade.

I traveled and met women and invited them back to the desert with the promise of the windblown trailer amid the tumbleweeds and the youngish author and his heeler who dwelled inside. Results were mixed. Like Merle put it: every front door found me hoping I would find the back door open.

My roots failed to sink into the soil. I lived in Alaska, Vermont, New York City, and finally, in the summer of 2005, Missoula, Montana, where a bunch of my friends had migrated. As I packed up some belongings in the trailer on the way to Montana, I gave Wendy a call. Turned out she was visiting her mother in Billings. She wanted one item: the cowboy painting. We met at the old ranch where her dad grew up, out on Hanging Woman Creek by Crow Agency. She introduced me to her daughter, who was three and looked just like her.

We walked along the creek under the cottonwoods. By now she was forty-five, and her eyes crinkled when she smiled. My face was dotted with sunspots, hair receding high on my forehead. Somehow the topic turned to having an affair. Not with each other, just in general. All these years later, it seems impossible that this turn wasn't suggestive or flirtatious, but that's not how I remember it. It was just Wendy talking bluntly about being married.

"It would just be too much work!" she said. "And such a hassle! I mean, we own these houses together, and boats, and a business, to say nothing of having a daughter. I just don't see how people could do it."

I asked her about the time she kissed me on the porch couch. I still wasn't clear how we'd missed each other. It should not have surprised me that, like Q, she had seen things more clearly than I had.

"I was interested," she said. "But you were running around with all these girls who were fifteen years younger than me. I just felt so old and silly."

I became an absentee landlord. I did only the bare maintenance on the trailer yet fretted about the foliage. A renter reported that the silver maple appeared sick, so I called a gardener friend; she reported that the drip emitter was merely clogged. Too late. The tree died. I'd email the tenants to say that a heat wave was on the way and could they check the lines and turn up the water. Or I'd call on a Friday night at nine and ask them to unhook the timers because I'd seen that it was supposed to freeze. I visited once or twice a year, beating back the tumbleweeds with a torch and rake. It was during these years that someone christened the place the Shinglewide. The name stuck.

My absence meant a low survival rate for the plants. I mourned each brittle twig choked by goatheads. In a devastating blow, my flowering plum tree with purple leaves—just outside the window, just beginning to cast shade on the shingles—died after a cold snap. My land seemed to reject efforts to settle it. Perhaps it sensed that my heart was elsewhere. But when I visited the next spring, in 2006, a small miracle had unfurled. The plum sent up a robust and mysterious new trunk, with green leaves instead of red. I learned that the ornamental species had originally been grafted onto a sturdier rootstock at the nursery. A new tree, not the one I thought I'd planted, was reborn.

I married a Montana girl. Not Wendy, of course, but one who'd grown up in a barn and been homeschooled in the woods, and who, every time she walked outside, seemed to pick up an arrowhead or an owl feather or a tiny toad.

By then I was close to forty and knew that you don't love someone merely for her story, but habits die hard and I couldn't resist the allure of her biography. A botanist by trade, Cedar could identify all the weeds and native grasses on the western range. She sang and fiddled and spat tobacco and also marched against the WTO in Seattle and wrote a book of poems about love and frost that made me swoon and crack. Biking along back roads, she stopped to carry roadkill birds and squirrels into the woods, where she covered them with leaves and pine needles and said small blessings. On our first date, we camped in a tepee in a town called Hot Springs, soaked for hours in the tub, walked to the bar in a drizzle, and two-stepped to Johnny Cash on the jukebox, then sat around the campfire, where she rolled cigarettes and we exchanged songs of marital homicide: "Delia's Gone" for me and "Cold Rain and Snow" for her. The first time she saw the trailer, she made wry comments about my attempts at horticulture.

When my fifteen-year-old dog lay down to die, Cedar suggested that we not take her to the vet. Instead she arranged a bed of blankets and pillows on the living room floor, where we sat for Sadie's last hours, burning candles and singing prayers. I was washing dishes when she called to me: "Come now. It's happening." We knelt and lay our hands on her coat as she drifted away.

Not long after that, as we skied through the backcountry, I bent onto one knee and proposed. In retrospect, I should have taken the skis off first, because the maneuver was awkward, and unlike in the movies, Cedar said she needed to think about it. Also unlike the movies, the precise inspiration for this spontaneous act was not a burst of romance but a welling irritation at my shallowness. I now knew that the love I'd sought wasn't something for which you waited and waited to arrive, but something you created when you made a promise.

In the fall of 2018, I drove up to Moab alone. Cedar and I had been together for a decade. We had trekked around Nepal twice, lived three months in our car on Mexican beaches, moved to Colorado for her poetry degree, and were now in Albuquerque, New Mexico, both teaching creative writing at a university. She was visiting a friend and would arrive the next day. I drove across the creek with those yellow leaves quivering overhead, and before unloading a single item, I hurried from shrub to tree, holding the leaves between my fingers, whispering words. Then I called Wendy.

I could tell by the upness of her tone that she had not heard the news.

"We had a baby boy," I told her. "He died the same day."

One reason I'd fallen in love with my wife was the mystical way she inhabited the spirit world, the calm and wisdom with which she faced death, but I did not think I would witness it with our own child. Even through the howling and weeping, the days where I just wanted to get rid of his body—cremate it, bury it, I didn't really care—she swaddled him in knit blankets, anointed him with oils, wrapped his wrists and neck with holy beads.

I had also learned a lot about my friends when my son died. Some disappeared. Some pointed fingers at the doctors and midwife. Others jumped on planes to grieve with me. And that was what I wanted. Not etiquette or "space" or outrage, but someone who could join me in the only place I inhabited: sorrow.

Wendy broke down and sobbed. I lowered myself to the splintered front steps and cried into my phone with her. She told me that before her daughter was born, when she was thirty-nine, she had miscarried. She had thought that was her one chance, her last chance, and then, not long after that, she was pregnant again.

Cedar arrived the next night. It was my forty-eighth birthday. On her way into town, she stopped for groceries. A lifelong vegetarian, she bought a steak. In the morning, she took a test. Another baby was on the way.

Out there on one of those cosmic plates, Silver's birth went differently: The cord did not get pinched, his heart did not stop, the machines saved him. He lives with his parents, toddling along the porch of the trailer.

Yes, they live in a trailer home.

The Shinglewide was vacant when the pandemic began. Our second son was nine months old. There had been no cases reported in Moab and only a handful in New Mexico, and yet it seemed that any day they could shut the borders between states. We drove up to Utah while we could.

On a warm March afternoon, we arrived with bags of rice and a twenty-pound burlap sack of pinto beans. We carried Bodie down through the cottonwoods and the thatch of Russian olives to the creek gurgling over mossy stones. The catalpa was thirty feet tall, ready to emit a thousand white flowers. The green-leafed plum was thriving. The sycamores were spindly, not hardy enough for the cold winters. I introduced him to the spirea, the skunk brush, the rabbit brush. No leaves had emerged yet, but I let him hold each stalk in his fingers. The Apache plume, forsythia, wisteria, privet. He clutched the white bark of the sycamore.

The forsythia blossomed first, early April, bright yellow flowers on bare branches. As the days warmed, we strung a hammock in the thicket by the creek and swung our son. The almond tree bloomed later that month, and still we did not go home to Albuquerque. I cannot say if our baby was at risk from the virus, but I could not be persuaded to take him out of isolation. He was safe here with us at the trailer.

As May began, before leaves had returned to most trees, a heat wave swept through. I pushed Bodie in his stroller along the bumpy dirt road to where it crossed the creek, then turned around and returned home, peeking under the canopy to see that he was asleep. I parked him beside the kitchen window, beneath the plum that had died and come back as another tree. I eased onto the cracked wooden steps and watched my son's chest rise and fall, his toes twitch, as he lay sheltered in the spreading shade.

Postscript

These essays collected here remain largely in their original state, stamped in a moment in time which has since passed. The situations I reported have since changed. My updates are here.

GREEN GREEN GRASS OF HOME

The Lake Powell Pipeline stalled during the process of federal approval and has not been built. Washington County insists that it "remains a viable part of Utah's long-term water supply plan." In 2022, as the megadrought entered its third decade, the Colorado River's primary reservoirs, Lake Mead and Lake Powell, dropped to record lows and approached "dead pool," the level at which the water would stop flowing through Hoover Dam and Glen Canyon Dam. At that point, hydroelectric production would cease, and no water would be delivered to Arizona and California. In 2023, the Biden administration reached a deal with Nevada, Arizona, and California to conserve 3 million acre-feet of water through 2026.

Growth in St. George continued to surge, with or without the pipeline. When I began reporting this story in 2017, Washington County's population was 166,000; by 2021 it was 191,000, estimated to reach 464,000 by 2060.

The Navajo Utah Water Rights Settlement was approved by the Congress in 2020, allocating $220 million for infrastructure projects to deliver 81,500 acre-feet of water to the Utah portion of the Navajo Nation. The Lake Powell Pipeline would cost ten times that amount to deliver roughly the same amount of water to Washington County, which is 78 percent white.

In a related 2023 case, the US Supreme Court ruled on a lawsuit filed by the Navajo Nation twenty years earlier, hoping to secure water rights that it claimed were promised in an 1868 peace treaty. In a five to four decision, the court ruled against the tribe, stating that the US was not required to secure water for the Navajos.

WHY NOAH WENT TO THE WOODS

Several months after this story was published, Noah Pippin's body was found by search crews near the Chinese Wall, close to where the previous search had been stopped by a storm. The Flathead County coroner ruled his death a suicide. The Pippin family disputed this; they maintain that Noah died of hypothermia. In a Facebook post from May 31, 2021, they wrote:

> Noah lost his life in an early winter snow storm in the
> mountains of Montana September 16, 2010 preparing
> solo for a deployment with his California National Guard
> unit scheduled to go to Afghanistan December of 2010.

UPRISING AT STANDING ROCK / LAST DAYS AT STANDING ROCK

Most of the resistance camp at Standing Rock was disbanded after the December, 2016, ruling by the United States Army Corps of Engineers, which withdrew the easement to drill under Oahe Lake. Shortly after Donald Trump was inaugurated the next year, he reversed that decision, and ordered the Corps to issue the permit.

The Dakota Access Pipeline was completed in April, 2017, and became operational in June. By 2021, the pipeline was able to ship 750,000 barrels of oil, accounting for 40 percent of the crude produced in the Balkan shale of North Dakota.

The Standing Rock Sioux's lawsuit persisted, and in 2020 a federal judge ordered the pipeline to be shut down and be emptied of oil until an environmental assessment was completed. The shutdown was quickly overturned on appeal. The review continues. The oil flows.

Despite the pipeline being built, the uprising at Standing Rock launched a new era of Indigenous power. One water protector in the camps, a single mom from Albuquerque named Deb Haaland, would become in 2018, along with Sharice Davids of Oklahoma, one of the first two Indigenous US congresswomen. In 2020, Haaland joined President Biden's cabinet as

Secretary of Interior—the first Indigenous person to oversee the Bureau of Indian Affairs—and launched the nation's first-ever investigation into abuses committed at Indian Boarding Schools. In Minnesota, Peggy Flanagan was elected lieutenant governor, making her the country's highest-ranking Native woman elected to executive office. (Another water protector at the Oceti Sakowin camp, a twenty-seven-year-old bartender of Puerto Rican descent from the Bronx, was inspired "from that crucible of activism" to run for congress. Her name: Alexandria Ocasio-Cortez.)

Indigenous people rose to the highest ranks of cultural influence. In 2019, when Joy Harjo became Poet Laureate of the United States, she was the first Native American to hold that position. A number of Natives were awarded Pulitzer Prizes in 2021, including novelist Louise Erdrich and poet Natalie Diaz (and editorial cartoonist Marty Two Bulls Sr. was named as a finalist). Composer Raven Chacon won the Pulitzer for music in 2022. Novelists Tommy Orange and Brandon Hobson were finalists for major book prizes in 2019, poet Jake Skeets won the 2020 American Book Award, David Treuer's sweeping history *The Heartbeat of Wounded Knee* was short-listed for the 2020 National Book Award, and essayists Terese Marie Mailhot and Robin Wall Kimmerer had *New York Times* bestsellers in 2018 and 2019. Since 2018, Diaz, Chacon, Kimmerer, artist/filmmaker Sky Hopinka, and artist Dyani White Hawk won MacArthur Foundation "genius grants." The hit FX series *Reservation Dogs* was the first major television show written and directed exclusively by Indigenous people.

For decades, the pressing issues in Indian country—broken treaties, tribal sovereignty, boarding schools—had been ignored in the national discourse. After #NoDAPL, influenced by the surge in racial awareness that followed the 2020 murder of George Floyd, they moved closer to the center. The Washington Redskins and Cleveland Indians dropped their mascot names after decades of pressure. And in 2020, the Supreme Court issued a landmark decision in a case called *McGirt v. Oklahoma*: By a vote of five to four, the court ruled that, because Congress had never disestablished five Indian reservations that it had created prior to Oklahoma statehood—and though most of that land had long since passed out of Indigenous hands—the owners of these lands were exempt from certain state laws. In essence, the court affirmed that tribes had sovereignty over their historical domains.

Overruling President Trump, President Biden re-instated the boundaries of Bears Ears and Grand Staircase–Escalante National Monuments in 2021. Lawsuits by the State of Utah and several counties in the south of the state were dismissed by a federal judge in 2023.

After a pandemic slump, visitation at Arches, Zion, Canyonlands, and Capitol Reef National Parks reached record highs in 2021. (Bryce Canyon has not yet matched its 2017 peak.) In 2022, Arches implemented a timed entry reservation system, ending the necessity to shut the gate.

The effects of the moratoriums on new hotels in Moab are still unclear. Grand County's ban expired after six months. As with many resort towns in the West, the pandemic sent the cost of housing skyrocketing. Zillow's Home Value Index for Moab jumped from $363,000 in 2020 to $581,000 in 2022. Grand County, comprised of 87 percent of mostly spectacular public land, will likely remain desirable and unaffordable into the future.

I returned with my family to live in our rickety trailerhouse during the pandemic. The few wondrous months of quarantine in which everything shut down was like riding a time machine to the nineties, after which the tourists returned, first in a trickle, then in a deluge. The town felt crowded and loud, the hostility simmering between exhausted locals and the off-highway vehicle mob, their go-carts now festooned with TRUMP 2024 and LET'S GO BRANDON pennants. We wished these man-children might one day tire of the dirty looks and say: This place sucks, Brandon. Let's go somewhere else.

Out at the trailer, little had changed, not the shallow floods that muddied its wheels nor the drifts of tumbleweeds piling against the rusty fence. With our one-year-old son we planted pear and peach trees, sand cherry and privet, cottonwood and sage and rabbit brush, and finally two sycamores that will one day cast shade over this dusty little compound that my heart calls home.

Acknowledgments

Thanks to the following publications, where some of the essays in this collection previously appeared:

— *The Believer*: "The Dropout in Your Inbox" and "The Man Who Would Be Jack London"
— *Blue Mesa Review*: "The Cave Dreamer"
— *Great God Pan*: "Too Much Fun for Just One State"
— *New York Times*: "Cave Men" (published as "Taking the Plunge in Oregon's Grand Canyon")
— *Outside*: "Why Noah Went to the Woods," "Green Green Grass of Home," and "Tinier Than Thou"
— *Popular Science*: "The Fortress of Nice" (published as "Welcome to Drone-Kota")
— OutsideOnline: "Uprising at Standing Rock," "Last Days at Standing Rock," "How the Mighty Have Fallen" (published as "Utah Wanted All The Tourists. Then It Got Them"), and "The Shinglewide" (published as "Notes from a Moab Trailer")